CORPS AND CLIENTELES

La grande despence me fait beaucoup de peine; mais il y en a de nécessaires

Great expenses cause me much pain, but there are those that cannot be avoided

(Louis XIV to Colbert, June 1683)

Corps and Clienteles
Public Finance and Political Change in France, 1688–1715

MARK POTTER
University of Wyoming, USA

LONDON AND NEW YORK

First published 2003 by Ashgate Publishing

Reissued 2019 by Routledge
2 Park Square, Milton Park, Abingdon, Oxon, OX14 4RN
52 Vanderbilt Avenue, New York, NY 10017

Routledge is an imprint of the Taylor & Francis Group, an informa business

© Mark Potter 2003

The author has asserted his moral right under the Copyright, Designs and Patents Act, 1988, to be identified as the author of this work.

All rights reserved. No part of this book may be reprinted or reproduced or utilised in any form or by any electronic, mechanical, or other means, now known or hereafter invented, including photocopying and recording, or in any information storage or retrieval system, without permission in writing from the publishers.

Notice:
Product or corporate names may be trademarks or registered trademarks, and are used only for identification and explanation without intent to infringe.

Publisher's Note
The publisher has gone to great lengths to ensure the quality of this reprint but points out that some imperfections in the original copies may be apparent.

Disclaimer
The publisher has made every effort to trace copyright holders and welcomes correspondence from those they have been unable to contact.

A Library of Congress record exists under LC control number:

ISBN 13: 978-1-138-70925-6 (hbk)
ISBN 13: 978-1-138-70923-2 (pbk)
ISBN 13: 978-1-315-19833-0 (ebk)

Contents

List of Figures		*vi*
List of Tables		*vii*
Preface		*ix*

PART I: ABSOLUTISM AND THE OLD-REGIME ELITE

| 1 | Introduction | 3 |
| 2 | Venality Entrenched: The Property Rights of Office Holding Under Louis XIV | 28 |

PART II: CROWN AND PROVINCE

| 3 | Estates and Ruling Coalitions in Burgundy | 51 |
| 4 | Royal Strategies and Elite Responses in Normandy | 100 |

PART III: CORPS AND CLIENTELES IN PUBLIC FINANCE

5	Lenders and Money Handlers	135
6	Intermediating Corps and Financial Clienteles	158
7	Conclusion	182

Appendix 1: Merchants and the Rouennais Town Council	*195*
Appendix 2: Privilege and Louis XIV's Divide-and-Rule Strategies	*200*
Appendix 3: Data Sources for Lending Clienteles	*203*
Bibliography	*205*
Index	*215*

List of Figures

1.1	Annual direct tax levels, 1688-1717	6
1.2	*Affaires extraordinaires*	9
2.1	Annual office transmissions, *généralité* of Rouen	44
3.1	Direct taxation levels in Burgundy, adjusted to 1679 livre	60
3.2	Annual revenues and sums borrowed against the *octrois de la Saône*	89
4.1	*Taille* levels, *généralité* of Rouen	105
5.1	Levels of involvement in extraordinary affairs	139
6.1	Comparative interest rates of rentes	160

List of Tables

2.1	Transmissions of offices in Burgundy and Rouen, sampling from 1680-1715	43
3.1	Triennial levels of *dons gratuits* agreed upon by Estates of Burgundy (000 livres)	58
3.2	Annual obligations of Estates of Burgundy (000 livres)	59
3.3	Attendance rates of deputies to the Estates of Burgundy at four successive meetings, 1694-1703	65
3.4	Principal due for *augmentations de gages* from superior courts, in livres	79
3.5	Borrowing by Estates of Burgundy to cover annual direct tax obligations (000 livres)	82
3.6	Borrowing by Estates of Burgundy to cover extraordinary obligations (000 livres)	84
3.7	Annual revenues collected from and sums borrowed against *octrois de la Saône* (000 livres)	88
3.8	*Octrois* accorded to and mortgaged by the Estates of Burgundy	91
4.1	Levels of *taille* and Capitation in *généralité* of Rouen, selected years, in livres	106
4.2	*Dixième* revenues from the *généralité* of Rouen, in livres	107
4.3	Comparison of direct tax levels in Burgundy and *généralité* of Rouen, nominal (000 livres) and per capita	108
4.4	Purchasers of new offices in Chamber of Accounts of Rouen	116
4.5	Status of *traités* in Rouen in 1713, grouped by years of origin of contracts	119
4.6	Total extraordinary obligations of municipality of Rouen	124

6.1	Borrowing by Estates of Burgundy	168
6.2	Sample of officer corps borrowing in Burgundy and Rouen	169
6.3	Sample of individual office-holder borrowing in Rouen	170
6.4	Lenders' contacts with borrowing corps	172
6.5	Lenders' contacts with officer corps, Burgundian versus Norman	173
6.6	Lenders' contacts with borrowing corps, two periods	175

Preface

Do we need yet another book on French public finances in the seventeenth century? Françoise Bayard, William Beik, Richard Bonney, James Collins, Julian Dent, Daniel Dessert and Alain Guéry have each covered this ground quite thoroughly, and because of their works our understanding of French finances in the Old Regime surpasses that of any other European country in the early modern era. Indeed, without the contributions of these historians, my work would not have been possible. I did not set out to revisit the findings of these scholars, nor, to be sure, was it ever my intention to reconstruct figures for the receipts and expenditures of the French crown. Instead, I seek here to fill an historiographical gap while charting some new ground in our understanding of the French absolutist state. The final decades of Louis XIV's reign have indeed been largely overlooked by historians of both French public finances and absolutist state development. In relying on the financial intermediation of privileged corps to pay for the costs of war, the French crown in this period embarked upon a political and financial experiment that, while short-lived in duration, affected the financial options and decisions of Louis XIV's successors through to the end of the Old Regime. It is thus from this vantage point that I am able ultimately to draw my conclusions regarding warfare and state development. My overriding interest in this work is to investigate how *both* historical *and* structural constraints interacted to shape the crown's options for financing war. It is that intersection of the historical and the structural, I argue, that guided political change in early modern France.

There are many to thank for lending help and support to this project, and my gratitude and appreciation extend far. Generous financial support provided by a Fulbright fellowship made possible the research that forms the foundation of this project. I was able to follow this up with further research funded by the College of Arts and Sciences at the University of Wyoming.

While in France, Alain Guéry, Robert Descimon, Anette Smedley and Gilles Postel-Vinay all took time from their own responsibilities to lend valuable guidance to my research, addressing everything from the most mundane questions that I had to the more complicated matters of reading, digesting and analysing a mass of archival sources.

In the U.S., I have been fortunate to find the support and expertise of a number of experienced scholars. The first incarnation of this work came in the form of my Ph.D. dissertation, and at that stage the contributions of my dissertation co-directors, Robert Brenner and Geoffrey Symcox, were valuable and irreplaceable, and their intellectual influences remain notable throughout this present work. While their comments, suggestions, and probing questions were instrumental to producing a quality dissertation, equally important was the high level of intellectual rigor that they demanded of me from the very beginning of my graduate career.

Jean-Laurent Rosenthal has been instrumental throughout the life of this project. By demonstrating his confidence in me at a very early stage of my academic formation and agreeing to form a lasting research partnership that has run parallel to this project, Jean-Laurent has helped me to develop the experience and skills, not to mention the confidence, necessary to undertake the distinct body of research that went into this work. His influence, too, can be found throughout this study, but I should note that Chapter Six in particular would not have been possible without his generous intellectual and material support. Likewise, Phil Hoffman and Naomi Lamoreaux gave generously of their time to read drafts and provide comments on this project at various points throughout its life.

Since I turned to the occasionally arduous task of transforming the dissertation into this present monograph, several scholars and colleagues have helped tremendously in the completion of the project. Bill Beik, Gail Bossenga, Al Hamscher, John Hurt, Sharon Kettering and Julian Swann each provided feedback, encouragement and advice at one point or the other. Much of that interaction came at the indispensable annual meetings of the Society for French Historical Studies. Colleagues at the University of Wyoming who took part in the Colloquium on History, Culture and Society also provided useful comments on drafts of chapters.

My cohort of French historians who completed their graduate studies at roughly the same time as I and who, like I, have been confronting the challenges of establishing themselves within the profession have given me both moral and intellectual support, without which I would have arrived at this point in my career only with great difficulty. These include Megan Armstrong, Sara Beam, Michael Breen, Greg Brown, Sara Chapman, Steve Miller and David K. Smith.

Tom Gray at Ashgate Publishing deserves my gratitude for giving this project the chance to see the light of day from within the world of published books.

For many years, I have looked upon my brother Jim as a model of academic rigor and accomplishment, and it is to him that I dedicate this book.

PART I
ABSOLUTISM AND THE OLD-REGIME ELITE

Chapter 1

Introduction

Warfare and its impact on the absolutist state is a topic that continues to merit investigation. At the expense of greater nuance and sophistication in their analyses, historians of French absolutism have tended to gravitate toward two schools of thought, neither of which is sufficient on its own. One group of historians, focusing particularly on eighteenth-century developments, has tended to characterize French absolutism as an unwieldy state system that handicapped France in the international arena.[1] The institutions and structures of absolutism, they argue, raised the costs of borrowing well beyond what France's rivals paid to finance war, and the proliferation of privilege erected political barriers to increasing taxation and reforming political institutions.[2] Alternatively, historians approaching absolutism from the perspective of the first half of the seventeenth century leave us with an image of the absolutist state responding to the exigencies of war by undermining privileges, erecting powerful new branches of government and violating provincial liberties all in a search for increased revenues.[3] Absolutism by

---

[1] Hilton Root, *The Fountain of Privilege: Political Foundations of Markets in Old Regime France and England*, (Berkeley and Los Angeles: University of California Press, 1994); Douglass North and Barry Weingast, 'Constitutions and Commitment: The Evolution of Institutions Governing Public Choice in Seventeenth-century England,' *Journal of Economic History*, 49 (1989): 792-821; Philip T. Hoffman and Kathryn Norberg, eds., *Fiscal Crises, Liberty and Representative Government, 1450-1789*, (Stanford: Stanford University Press, 1994), p. 306; Richard Bonney, 'The Struggle for Great Power Status and the End of the Old Fiscal Regime,' in Richard Bonney, ed., *Economic Systems and State Finance*, (Oxford: Clarendon Press, 1995), pp. 318 and 338.

[2] Bonney, 'Struggle'; Michael Kwass, *Privilege and the Politics of Taxation in Eighteenth-Century France: Liberté, Égalité, Fiscalité*, (Cambridge: Cambridge University Press, 2000); David Bien, 'Offices, Corps, and a System of State Credit: The Uses of Privilege under the Ancien Régime,' in Keith M. Baker, ed., *The French Revolution and the Creation of Modern Political Culture*, (Oxford: Pergamon Press, 1987), 1: 89-114; Peter Mathias and Patrick K. O'Brien, 'Taxation in England and France, 1715-1810,' *Journal of European Economic History*, 5 (1976): 601-650.

[3] Roland Mousnier, *La monarchie absolue en Europe du Ve siècle à nos jours*, (Paris: Presses Universitaires de France, 1982), pp. 141-150; Georges Pagès, *La Monarchie d'Ancien Régime en France (de Henri IV à Louis XIV)*, (Paris: Armand Colin, 1928), pp. 96-109; Richard Bonney, *Political Change under Richelieu and Mazarin, 1624-1661*, (Oxford: Oxford University Press, 1978); Niels Steensgaard, 'The Seventeenth-century Crisis,' in Geoffrey Parker and Lesley M.

one account was weak and inflexible; by the other it was an unconstrained Leviathan.[4]

Neither understanding of absolutism is satisfactory. I argue instead a third view. Absolutist kings *were* constrained in their options, both by the underlying structures of privilege that lay at the root of society and by the particular conditions passed on from previous times of financial squeeze. Yet while constrained, absolutism proved capable of responding to international exigencies with a surprising degree of flexibility, at times using those very structures of privilege to its advantage. The result was political change over the course of the seventeenth and eighteenth centuries that belies any notion of absolutism as ossified.

The object and scope of this study comprise Louis XIV's financial strategies during the final 26 years of his reign and the political impact they had. I approach this topic from several perspectives: within the international arena I consider French developments during a time of intense military competition on the European stage. I also trace changes on a 'national' level as Louis XIV sought financial support for his wars, and finally I consider provincial particularities in the evolution of financial and political arrangements. The period 1688 to 1715 was one in which both France and her rivals undertook resource mobilization on a scale unprecedented in European history. Across Europe, the different strategies chosen to meet the costs of war conditioned later developments well into the eighteenth century. This was truly a time that brought political change in France and throughout Europe. Furthermore, absolutism certainly did not cripple France's abilities of resource mobilization. France competed respectably against broad coalitions of European powers in two long-lasting and costly wars, the Nine Years' War, which lasted from 1688 to 1697, and the War of the Spanish Succession, 1701-1714.[5] On the other hand, the difficulties she would face in later eighteenth-century conflicts did indeed stem from the legacies of Louis XIV's financial strategies. Thus, I argue, the structures of absolutism in themselves do not explain France's difficulties in the eighteenth century; rather the particular path that French absolutism followed coming out of Louis XIV's wars do. Again, we are faced with the challenge of understanding the intersection between warfare and political change under absolutism.

Warfare and the efforts involved in waging war were a near constant feature driving political change in old-regime France, and two periods of long-lasting and costly warfare particularly marked the seventeenth century. The first of these comprised France's involvement in the Thirty Years' War. After several years of covert support, Louis XIII entered the war in 1635, and then following upon the Peace of Westphalia in 1648, France and Spain continued to fight until terms were reached in 1659 at the Peace of the Pyrenées. The second major period of warfare

---

Smith, eds., *The General Crisis of the Seventeenth Century*, (London: Routledge, 1978), pp. 44-48.
[4] An important revisionist view of absolutism has arisen in recent decades, but it has little to say about patterns or processes of political change. I examine this revisionist school below.
[5] John A. Lynn, *The Wars of Louis XIV, 1667-1714*, (New York: Longman, 1999), p. 46.

then spanned the above-mentioned final two wars of Louis XIV.[6] While the latter period of warfare is our focus in this study, it is my argument that previous wartime financial strategies along with the responses to them conditioned later approaches to war finance. Thus, with regard to warfare in the seventeenth century, strategies to pay for the Thirty Years' War and the fallout from them determined in part the options Louis XIV had when it came time to finance his final two wars. In particular, recourse to extraordinary financial measures in the first period of warfare shaped how Louis XIV sought extraordinary support in the second.

Neither Richelieu and, succeeding him as First Minister, Mazarin nor Louis XIV could pay for their involvement in war strictly through ordinary revenues. In both periods, taxation quickly ran up against structural limits at the initial stages of warfare.[7] Indeed, as Figure 1.1 suggests, direct taxation actually fell in real terms during the final two wars of Louis XIV.[8] In both cases, therefore, the crown turned to extraordinary means, or *affaires extraordinaires*, to finance war. By their very nature, these measures overwhelmingly targeted members of the privileged elite who by virtue of their status avoided paying many of the ordinary tax obligations. Their responses to such measures could determine the success of overall financial strategies, and in this regard, important differences separated the extraordinary affairs of the Thirty Years' War from those of Louis XIV's wars.

Richelieu's measures elicited contention and widespread opposition in large part because they targeted *en masse* the elite. In 1634, for example, Richelieu defaulted on all outstanding *droits aliénés*, rights to anticipated surtaxes held primarily by financial officers in return for their prior advances to the crown. The crown then required towns and office holders to lend additional sums to the Royal Treasury in 1637.[9] To make matters worse for local notables, Louis XIII and his ministers coupled their financial measures with political changes intended to rationalize financial administration and reduce the costs and delays of raising money. In particular, the crown systematized the use of intendants. With their powers defined by royal commissions, these crown-dependent agents wrested many of the cherished public functions from local notables in both the judicial and financial branches of government. Then, with the strong support of Michel de

---

[6] Louis XIV also fought two wars prior to the outbreak of the Nine Years' War: the War of Devolution, 1667-1668, and the Dutch War, 1672-1679, but in terms of their financial costs, these wars do not belong in the same category as our two major periods of warfare.

[7] John Lynn (*Wars*, p. 25) writes: '...warfare quickly outstripped the level of moneys produced by taxation. Driving up tax rates during wartime could at best only cover part of the increased demands of warfare, and at worst higher taxes could bring resistance and rebellion.' On the limits of direct taxation during France's involvement in the Thirty Years' War, see James B. Collins, *Fiscal Limits of Absolutism*, (Berkeley and Los Angeles: University of California Press, 1988).

[8] A.M. de Boislisle, *Correspondance des contrôleurs généraux des finances avec les intendants des provinces*, 3 vols., (Paris: Imprimerie Nationale, 1874-97), 1: 589-597 and 2: 583-599.

[9] Collins, *Fiscal Limits*, p. 100; Madeleine Foisil, *La Révolte des Nu-Pieds et les révoltes normandes de 1639*, (Paris: Presses Universitaires de France, 1970), pp. 63-65.

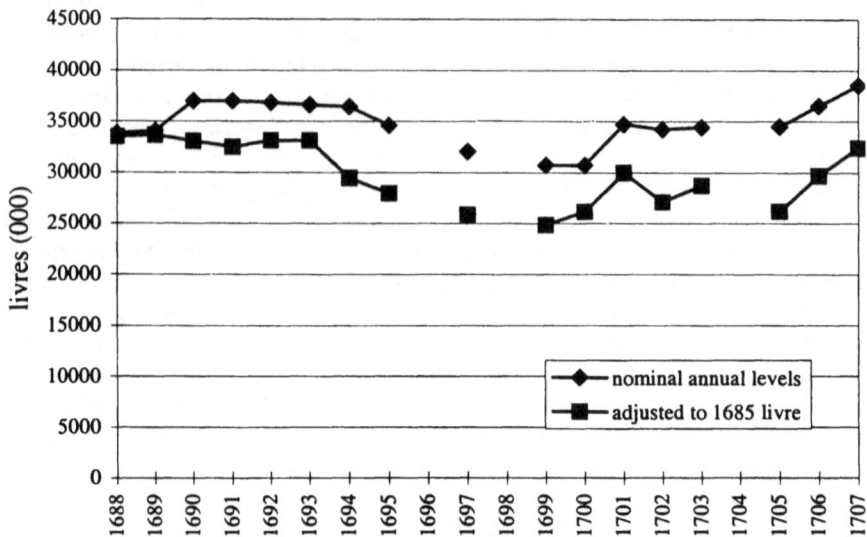

Figure 1.1 Annual direct tax levels, 1688-1717

Marillac, keeper of the seals, Louis XIII leveled an attack on the financial independence of privileged provinces, or *pays d'États*. Finally, in 1648, Mazarin threatened to revoke the heritability of offices in order to gain political and financial concessions from the judicial and financial elite.[10] Throughout, the crown created and sold new offices, which placed downward pressure on the market prices of those offices in which private individuals had already invested. *Traités*, or the contracts by which the crown sold the rights to market new offices or collect extraordinary taxes, peaked in value in 1635 at around 76 million livres. They then remained at a rough plateau, slightly lower than the 1635 peak, until 1648.[11]

Such widespread attacks against the political and financial interests of the elite alienated crucial pillars of support for royal authority and thereby contributed to waves of political and social unrest from the 1620s to the mid-1650s. Widespread peasant uprisings presented a significant challenge to both royal authority and social order. The most serious of these were the Croquants uprisings in southwest

---

[10] Bonney, *Political Change*, pp. 29-56; J. Russell Major, *From Renaissance Monarchy to Absolute Monarchy: French Kings, Nobles, and Estates*, (Baltimore: The Johns Hopkins University Press, 1994), pp. 220-303; Sharon Kettering, *Judicial Politics and Urban Revolt in Seventeenth-century France*, (Princeton: Princeton University Press, 1978), pp. 51-109.

[11] Françoise Bayard, *Le Monde des financiers au XVIIe siècle*, (Paris: Flammarion, 1988), pp. 198-200. On the crown's readiness to pressure office holders in this period, see Richard Bonney, *The King's Debts*, (Oxford: Clarendon, 1981), p. 179.

France that within two years, from 1636 to 1637, covered nearly a quarter the area of France, and the Nu-Pieds revolt that struck Normandy in 1639. Urban revolts also plagued the political scene in these decades, erupting in Dijon (1630), Aix (1631), Lyon (1632), Bordeaux (1635), and Rouen (1639). This period of unrest culminated with the collapse of royal authority and the outbreak of civil war during the Fronde, from 1648 to 1653.

A number of interpretations have been offered to explain the nature and dynamics of these uprisings.[12] What is important for our purposes is that local elite groups played roles in these uprisings that ranged from passive acquiescence to active leadership. Despite their responsibilities for maintaining order, they often allowed popular disturbances to spread unrepressed until it became clear to them that the uprisings posed serious threats to social order.[13] Conflict between the crown and provincial elites that began with Richelieu's wartime financial measures thus rendered a coordinated and effective suppression of popular revolts beyond the reach of royal authority. As a result, the crown and the privileged elite together opened the door to what would be the collapse of centralized authority upon the outbreak of the Fronde in 1648. Without political and financial coordination and cooperation, the effective exercise of authority and the preservation of social order proved impossible.

Resistance to royal financial measures along with the collapse of authority and order during the Fronde deepened the 'crisis' in royal finances.[14] Alongside royal authority, the ability to raise revenues through *traités* all but collapsed between 1648 and 1653. Beyond this short-term collapse, though, was a longer-term crisis in the financial returns from the creation and sale of offices. Contracts for the right to market offices diminished as a proportion of total *traités* beginning in 1638, and the total income that the crown gained from offices, including returns from their sale along with mutation fees levied as they changed hands, fell from around 36 million livres in 1639 to under a million in 1661.[15] Elite resistance to the sale of

---

[12] Boris Porchnev, *Les soulèvements populaires en France de 1623 à 1648*, (Paris: S.E.V.P.E.N., 1963); Roland Mousnier, 'Recherches sur les soulèvements populaires en France avant la Fronde,' *Revue d'histoire moderne et contemporaine* 5 (1958): 81-113; Yves-Marie Bercé, *Croquants et nu-pieds: les soulèvements paysans en France du XVIe au XIXe siècle*, (Paris: Gallimard, 1974); William Beik, *Urban Protest in Seventeenth-Century France: The Culture of Retribution*, (New York: Cambridge University Press, 1997).

[13] Urban anti-fiscal insurrections often gained momentum from the belief that local magistrates or civic leaders supported their causes. According to Porchnev, local notables often did little, at least initially, to dispel such assumptions. In the August 1648 uprising in Paris that marked the beginning of the Fronde, for example, only after the insurrection became truly popular, and thus uncontrollable, did local leaders make clear their opposition to the movement. See *Soulèvements populaires*, p. 283. See also Beik, *Urban Protest in Seventeenth-century France*, (Cambridge: Cambridge University Press, 1997), pp. 95-115.

[14] Julian Dent, 'An Aspect of the Crisis of the Seventeenth Century: The Collapse of the Financial Administration of the French Monarchy (1653-61),' *The Economic History Review*, 2nd Series, 20 (1967): 241-256.

[15] Bayard, p, 200; Dent, 'Aspect,' p. 247.

new, often redundant, offices likely combined with an exhaustion of market opportunities to produce this decline. As a result, the crown in the 1650s increased its dependence on short term loans which Nicolas Fouquet, superintendent of finances, secured from his personal clientele of friends and family.

Louis XIV's persecution of Fouquet upon assuming personal rule gave signal of his desire to change the way the crown did business. A clientele under the control of Colbert replaced that which had been loyal to Fouquet; Louis began to assert greater personal control over finances; and, as our period of warfare ultimately unfolded and the crown found itself once again increasingly more dependent on extraordinary financial means, Louis XIV showed himself to be particularly adept at raising money by creating for sale an array of offices, privileges, monopolies and surtaxes.[16] These measures brought to the Treasury important sums that responded to the crown's wartime needs (the years 1709 and 1710 are an exception), and, unlike during the Thirty Years' War, the sums mostly kept pace with the demands generated by warfare, reaching their peak well into the war years, in 1705.[17] (See Figure 1.2). Thus, the turn to *affaires extraordinaires* as a means of war finance proved more successful for Louis XIV than they had been during French involvement in the Thirty Years' War. Not only were such measures more responsive to meeting the needs of warfare over a longer period of time, but in addition Louis XIV was able to sidestep the resistance that Richelieu and Mazarin had faced in response to their measures.

What explains Louis XIV's relative success at using *affaires extraodinaires* to finance his wars, when such methods had been met with resistance and when the sale of offices in particular had failed to keep pace with wartime needs earlier in the century? One possible explanation points to Louis XIV's strategy of 'divide-and-rule'.[18] Rather than attacking members of the elite *en masse* as Richelieu and Mazarin had done, Louis succeeded in playing off of one another groups concerned with protecting their particular privileges. In so doing, he secured their acquiescence in the face of forced loans and other extraordinary measures.

This 'divide-and-rule' strategy was certainly integral to Louis' relative success, but the model is incomplete for two reasons. First, such a 'divide-and-rule' stance implies a strong crown with considerable leverage over an elite lacking its own power bases and initiative. A large body of recent literature has countered such a view and has emphasized instead the limits of absolutist royal power and the need for kings to rule through accommodation with elite interests.[19] While this historiographical trend has tended to overlook the final decades of Louis XIV's

---

[16] Bonney, *King's Debts*, pp. 265-266.

[17] Dessert, *Argent*, p. 167.

[18] About Louis XIV, William Beik writes: 'Once again we see the value of the inherited ideology of inequality and the need for a king who could make it work.' See 'A Social Interpretation of the Reign of Louis XIV,' in Neithard Bulst, Robert Descimon, and Alain Guerreau, eds., *L'État ou le Roi*, (Paris: Éditions de la Maison des sciences de l'homme, 1996), pp. 145-160. See also Richard Lachmann, *Capitalists in Spite of Themselves*, (New York: Oxford University Press, 2000), p. 133; Major, *Renaissance*, p. 344.

[19] I will examine this 'revisionist' historiography in the following section.

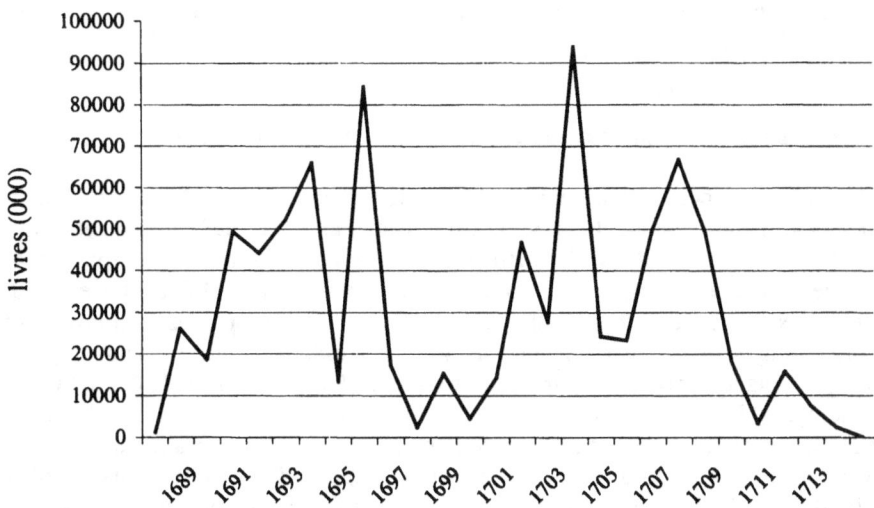

Figure 1.2 *Affaires extraordinaires*

rule when accommodation would have had to survive the push and pull of war-driven financial squeeze, we must nonetheless assume that an *underlying* need for a broad accommodation continued to guide political and financial dealings between the crown and members of the privileged elite. Second, regardless of the degree of leverage that Louis was ultimately able to wield, the kingdom's elite still faced their own personal budget constraints in this time of economic crisis. Market saturation limited the returns from the sale of offices and privileges, just as they did during the Thirty Years' War, and the holders of offices or privileges could only agree to so many unsecured forced loans before the risks and costs of subscribing to them outweighed the benefits of holding onto their positions.[20] 'Divide-and-rule' could not have been a sufficient mechanism on its own to elicit the extraordinary financial support of the kingdom's elite.

There is thus an element missing in our equation to explain Louis' relative success, and it is to be found in the rise of privileged corps as financial intermediaries. By compelling corps to borrow for the King, Louis was able to develop a financial strategy that appealed both to the particularistic desires of the elite to preserve their specific privileged positions and to the underlying need for both the crown and elite groups to adhere to a general accommodation that revolved around mutual interests. Finally, intermediation by privileged corps

---

[20] As I present in Chapter 2, some 'lower' offices were abandoned for this very reason. For the theoretical underpinnings to this constraint on royal power, see R.H. Coase, 'Durability and Monopoly,' *The Journal of Law and Economics*, 15 (1972): 143-149.

Absolutism and Corporate Society in the Seventeenth Century

Old-regime France was a society of privileged corporations.[21] In juridical and financial matters, inequality was the rule of law, as the French crown sat atop an incalculable number of legally distinct groups, or *corps*. Territorial corps included villages, municipalities, and in some cases provinces. Professions were divided into corps as well, and these included guilds, merchant companies, and law courts. Corps enjoyed their own financial as well as juridical identities, and they each enjoyed sets of privileges particular to them. Thus, an individual's privileged standing, which could include exemption from certain taxes, legal rights to have cases heard in specific courts, or ceremonial rights to wear certain status markers or to precede others in public processions, depended in part on his corporate affiliation.[22] Furthermore, corps enjoyed rights of self-governance along with, in many cases, remunerative political prerogatives. Corps, and the rights and privileges attached to them, were thus an important element in that complex matrix that shaped identity in early modern France.

Kings, for their part, were expected to respect and uphold the customary privileges of corps. For this reason, the traditional confirmation of a province's, town's, or a profession's privileges was eagerly awaited following a king's ascension to the throne.[23] Yet at the same time, a corps' privileges were not inviolable, and this became especially clear over the course of the seventeenth century.[24] Privilege was, after all, a 'politically constituted' form of property in old-regime France.[25] In other words, it bound members of the elite to the crown in

---

[21] For more on the corporate society of old-regime France, see François Olivier-Martin, *Organisation corporative de la France d'Ancien Régime*, (Paris: Receuil Sirey, 1938).

[22] One's titled status also determined such privileges, although that titled status itself could depend upon corporate affiliation. The title *'bourgeois de statut'*, for example, depended upon length of residence in a particular town and thus upon affiliation with a territorial corps.

[23] Gail Bossenga, *The Politics of Privilege*, (New York: Cambridge University Press, 1991), pp. 1-21.

[24] For example, Robert Descimon writes that in the seventeenth century, parlementary magistrates began to conceive of their nobility not as inherent in their own dignity, but as a privilege, and thus a creation of the monarchy. See 'The Birth of the Nobility of the Robe: Dignity versus Privilege in the Parlement of Paris, 1500-1700,' in Michael Wolfe, ed., *Changing Identities in Early Modern France*, (Durham: Duke University Press, 1997), pp. 95-123.

[25] Robert Brenner defines 'politically constituted forms of private property' as that property which made possible an extra-economic lordly take from peasant revenues, either directly, as in the case of revenues from seigneuries and lordships, or indirectly in the case of

complex ties of interdependence. Crown and elite strove in common to protect politically constituted forms of property generally while eyeing each other as rivals for the specific income streams extracted through that property. Further, French kings in particular had the authority, unchecked by any competing sovereign body, to create value in privileges and then expect services and support in return for that value.[26] The crown's role as protector of customary privileges thus ran up against its potential to violate those same privileges as it sought an increasing share of the extracted income. Recent research has underscored the practical limits of unilateral action on the part of the King. Kings governed best when they coordinated their interests with those of privileged groups. Still, the King clearly reserved the final say in matters of privilege, and if Louis XIV might have been reluctant to attack the elite *en masse*, he could, through his divide-and-rule strategy, underscore the insecurity of particular privileges.

A tension thus existed within otherwise broad lines of cooperation between crown and elite, and this interplay manifested itself in the political and financial dealings between crown and corps. Members of corps were eager to do what was necessary to preserve their privileged status, even as they came under increasing pressure from a revenue-seeking crown. Under Louis XIV, an accommodation arose whereby corps could stave off attacks against their privileged status by borrowing for the crown and pledging either their property in offices or their crown-granted revenues to guarantee those loans. Holders of venal offices, for example, were well placed to borrow against their privately possessed government offices, passing the capital on to the crown and servicing their debts with increased incomes, or *augmentations de gages*, from those same offices. As David Bien has demonstrated, corps of venal office holders were some of the most important financial intermediaries for the crown. By tapping their potential as intermediaries, the crown gained access to high volume borrowing at relatively low costs. Venal officer corps were better risks as borrowers than the crown and could therefore borrow from the public at lower interest rates. The amount in *gages* that the crown

---

revenues from offices. We could add to the list monopolies and loans to the crown as forms of property that made possible indirect surplus extraction. As a counterexample to the French case, Brenner notes that the English landed elite by the seventeenth century had largely secured an absolute and unconditional hold over their landed estates. They thus secured a source of income independent of the state through the commercial exploitation of their holdings. The English landed classes' political needs were therefore for a unified state that could protect the integrity of private property – not for a state along the lines of the French 'tax/office' system that provided the means of ruling class reproduction through the granting of politically constituted forms of property. See *Merchants and Revolution: Commercial Change, Political Conflict, and London's Overseas Traders, 1550-1653*, (Princeton: Princeton University Press, 1993), pp. 642 and 652.

[26] '...the crown used its political power to create nonseigneurial sources of income, but then it appropriated much of that income for the royal account.' Lachmann, *Capitalists*, p. 123. Hilton Root writes of the bargaining process by which groups sought to gain royal protection of their privileges and property rights. See *The Fountain of Privilege*, (Berkeley and Los Angeles: University of California Press, 1994), pp. 21-57.

paid the corps to cover these payments, then, was less than what the crown would have paid in interest by borrowing directly. Venal office holders, for their part, benefited from the implicit understanding that the crown would not sell redundant offices and would thereby maintain intact the privileges of officers and the value of the investments in their offices. This appears, at least on the surface, to have been a win-win situation for both crown and privileged corps. Lacking in this analysis, however, are the tensions between the crown and office holders that must have been present.

Bien's model, as he posits it, assumes a broad political equilibrium based on mutual assent between crown and corps.[27] Such a view ignores two potential openings for tension and conflict. The first of these arose as the crown leaned on corps to borrow. Bien characterizes much of the extraordinary sums demanded of officers as informal taxation, either to capture the market gains of offices or to tap the wealth of members of the elite otherwise exempt from ordinary direct taxation. In cases where demands exceeded what could be supported by market gains, the debts incurred by office holders to raise the sums demanded of them were presumably covered by the crown in the form of increased *gages* payments. In such cases, though, there was an important transfer of risk as corps, liable to their creditors, depended on the crown to honor its *gages* obligations.[28] Office holders surely did not assume these risks willingly, hence the crown's need to accompany its appeals for capital infusions with threats, either explicit or implicit, to create competing offices or to manipulate privileges.

The second potential opening for conflict arose once the corps actually borrowed money for the crown. In doing so, they took on the role of guarantors of loans, yet they continued to depend on royal good will to be able to service those debts. A royal induced default could thus expose them to the legal actions of their creditors. Office holders had some leverage, though, to defend their positions against such forced defaults. Insofar as they held politically prominent posts, they could use the threat of withdrawing their public services in order to hold the King to his commitments.

---

[27] Indeed, Bien more than once likens the financial intermediation of venal officer corps to English Constitutionalism, implying both that the relationship was mutually beneficial for crown and corps and that it was financially efficient. Such a comparison, though, confuses the *decrease* in risk as the post-1688 English Parliament secured sovereign control over fiscal matters and the *transfer* of risk in the French case to the venal officer corps. See Bien, 'Secrétaires du Roi,' pp. 158-159; idem, 'Offices and State Credit,' p. 108.

[28] Bien admits that the crown's record of honoring its *gages* payments was quite poor, but dismisses the risk transferred to office holders as 'perhaps not excessive' and 'fairly well defined,' referring to the limited liability of the office holder who, having mortgaged his office, remained liable only up to the value of that office and who could divest himself of that responsibility by simply selling the office. Still, offices often represented significant investments with financial, political, and social returns. Office holders wanting to avoid foreclosure thus had to make up from their own reserves any interest payments not covered by the crown, and a delinquent debt attached to an office would certainly have significantly undermined its value. See 'Offices and State Credit,' p. 106.

Neither of these potential points of tension figure prominently in Bien's analysis of intermediation by privileged corps. For the most part, Bien has focused on intermediation by the corps of *secrétaires du roi* in the eighteenth century, and the scope of his studies has shaped his findings. Indeed, from the end of Louis XIV's reign in 1715 to the fall of the Old Regime in 1789, the total capital debt held by venal office holders remained roughly level, so there was no great and sustained pressure placed upon office holders over the course of that century to increase significantly their exposure to the risks of intermediation. Furthermore, as holders of mere sinecures, *secrétaires du roi* were hardly in a position to withhold their services as a means of protecting against royal induced default. Thus, the contours of the relationship between crown and intermediating corps, having evolved within this intersection between tension and broad lines of cooperation, can be best uncovered by incorporating several types of corps into the analysis and by shifting the focus to the period 1689 to 1715 when there was significant expansion of such arrangements.

Indeed, the latter half of Louis XIV's reign was particularly marked by recourse to financial intermediation by privileged corps. Not only officer corps, but practically all privileged corps undertook intermediation for the crown in this period.[29] A rough estimate of total borrowing by privileged corps in the period 1689 to 1715 suggests that such arrangements made up one-third of total war finance. The total debt incurred by the crown in this period through its direct solicitation of loans was 1.537 billion livres.[30] In addition, William Doyle has estimated that venality brought the crown approximately 700 million livres during the final two wars of Louis XIV. Ordinary taxes on office holding, such as mutation fees and payments to guarantee succession rights, account for about 61 million of this sum; the remainder derived from sales of new offices and extraordinary payments demanded of office holders for which they would likely have borrowed. Meanwhile, the four 'largest' provincial estates – Burgundy, Brittany, Languedoc, and Provence – borrowed an estimated 55.4 million livres in extraordinary support for the crown.[31] The net increase in royal debt thus amounted

---

[29] Bien rightly points out that any privileged corps could act as a financial intermediary for the crown, but he never considers the political implication of their financial activities in a comparative light.

[30] Robin Briggs (*Early Modern France*, [New York: Oxford University Press, 1977], p. 220) puts the debt in 1683 at 240 million livres; outstanding debt in 1719, according to one source, was 1.777 billion. See Joel Félix, 'Les Dettes de l'État à la Mort de Louis XIV,' in *Comité pour l'histoire économique et financière de la France: Études et Documents*, 6 (1994): 606-608.

[31] Doyle, *Venality*, (New York: Oxford University Press, 1996), p. 51; Boislisle, *Correspondance*, 1: 583-597 and 2: 583-605. The precise amount borrowed by the Estates of Burgundy was 12,191,030 livres. Marion (*Histoire Financière*, 1: 52-58) offers figures for the total debts held by these four provincial estates in 1789, debts which they had incurred specifically for the purpose of extraordinary support to the crown. I have applied the proportions derived from the 1789 figures to the known figure of borrowing by the Burgundian estates to arrive at my figure for all four between 1689 and 1715. Such

to 2.231 billion livres, of which 28.6 per cent came through the intermediation of venal officer corps and 2.5 per cent from four provincial estates. The assumptions behind the figure for borrowing by venal officer corps creates a slight overestimation;[32] I have not, however, accounted for the financial intermediation of guilds, municipalities, and the financially important Assembly of the Clergy.[33] One-third is thus a conservative estimate of the proportion of extraordinary borrowing attributed to privileged corps.[34] In short, borrowing by privileged corps provided a key source of wartime financial support.

Yet was there anything new with this use of privilege as a means of eliciting financial support in times of need? Renaissance kings had sold offices to finance their wars, and *augmentations de gages* were by no means an innovation of Louis XIV and his ministers. Both Richelieu and Mazarin had made wide use of them as financial measures during the first half of the seventeenth century. The distinction, indeed, lies in that throughout most of the seventeenth century, forced loans were typically financed directly by individual office holders with their own savings, and it was not until the last two wars of the Sun King's reign that corps of venal officers began borrowing collectively on a systematic basis to finance these capital transfers.[35] Likewise, provincial estates had borrowed only on an occasional and ad hoc basis for the crown earlier in the century; now such activity took on a regular and permanent quality. By focusing on the period 1689 to 1715, we are centering on not only the *formative* but the only truly *expansive* period of intermediation by privileged corps.

This rise of privileged corps as intermediaries altered the political balance of the kingdom. Corps had to offer their lenders assurances that their loans were safe. Such assurances required a shift in authority away from the crown to intermediating corps; lacking such a shift, loans to privileged corps would have

---

backward extrapolation, of course, leaves us with only a very rough estimate, but my present interest is merely to suggest the approximate weight of financing through such intermediation.

[32] We can expect most, though not all, of the extraordinary sums paid by office holders to have been borrowed by venal officer corps acting as financial intermediaries. According to Robin's study of the corps of *secrétaires du roi* (*Compagnie*, pp. 108-110), the transition to borrowing through corps, rather than meeting exactions from personal assets, was abrupt and virtually total with the outbreak of war in 1689.

[33] The Assembly of the Clergy, for example, borrowed 5.5 million livres in 1690 to help pay for a 'free gift' to the king of 12 million. See Claude Michaud, *L'Église et l'Argent sous l'Ancien Régime*, (Paris: Fayard, 1991), pp. 345-348.

[34] Bien agrees: 'Together with the rest of the debt resting on privilege, it (the debt represented by offices) was perhaps one-third of the total royal debt.' See 'Property in office under the *ancien régime*: The case of the stockbrokers,' in John Brewer and Susan Staves, eds., *Early Modern Conceptions of Property*, (New York: Routledge, 1996), p. 484.

[35] Philippe Hamon, *'Messieurs des finances': Les grands officiers de finances dans la France de la Renaissance*, (Paris: C.H.E.F.F., 1999), pp. 14-16. According to Pierre Robin (*La Compagnie des Secrétaires du Roi* [Paris: Recueil Sirey, 1933], pp. 109-110), 1689 marks the turning point for secretaries of the king when they ceased funding *augmentations de gages* individually and began borrowing as a corps. See also Doyle, *Venality*, pp. 37-42.

offered no greater guarantee than loans made directly to the King. The turn to intermediation under Louis XIV, therefore, brought about a necessary devolution of power away from the center and actually strengthened the ties of interdependence between crown and elite.

Indeed, the changing political balance brought about by the increased recourse to intermediation by privileged corps accords with recent 'revisionist' trends in scholarship emphasizing the co-optation of elite groups by Louis XIV into cooperative governing relationships. According to scholars such as Albert Hamscher and William Beik, Louis XIV's governing strategy entailed clearly defining and securing the rights and privileges of elite groups.[36] Political change in the latter half of the seventeenth century, the argument goes, entailed the coming of a new era in which members of the elite would 'bask in the sun' of the King by running to his side and assuming collaborative and cooperative roles. Local notables *chose* to cooperate with the crown because Louis XIV made the incentive structure clear – social, economic, and political prosperity lay with personal loyalty to the King.[37] The King's far reaching gaze recognized and rewarded noble concepts of meritorious service and standing.[38] Even as wartime financial pressures in the latter half of Louis' reign threatened to revive conflicts between crown and elite, and even as the potential for conflict inhered within the financial strategy itself, the turn to intermediation by privileged corps preserved the broad lines of this accommodation.

Yet, as our focus on intermediation will demonstrate, how these broad lines of accommodation were preserved contrast with how this recent literature on absolutism would predict. Central to Louis' ability to coopt and govern successfully was his personal command of the patron/client networks that traversed the kingdom. Sharon Kettering, William Beik and J. Russell Major have all emphasized Louis' *personal* rule, implying not just that Louis governed without a First Minister after 1661, but that he managed to center patron/client networks upon himself and *personally* manage them.[39] Clearly, as this body of research has shown, command of clienteles was important to the functioning of government. Yet institutions also shaped Louis' rule in our period of warfare. The shift in power that occurred as a result of financial intermediation by privileged corps was not uniform. Corps differed in their ability to intermediate finances. For reasons explored throughout this work, provincial estates were particularly well suited to borrowing money, guaranteeing their loans, and managing a permanent debt.

---

[36] Beik, *Absolutism*; Albert Hamscher, *The Parlement of Paris after the Fronde, 1653-1673*, (Pittsburgh: University of Pittsburgh Press, 1976). See also Sharon Kettering, *Patrons, Brokers, and Clients in Seventeenth-Century France*, (New York: Oxford University Press, 1986).
[37] Beik, *Absolutism*, pp. 303-339. For an opposing view, see John J. Hurt, *Louis XIV and the Parlements*, (Manchester: Manchester University Press, 2002).
[38] Jay M. Smith, *The Culture of Merit*, (Ann Arbor: University of Michigan Press, 1996), pp. 151-164.
[39] Kettering, *Patrons*; Idem, 'Brokerage'; Beik, *Absolutism*, pp. 223-244; Major, *Renaissance*, pp. 335-366.

Overall, as we will find, the presence of provincial estates affected the politics of finance in many ways, including the extent to which Beik's model of cooperation between crown and elite under Louis XIV held up. Institutions (for which we can take privileged corps as a proxy) and clienteles were thus *both* essential to shaping the options and the outcomes in negotiations between the crown and local elite groups. The present study sets out to redress the balance in our understanding of the old-regime state by reconsidering the role of institutions in the politics of finance.

French Absolutism on the European Stage

We have seen, thus, that the mechanics of intermediation by privileged corps led to a devolution of power within Louis XIV's kingdom, and that the shape and extent of this devolution depended at least partly on institutional variables. In order to proceed from these mechanics to a theory of political change, we need to examine France in comparative terms on the European stage. Borrowing from Marjolein t'Hart, we can identify four major trends in the development of state structures across Europe in the seventeenth century. First, the financial burdens that warfare posed upon states rose dramatically. Secondly, states consolidated both their authority and their capabilities to tax.[40] Thirdly, a stable long-term public debt became an increasingly important means of financing war for the more belligerent states. Finally, the increased reach of revenue-hungry 'states' into 'society' subjected to revision both property rights and rules for participation in statemaking, thereby increasing the chance for domestic conflict.[41]

Numerous works trace these trends as they pertain (or not) to different polities at various stages of development.[42] Here, I seek to explore the interactions between the four trends and how those interactions shaped state development. Two 'traditional' views have dominated the historiography and informed our

---

[40] This second trend refers to the so-called transition from the 'domain state' to the 'tax state.' See Bonney, *Rise*, passim.

[41] As t'Hart clarifies, 'these trends were not exclusive to this age: they had begun in the late Middle Ages and were to continue throughout the last phase of *ancien régime* Europe. Yet they took on a definite shape in the course of the seventeenth century.' See 'The Emergence and Consolidation of the "Tax State". The Seventeenth Century,' in Richard Bonney, ed., *Economic Systems and State Finance*, (Oxford: Oxford University Press, 1995), p. 281.

[42] Richard Bonney, ed., *The Rise of the Fiscal State in Europe c. 1200-1815*, (Oxford: Oxford University Press, 1999); Kersten Kruger, 'Public Finance and Modernisation: The Change from Domain State to Tax State in Hesse in the Sixteenth and Seventeenth Centuries. A Case Study,' in Peter-Christian Witt, ed., *Wealth and Taxation in Central Europe: The History and Sociology of Public Finance*, (New York: Berg, 1987), pp 49-62; P.G.M. Dickson, *The Financial Revolution in England: A Study in the Development of Public Credit, 1688-1756)*, (New York: Macmillan, 1967); James Tracy, *A Financial Revolution in the Habsburg Netherlands*, (Berkeley and Los Angeles: University of California Press, 1985).

understanding of early modern state development. The first view is that the costs of war (trend one) drove the development of the fiscal state (trend 2). The second suggests that a monarch's ability to reach down into society and rewrite property rights and the rules of statemaking (trend 4) adversely affected the chances to develop a stable long-term public debt (trend 3). Taken together, these views suggest that warfare drove the development of modern state structures, but that constitutional regimes in the end proved more capable than their absolutist counterparts in meeting the costs of war by developing institutions of public credit.

The experience of France between 1689 and 1715 calls into question both of these views. First, warfare in early modern Europe did not set the French state on a unidirectional course toward modernization. The 'traditional' argument holds that the pressures of international competition and the increasing costs of raising and provisioning standing armies brought about a strengthening of royal power in certain advantaged monarchies through a process of 'survival of the fittest.' The political history of seventeenth-century France has long been framed in just these terms. Roland Mousnier, for example, argues that it was in response to international conflict that the French crown both increased taxes and strengthened the bureaucratic apparatus needed to collect those revenues. Involvement in the Thirty Years' War in particular led the crown to 'violate provincial and local liberties and privileges in order to find money, and it [the crown] even created a sort of revolutionary administration – staffed by tax farmers, ... supplemented by royal commissioners... and soldiers – which replaced the ordinary officials in the execution of royal power.' Mousnier's view, therefore, is that a cadre of officials working in the name of royal power, committed to the interests of the state, or *raison d'état*, was, in response to the exigencies of war, overriding local traditional bodies of power.[43]

Similarly, historical sociologists, inspired by the works of Max Weber, look toward warfare and international competition as important forces of change in the early modern world. Brian Downing adopts such a view in his exploration into the early modern antecedents of 19th and 20th century regimes. One of the barriers to liberal democracy, he argues, was the rise of what he terms military-bureaucratic absolutism, such as existed in France in the seventeenth century and Prussia in the eighteenth. He defines military-bureaucratic absolutism in part as the overturning of medieval constitutionalism by an increasingly powerful monarchy, a development which entailed stripping representative institutions (estates or diets, for example) of their prerogatives. Echoing Mousnier, Downing argues that in the case of France, such developments came about in the midst of and in response to involvement in the Thirty Years' War. Having entered the war in 1635, he states, French ministers had 'only one alternative to defeat: rapid mobilization of French resources. This, they knew, meant constitutional crisis and political change... New

---

[43] Roland Mousnier, 'The Fronde,' in Robert Forster, ed., *Preconditions of Revolution in Early Modern Europe*, (Baltimore: The Johns Hopkins University Press, 1970), p. 133.

taxes and political institutions came into *direct and fierce conflict* with the parlements, estates, and towns.'[44]

This 'direct and fierce conflict', or what we can think of as a wedge driven between the crown and elite by the pressures of warfare, is central to historical sociologists' understanding of political change. Theda Skocpol, to take another example, focuses her analysis on the intersection between international competition and the potential autonomy of administrative states. In the case of old-regime France, she writes, the 'medieval rubbish' of estates, municipalities, parlements and other corporate bodies stood in the way of the 'efficient functioning of royal absolutism'; state-led efforts at reform thus ran up against 'a socially consolidated dominant class.'[45]

Indeed, for Skocpol, a 'cumbrous collection of institutionalized and politically guaranteed local, provincial, occupational, and estate rights and corporate bodies' both depended on the monarchical regime for their survival and stood in the way of the same regime's search for revenues needed to survive in the dangerous world of the eighteenth century. Here, she differs only in chronology with many of the more traditional historians of seventeenth-century France, like Mousnier, who all too often see the schism between crown and privileged corps as resolved in the crown's favor by the end of that century. For many, this is the very measure of absolutism – could the King dispense with estates, with representative institutions, in governing the kingdom, in setting and raising taxes? J. Russell Major, for one, speaks of a transition from Renaissance monarchy to absolute monarchy in the 17th century where provincial estates no longer resisted the fiscal demands of the crown.[46]

'Revisionist' notions of absolutism, as detailed above, cast doubt upon such views of state development as pitting reform-minded monarchs and their ministers against entrenched privileged interests. Not the least problematic for Skocpol's thesis are the indistinct lines separating old-regime state and society, rendering a regime-ending schism between crown and elite difficult if not impossible.[47]

This present study seeks to take the 'revisionist' argument one step further in an attempt to incorporate an understanding of political change. Much of the recent literature on absolutism stresses the limits of royal authority, implying that royal interests ran up against elite interests and that the crown thus had no choice but to

---

[44] Brian Downing, *The Military Revolution and Political Change*, (Princeton: Princeton University Press, 1992), p. 123. Emphasis added.

[45] Theda Skocpol, *States and Social Revolutions*, (New York: Cambridge University Press, 1979), pp. 64 and 178. Charles Tilly also views international competition as a catalyst for political consolidation of central governments, though the precise shape of the outcome in his case depends on the particular historical context: 'War drove the European network of national states, and preparation for war created the internal structures of states within it...' See *Coercion, Capital and European States, A.D. 900-1992*, (New York: Oxford University Press, 1992), pp. 82-83.

[46] Major, p. 375.

[47] James Collins, *The State in Early Modern France*, (New York: Cambridge University Press, 1995), pp. 46 and 54; Beik, *Absolutism*, pp. 12-17.

back off from designs at reform and governmental rationalization. Again, the implication is that a stable equilibrium between crown and elite set in. Collins, for example, writes:

> Seventeenth-century French society was the scene of a bitter conflict between local elites and the central government for control of the country. There can be little question that the central government never achieved absolutism in any real sense of the term. The main reason for its failure to do so was that it could never raise enough money to pay for all it wanted to do. The king could not tax 'à volonté.' There were limits to how much he could raise, and those limits restricted his ability to extend his power in other ways.[48]

This view of 'absolutism constrained' errs in the same way as do those that emphasize the rise of a military-bureaucratic state, in assuming that the crown was a revenue maximizer and that privileged bodies were revenue minimizers in all instances, and that a breach, or at least the potential for a breach, developed as warfare drove the monarchy to seek revenues. As the following pages will demonstrate, involvement in the wars of Louis XIV did not necessarily promote centralization and a stronger monarchy, insofar as 'strong monarchy' is taken to mean a state that could and would undermine liberties and privileges in order to maximize revenues, or one that would hold off from doing so only in response to political calculations. We would be mistaken to focus solely on that which limited Louis XIV from increasing taxes and rationalizing administration. Rather, his financial strategies set the French polity on a number of divergent paths of development. As mentioned above, intermediation by privileged corps caused power to shift away from the crown. At the same time, initiatives such as the establishment of the *dixième* laid the groundwork for an entirely new relationship between state and citizen/tax payer.[49] The wars of Louis XIV would bequeath to his successors both enhanced bureaucratic powers in certain limited areas and a monumental political shackle in the form of devolved power to privileged corps that acted as guarantors of public debt. Far from driving a wedge between crown and elite, these latter arrangements, initiated and upheld by the crown, enhanced

---

[48] Collins, *Limits*, p. 220. Christopher Storrs frames political developments in the Savoyard state in similar terms. Warfare, he writes, drove Savoyard administrative structures to become 'larger, more specialized and more sophisticated,' but, he cautions, traditional structures constrained such developments from reaching their culmination: 'The Savoyard state was not a "bureaucracy", governed and held together by its central administration, before or by 1713 (or 1720) – although it was more clearly set on that road.' See *War, Diplomacy and the Rise of the Savoy, 1690-1720*, (New York: Cambridge University Press), p. 186.
[49] Kwass, *Privilege*, pp. 47-61. The process was hardly complete, though, at the end of Louis XIV's reign, and in fact, the regency revoked the *dixième* in the face of elite opposition. See Bonney, "Secret", pp. 383-385. Military administration, crucial for the actual execution of warfare, is another of those areas that experienced greater bureaucratization as a result of the pressures of warfare. See Lynn, *Wars*, pp. 17-18.

the power and prestige of elite groups while promoting their economic, social and political interests.

With regard to our second 'traditional' view – that unconstrained absolutism retarded the development of the mechanisms of public debt – the absolutist state in France itself provided the social structural and institutional foundation to develop stable long term funded debts. The privileged corps that proved most capable of intermediating loans to the King were not sovereign representative institutions along the lines of the post-1688 English Parliament, and any political change that ensued from intermediation by privileged corps certainly did not entail a shift toward consitutionalism. Yet, much of the literature on the early modern financial revolutions experienced by the Dutch and the British suggest that there were indeed constitutional preconditions for efficient public borrowing. Douglass North and Barry Weingast argue that regimes had to be constitutionally bound to honor their own commitments and to uphold property rights in order for there to develop sustained economic growth, capital markets and efficient mechanisms of public borrowing. Accordingly, the post-1688 British parliamentary regime, with its built-in checks and balances, was ideal for its credible commitment to upholding property rights. Likewise, James Tracy argues that an essential element of a financial revolution was the creation of a legislature in which the members 'obligate themselves in their collective capacity' to honor its debts, thereby engendering confidence among potential creditors. This was achieved in the decentralized states system of the Habsburg Netherlands in the 1540s when the provincial estates, particularly those of Holland, began to fund long-term debt with specific earmarked revenues. In so doing, they succeeded in lowering the costs of borrowing to around 3 per cent.[50]

Implicit in these arguments is the idea that absolutism was constitutionally incompatible with the conditions necessary for low-cost, long-term, borrowing. Only after parliamentary sovereignty was firmly established in the Glorious Revolution of 1688 was there sufficient 'credible commitment'; likewise the almost total devolution of power to states and towns in the Netherlands in the sixteenth century created the constitutional preconditions for a financial revolution. Conversely, Tracy argues that in sixteenth-century France, the institutions were absent that would have allowed for a financial revolution in that kingdom since the Estates-General no longer took a leading role in setting taxes, and 'parliamentary bodies were thus in no position to act as guarantors of the royal debt.' Without constitutional checks, the argument goes, kings tended to renege on contracts, sell privileges and monopolies, and manipulate property rights. Short-term loans, often coerced, and never realistically guaranteed, were typically chosen over voluntary, long-term, funded debt. Not even a concern for preserving a creditworthy

---

[50] North and Weingast, 'Constitutions,' pp. 803-808; Tracy, *Financial Revolution*, pp. 1-3, 45, and 71-107. John Brewer (*The Sinews of Power*, [New York: Knopf, 1989], pp. 88-91) also writes of the constitutional significance of the Glorious Revolution of 1688, but he adds that the financial revolution that followed would not have been possible without as well effective and competent tax collection by the government bureaucracy.

reputation was sufficient to prevent confiscatory practices in all instances, since the immediate needs of war often pressed statesmen to sacrifice future opportunities for immediate gain.[51]

This study will demonstrate that French finances under Louis XIV were not bound to stark choices between 'standard' absolutist policies and 'innovative' constitutionally distinct arrangements. Through financial intermediation by privileged corps, and in particular through intermediation by provincial estates, certain of the advantages enjoyed by the Dutch and the English developed in France: Voluntary, long-term, funded debt backed by privileged corps made possible reduced rates of borrowing. And yet, while important political shifts set in, there were no fundamental constitutional changes in old-regime France. Indeed, privilege, so anathema to parliamentary ideology, continued explicitly to underpin the whole system of French public finance.[52]

French experiences from 1689 to 1715 thus cast doubt on the two pillars of our 'traditional' understanding of political change in the early modern world. The search for revenues to finance warfare did not translate into revenue maximization at the political center. Rather, a devolution of power within the framework of absolutism laid the conditions for raising the sums needed through intermediation by privileged corps.

While comparison with post-1688 England is one of the most common tropes in the historiography of the French state under Louis XIV and his successors, it is perhaps more useful to compare French developments with those of Prussia. Whereas in France fiscal and financial authority devolved to local bodies during the wars of Louis XIV, in Prussia, negotiations between elector/king and elites produced the opposite result. There, central government solvency (we can speak of 'royal' solvency after 1701) strengthened, along with noble oversight of landed estates, at the expense of peasants and towns. As a result, the Prussian state was able to extract approximately twice as much revenue per capita as the French state, and a greater proportion of those revenues were available to the central government, not having been skimmed off by tax farmers and other middle men. This evolution of fiscal authority toward the center allowed Prussia to make it through the wars of Louis XIV and then those of the eighteenth century without assuming crippling debt charges.[53] Elements of political compromise framed both the Prussian and the French responses to war finance, but the divergent shapes of those compromises, which saw fiscal authority evolving to the Prussian center while financial authority devolved in the French case, underscore the importance of understanding political change in terms specific to each polity's historically conditioned set of relationships between central authorities and elites. This study,

---

[51] North and Weingast, 'Constitutions,' p. 807; Tracy, *Financial Revolution*, p. 21.
[52] For parliamentary ideology with regard to trading and securing privileges, see Root, *Fountain*, pp. 41-52.
[53] Downing, pp. 84-112; Perry Anderson, *Lineages of the Absolutist State*, (London: Verso, 1974), p. 244; C.B.A. Behrens, *Society, Government and the Enlightenment*, (London: Thames and Hudson, 1985), p. 80.

by focusing on the interactions between various provincial elite groups and the monarchy, takes just such an approach to understanding political change in France.

How, then, can we account in these terms for political change in France over the course of the seventeenth and eighteenth centuries? Warfare, to be sure, induced important and lasting transformations in the crown/elite relationships. Generally, the financial conditions of the French monarchy underwent war-driven cycles in which times of war, financial crisis and a turn toward the elite for financial support alternated with times of relative peace, financial ease and a lessening of pressure on the elite.[54] But beyond these war-driven financial cycles, the strategies chosen by the crown to secure elite support in times of financial need and the responses of elite groups to the crown's demands had lasting political effects that conditioned those very relationships into the future.

In short, I argue that kings operated on a learning curve, and, judging from their strategies, they desired to avoid the political costs that their predecessors faced as they attempted to finance war. The political/financial crisis of the 1630s and 1640s that provoked uprisings and, ultimately, civil war thus conditioned the crown/elite relationship into the first decades of Louis XIV's personal reign. Having experienced first hand the extent of opposition and the collapse of royal authority from 1648 through 1653, Louis XIV ushered in an entirely new strategy upon assuming personal rule in 1661 that effectively avoided a return to the costly politics of contention.[55] These political changes did not merely reflect the improved financial conditions brought about by Colbert's effective management of revenues. Even with the outbreak of war in 1689, Louis XIV avoided a frontal assault on property and privilege similar to that conducted by Richelieu and Mazarin. The long-term result of Louis' strategies, as the following chapters demonstrate, was an increased dependence on privileged corps for their financial services and a deeper entrenchment of privilege on the French political landscape. These arrangements, then, would have their own set of costs and consequences that conditioned the choices available to Louis' successors in the eighteenth century.

The period 1689 to 1715 thus formed a pivotal stage in the development of absolutism. In examining this period, this study will tie the choices available to Louis XIV with the structures and institutions that he inherited from his predecessors, while setting his approach apart from that of Richelieu and Mazarin. In doing so, this book argues that absolutism under Louis XIV was neither ossified nor in crisis, but rather dynamic and flexible, and that the participation of

---

[54] Richard Bonney (*The King's Debts*, p. 280) offers such a cyclical view of political change: 'It is significant that the periods of reform occurred in the first and sixth decades of the seventeenth century, when France enjoyed relative peace.'

[55] Indeed, Louis XIV's style of learning emphasized those lessons that could be drawn from practical experience, and one of his most formative experiences was the Fronde of his early childhood. These 'terrible disorders throughout the kingdom' are mentioned prominently in the opening passages of his *Mémoires for the Instruction of the Dauphin* (p. 23), and John Wolf has likewise emphasized the centrality of this experience in Louis' formation. See Wolf, *Louis XIV*, (New York: Norton, 1968), p. 75.

privileged corps as financial intermediaries made possible the accommodation between heightened royal needs and continued protection of elite interests.

The Early Modern Elite

Before examining how the relationship between the crown and the kingdom's elite evolved over this period, it is first necessary to identify this group in the early modern context. By its very nature, though, the old-regime elite is not easily identifiable as a coherent social group. While some core values and attitudes and some common interests were shared by much of the elite, lines of division and competition produced at the same time a striking heterogeneity.[56]

Whereas a variety of attributes served to determine elite status, for our purposes it is useful to define the elite simply as the politically powerful. The elite enjoyed a standing that conferred either a degree of political participation on a kingdom-wide level or power and status on the local level. Such power and status could derive from an array of factors including wealth, profession, patron-client ties, titled status and dignity. Symbols and lifestyle, the outward displays of noble status, were at least as important to maintaining one's position within the elite as were such material considerations as inheritances and financial solvency. Not all nobles and not all officials, however, held a meaningful degree of influence over matters of state finance and politics. In order to concentrate on those who did, this study limits its focus mainly to those members of the elite whose presence in privileged corps (estates, judicial courts, town councils, etc.) or whose activity handling public funds, placed them in positions of frequent financial negotiation with the crown.

A common socio-economic foundation underpinned the elite. This group of the 'politically powerful' lived either directly (from rents, tithes or seigneurial dues), or indirectly (from the incomes of offices and royal pensions), from the produce of the peasantry.[57] One exception belongs to merchants who constituted a significant portion of the elite in some provinces and whose wealth was mostly generated from commercial activity. Even merchants, however, invested much of their wealth in land or in politically constituted forms of property, and they were well enmeshed in the world of crown-conferred privileges.

Yet it would be a mistake to overemphasize elite cohesion. Beyond the common socio-economic underpinnings, vertical lines of competition traversed a largely heterogeneous elite. Degrees of dignity and lifestyle, the extent to which

---

[56] Jonathan Dewald discusses the internal contradictions of the nobility as a group characterized by shared interests and values on the one hand and competition and divisions on the other. See *The European Nobility, 1400-1800*, (New York: Cambridge University Press, 1996), p. 114. Beik takes a similar approach to describing the seventeenth-century French elite. See *Urban Protest*, pp. 18-22.

[57] Denis Richet, *La France moderne: l'esprit des institutions*, (Paris: Flammarion, 1973), p. 102; Beik, 'Social Interpretation,' pp. 148-149.

one lived nobly, set groups within the elite apart from one another. Symbols and outward displays of status preserved distinctions both between and within orders.[58] Corporate affiliation also acted as a divisive force. Magistrates, merchants and municipal leaders, among others, identified with their corps, and contests ensued between these legally distinct groups over matters of jurisdiction or status. Likewise, interests within corps might divide those occupying different levels of authority and status.[59]

Finally, differences existed over how members of the elite supported themselves, where their interests lay and what their positions were regarding royal financial and fiscal policies. Most of the wealth of the elite was invested in land or in seigneurial rights and in such politically constituted forms of property as offices, royal pensions or royal bonds (*rentes*). Landed revenues clearly formed a primary source of wealth for much of the elite, though more so in some provinces, especially those with a historically strong lordly hold over the land, than others. The importance of land-holding for maintaining elite standing surely translated into an interest on the part of the elite to keep land taxes (that is, taxes on their tenants) to a minimum. Yet in other cases, and again differences existed from region to region, elite groups, particularly merchants, had a greater interest in keeping indirect taxes (that is, taxes on commercial activities) to a minimum. Also, members of the elite who held property in venal offices or who advanced money to the crown held an interest in protecting the specific revenues that funded their incomes. Where different privileged corps identified with the specific taxes on which they depended, rivalries could transform into conflicts over tax policy. In pre-Fronde Languedoc, for example, the Parlement of Toulouse promoted its own political prominence by accusing the estates of not sufficiently protecting the province's *taillables* against heavy burdens. The estates, on the other hand, enhanced their own image by rallying the public against indirect taxes which, not coincidentally, funded the parlementaires' *gages*.[60] Distinct propertied and privileged positions within the elite thus created complex allegiances and divisions regarding royal finances.

Its very heterogeneity suggests that the elite could not act as a monolith in its financial and political dealings with the crown. Divisions ran through the elite along lines of privilege and economic interests, setting distinct corporations and orders off from one another. As I present in the following chapters, these lines of

---

[58] Robert Darnton offers a useful description of social distinction between and within orders from the perspective of an eighteenth-century bourgeois. See 'A Bourgeois Puts His World in Order,' in *The Great Cat Massacre and Other Episodes in French Cultural History*, (New York: Vintage, 1984), pp. 107-143. The elite of the seventeenth century were equally interested in preserving distinctions among themselves during processions, assemblies and other public forums. See Dewald, *European Nobility*, p. 114.

[59] James Farr examines such privileged distinctions within artisan communities and the extent to which such distinctions precluded cohesive action in defense of common interests. See *Hands of Honor: Artisans and Their World in Dijon, 1550-1650*, (Ithaca: Cornell University Press, 1985).

[60] Beik, *Absolutism and Society*, pp. 159-178.

division made possible Louis XIV's strategy to use privilege and access to resources as bargaining chips for financial support. Yet the relationship was not one of clear royal dominance over the elite. This study identifies spaces within the body politic where coalitions could form to protect underlying socio-economic and political interests. With varying degrees of success, segments of the elite were able to form cohesive political blocs under Louis XIV to promote their own interests in relation both to the crown and to the non-elite. Again, though, differences abounded. As I demonstrate in the following chapters, how elite groups were able to organize and which groups in particular were able to most successfully promote their interests depended in large part on both the historically determined privileged status of the province and on the provincial institutions around which the local elite could coalesce and promote their interests.

Crown and Elite in Burgundy and Normandy

A comparative study spanning the elite groups of distinct provinces is thus ideal for understanding the impact of elite heterogeneity on political developments. The scope of this work allows for such a comparative examination. Specifically, I focus on the financial relationships between the crown and members of the provincial elite in Burgundy and Upper Normandy. In both regions, a venal office-holding elite was prominent. Both Dijon in Burgundy and Rouen in Upper Normandy were home to several law courts, including in each case both a parlement and a chamber of accounts. In terms of the centrality of venal office holding in shaping the local elite, only two other provinces surpassed either Burgundy or Normandy.[61]

But important differences also separated Burgundy from Upper Normandy in their financial relations with the crown. Rouen was an important port city, and in addition to the traditional elite groups – the landed nobility, the clergy and the office-holding robe nobility, a commercial elite dominated parts of the political landscape in Upper Normandy. Commercial interests were not as prevalent in Burgundy where robe and sword nobilities, both with strong ties to the land, dominated local power structures. In addition, these two regions had, by Louis XIV's personal reign, distinct institutional relations with the crown in financial matters. Burgundy was a *pays d'États*. By royally conferred privilege, an assembly called the Estates of Burgundy met every three years in Dijon to negotiate the province's tax levels. The estates were then responsible for apportioning the tax burden, collecting the taxes and transferring the payments to the crown. There was thus an important degree of financial autonomy at the regional level in Burgundy, and the estates played an important role in shaping the financial ties between the

---

[61] Only in Brittany and Languedoc might venal office holders have been more important in shaping the local elite groups.

crown and the Burgundian elite.[62] Normandy, on the other hand, lost its estates around the middle of the seventeenth century following on the heels of the Nu-Pieds uprising of 1639, though it is true that they were already well on their way to obsolescence prior to that revolt.[63] By the time Louis XIV began his personal rule, the last meeting of the estates had come and gone (1655), and Normandy was for all intents and purposes a *pays d'élection* taxed directly by the crown. As a result, not only was the crown free of formal constraints in setting tax levels for Normandy, the potential for local autonomy in financial matters had greatly diminished.

To begin this investigation, I focus in Chapter Two on the property rights of office holding and on the negotiations between the crown and venal officers over the heritability of offices. Since the power vested in venal offices was an extension of royal power, the King retained the legal prerogative to alter such crucial rights as that which allowed holders to bequeath offices to their heirs. Nonetheless, as offices became an important source of extraordinary financial support for the crown, the property rights of office holders became more firmly established in a *de facto* manner. While the crown continued to conduct the regular negotiations over extending the heritability of offices, the outcome of the negotiations came to be predictable, and the property rights over offices became increasingly transparent and stable. As a result, offices also became mortgageable, and Louis XIV could place greater pressure on office holding notables to borrow for the crown.

This pressure brought upon office holders to mortgage their property for the crown suggests that despite the *de facto* strengthening of their property rights, office holders were not free of all royal encroachment on their interests. Indeed, not only office holders, but the privileged elite in general continued to depend on royal good will to uphold the value of their privileges. As war broke out in 1688, Louis XIV began to balance the long-term necessity of protecting the property, privileges and status of his politically endowed supporters with a strategy of using privilege as a bargaining chip to solicit the financial support of the elite. The result was ever-closer financial ties between the crown and the elite groups as privileged corporations of all types acted as financial intermediaries for the crown. Chapter Three focuses on the ongoing negotiations between Burgundian corporations and the crown, focusing particularly on the estates. As a privilege conferred on the province and thus shared among Burgundians, the estates stood apart from venal officer corps in which members privately possessed their privileged positions. The estates provided an ideal arena for coalition building among the province's elite, and they thus played an important role in shaping the financial and political relationships between the crown and the province.

Chapter Four addresses the evolving relationship between Norman elite groups and the crown. Where estates no longer provided a forum in which

---

[62] The definitive study of the Estates of Burgundy is sure to be Julian Swann's forthcoming *Provincial Power and Absolute Monarchy: The Estates General of Burgundy, 1661-1790*, (Cambridge: Cambridge University Press, 2003).
[63] Bonney, *Political Change*, pp. 354-360; Foisil, *Nu-Pieds*.

members of the province's elite could coalesce to negotiate with the crown, Louis XIV was better able to follow a divide-and-rule strategy by which venal officer corps or merchant groups found themselves singled out and pressured to protect their privileges and prerogatives. As a result, there developed such arrangements whereby merchant groups controlled (and borrowed against) indirect tax revenues levied on their own commercial activity. As Louis would find, however, these 'smaller' local corps did not have the organizational capability and reputation necessary to attract lenders with the success that provincial estates had.

Chapters Five and Six then focus on the different institutions and clienteles on which Louis leaned to provide financial support, and they further examine how specific institutions and networks of personal relationships shaped the elite's responses to the crown's demands. The Estates of Burgundy made possible a greater degree of local financial autonomy and opened opportunities for members of the Burgundian elite to profit from the management of revenues. Such opportunities no longer existed in Normandy where outsiders, for the most part Parisians, organized and benefited from much of the tax collection and many of the extraordinary affairs. The Estates of Burgundy also borrowed from a much wider clientele of creditors than did most other corporations, suggesting again a greater degree of financial autonomy and political independence accorded to Burgundians by this institution. Finally, by way of conclusion, I examine both the short-term developments of the crown/elite relationship in the years following Louis XIV's death and some of the longer-term political effects of Louis' financial strategies and the implications for royal finances through the remainder of the Old Regime. French absolutism, like the state systems of France's rivals, saw its developmental path change as a result of involvement in warfare during the period 1689 to 1715. Yet France did not follow a pre-ordained path common to the European experience or even to an absolutist experience. Rather, France followed a path specific to her historical circumstances, paved by previous forays into warfare and bounded by the specific institutional landscape of the kingdom.

Chapter 2

Venality Entrenched: The Property Rights of Office Holding Under Louis XIV*

Historians of early modern France have long recognized a connection between warfare and the venality of offices, or the practice of raising revenues by creating public offices for sale to private individuals. Periods of long lasting and costly war, such as during the reigns of Francis I and Louis XIV, brought remarkable expansion to the venal office system. Such periods of expansion were then typically followed by efforts to rein in venality. On close inspection, however, the precise correlation between warfare and venality is not so clear. A number of options existed for a sovereign power that did not recognize legal constraints on its authority. Kings and their ministers might just as well have used warfare as an occasion to attack venality, and in addition to adjusting the *scope* of venality to respond to wartime needs, kings could manipulate the *shape* of venality, or the property rights of venal office holding. On the other hand, extra-legal constraints, both structural and historical, acted to restrict options. The nature of venal offices themselves and the political costs borne from previous wartime attempts to rewrite the rules of venality together weighed upon kings' approaches to venality and war finance.

This confrontation between options and constraints drew its complexity in part from the multi-dimensional nature of offices as a form of property. First and foremost, offices served as financial instruments that were particularly attractive to a crown saddled by limited abilities to tax. In exchange for a principal sum paid to the crown, one could acquire a newly created office along with the various incomes accruing to that office. Similar to the royal debt held in perpetual bonds, or *rentes*, the sums raised by selling offices did not constitute term debt for the crown. The lenders (office holders) could not demand repayment of the principal originally lent; instead the crown reserved the prerogative to reimburse principal sums owed to office holders and buy back their offices at its discretion. Also like bonds, offices and the incomes accruing to them could be traded on a secondary market,

---

* A slightly different version of this chapter has appeared as War Finance and Absolutist State Development in Early Modern Europe: An Examination of French Venality in the Seventeenth Century, *Journal of Early Modern History*, 7 (2003).

though only to qualified individuals, and over the course of the sixteenth and seventeenth centuries holders attained the rights to bequeath offices to their heirs.

The holder of an office received a set of various revenues and privileges that were specific to the office's functions and social standing. Holders of the most politically prominent and financially valuable offices received an annual payment from the crown called *gages*. *Gages* served as the interest payment made by the crown against the capital value of the office. Rates varied from office to office, and they tended to move with the legal interest rates for *rentes*. The *gages* paid to *secrétaires du roi*, for example, amounted to about ten per cent of principal in 1672, but only about two per cent by the 1720s.[1] In addition, office holders collected revenues from the exercise of their functions. For holders of judicial posts, these came in the form of *épices*, or fees that litigants had to pay courts at the conclusion of their lawsuits. Financial officials retained a portion of the funds that they handled, and many administrative officials collected surtaxes related to their functions. The returns on office holding were not merely financial, however. Offices conferred upon their holders status, and they offered the benefit of numerous privileges and fiscal exemptions. Many office holders, especially in the judiciary, gained exemption from the *taille*, the principal land tax in the Kingdom, though it is true that many were already free of that obligation by virtue of their privileged standing prior to their purchase. Venality also represented an important avenue to achieving noble status, with hereditary nobility often coming in the third generation of office holding.[2]

Offices were thus much more than financial instruments. They were also a form of feudal property, and as such the development of the venal office system had important political as well as financial implications. Two distinct, though interrelated, qualities lent offices their 'feudal' aspect. First, they were characterized by overlapping and competing claims.[3] Like fiefs, venal offices embodied the private possession of public power, the source of which was the King. Office holders thus laid claims to public power that overlapped with the King's rights. Secondly, as a politically constituted form of property, offices bound their holders to the grantee (the King) in important ways, enhancing holders' stakes

---

[1] Bien, '*Secrétaires*', pp. 153-168.
[2] Mousnier, *La Vénalité des offices sous Henry IV et Louis XIII*, (Paris: Presses Universitaires de France, 1971), pp. 455-465; Doyle, *Venality*, pp. 11-13; John J. Hurt, 'Les Offices au Parlement de Bretagne sous le régne de Louis XIV: aspects financiers,' *Revue d'histoire moderne et contemporaine*, 23 (1976): 3-31.
[3] Robert Gordon contrasts what I am calling feudal property rights with rights of absolute dominion. He describes the former as 'property rights fragmented and split among many holders...; property relations of dependence and subordination; property subject to arbitrary and discretionary direction or destruction...; property surrounded by restrictions on use and alienation; property qualified and regulated for communal or state purposes; property destabilized by fluctuating and conflicting regimes of legal regulation.' Each of these descriptions applies to venal offices. See Gordon, 'Paradoxical Property,' in Brewer and Staves, eds., *Early Modern Conceptions*, p. 96.

in the regime. From its first use of venality as a financial tool, the crown also used offices as political instruments for securing alliances and extending networks of personal servitors.[4] Yet the ensuing political relationships did not simply subordinate office holders to positions of dependence on and loyalty to the crown.

Venal office holders possessed, through a complicated legal construction, the very political power that was deemed royal. Their interests thus lay in preserving their hold on that authority and in ensuring that their positions brought lucrative returns. In times of heightened royal need, such an overlap could lead to conflict over financial and political questions, with magistrates and financial officials more concerned with protecting their privileges and property than with enforcing royal positions damaging to their or their constituents' interests. Or, such an overlap might conversely highlight the convergence of interests between the crown and the venal office holding elite, interests dictated by the politically constituted nature of the very property on which the elite depended for much of its political and financial standing. France witnessed just such a period of heightened royal need alternating with relatively flush royal accounts in the seventeenth century. The evolution of the property rights of office holding over the course of this century thus offers a useful barometer of this political spectrum that runs from conflict to cooperation.

Two periods have been undeniably influential in informing our understanding of the political history of France in the seventeenth century. The first of these is the period that surrounds France's involvement in the Thirty Years' War during the ministries of Richelieu and Mazarin. The second comprises the first decades of Louis XIV's personal reign, roughly 1661-1680, when Colbert's influence shaped far-reaching policy initiatives. The lessons drawn from these periods regarding venal offices in particular are that 1) warfare in the first half of the century forced a rift between crown and venal office holding elite and 2) the crown followed up on this rift with peacetime reform attempts to diminish the scope and weaken the strength of venality.[5] The historiographical tendency to draw broad conclusions from these two periods leaves untouched important changes that followed Colbert's ministry. There is a strong tendency indeed to view the financial measures taken in 1689 as simply a return to those that the crown adopted during the Thirty Years' War. Such views ignore what amounts to a turning point in negotiations between the crown and office holders.[6]

As the 1688 outbreak of war drew near, rather than simply undermining the interests of venal office holders, Louis XIV followed a dual-edged approach, securing their property rights while squeezing financial support from them. This combination of measures, which contrasted with established practice up to then,

---

[4] Mousnier, *Vénalité*, pp. 85, 117-124; Doyle, *Venality*, pp. 9-10.
[5] Doyle, *Venality*, pp. 11-13 and 19-20.
[6] Doyle (*Venality*, p. 27) writes: 'Those (financial measures) of France, at war more years than not since 1635, were better tried and tested than those of her enemies, and they came smoothly into action as soon as the fighting began (in 1688). Among the most reliable was the sale and manipulation of offices.'

came about not *despite* the coming of war, but *because* of the financial push and pull of warfare. In other words, the broad political accommodation laid out by Louis XIV beginning in the 1660s survived by certain measures the financial pressures of warfare. Indeed, Louis' wartime strategies strengthened particular elements of that accommodation, as the crown and elite groups settled upon intermediation by privileged corps as a means of financing war. Intermediation by corps of venal office holders in turn necessitated the strengthening of property rights in venality.[7] But before examining these important shifts under Louis XIV, we need first to survey the property rights of office holding as they evolved over several centuries.

The Evolving Property Rights of Office Holding

In 1786, a time at which 'venality seemed as fixed as ever into the nature of things,' a team of jurists led by the magistrate Pierre Jean Jacques Guillaume Guyot wrote what they hoped would become the definitive guide to the laws concerning royal offices.[8] The authors of this treatise defined venality of offices as the system by which the King conferred upon individuals 'the ability to sell, to give, to exchange and to transmit to heirs' their offices.[9] This conception of the venal office system in which the aspect of heritability constitutes an essential element is particular to the historical context in which Guyot et al. formulated it. The term venality in its most generic sense simply implies an exchange for money. According to this rather broad meaning, venality existed as early as the thirteenth century when the crown typically leased or farmed to private individuals lower judicial offices or offices attached to the royal domain.[10] This initial delegation of public power in exchange for money did not create property in offices, however, as the King could alter the terms of leases or revoke offices upon expiration of their leases. Guyot's eighteenth-century definition, on the other hand, implies much stronger property rights, with offices entering into families' patrimonies from where they then passed from generation to generation. Indeed, three distinct qualities combined to constitute the property rights of venal office holding as Guyot described them toward the end of the eighteenth century – the simple exchange of the public function for money, the life tenure, or *inamovibilité*, of the holder, and the heritability of the office. The development of these 'rights', which, as I will demonstrate below, remained legally tenuous by virtue of the feudal nature of

---

[7] Doyle recognizes the novelty of the crown drawing on the collective credit of venal officer corps beginning in 1689, but does not draw the connection to strengthened property rights. See *Venality*, p. 37.

[8] Ibid, p. 267.

[9] Pierre Jean Jacques Guillaume Guyot, ed., *Traité des droits, fonctions, franchises, exemptions, prérogatives et privileges annexés en France...*, 4 vols., (1786-87), 3: 22.

[10] Paul Louis-Lucas, *Étude sur la vénalité des charges et fonctions publiques*, 2 vols., (Paris, 1882), 2: 15-21.

offices, paralleled changes in monarchical power and in the financial strategies of the crown toward members of the kingdom's elite.

The first widespread use of offices as financial tools came in the fifteenth century. By the end of the seventeenth century, the expansion of the venal office system, in terms of both numbers of offices created and the status of their property rights, was largely complete. Yet the growth and development of the venal office system over these more than two centuries was not at all linear. Continuity of policy from one reign to the next was rare, and any strengthening of the venal office system faced strong opposition from different elite groups until well into the seventeenth century. After Charles VII declared himself formally opposed to venal offices in 1450 and embarked on a campaign to reduce their scope, his son Louis XI reversed that stance and found in offices a convenient source of revenue. His successors, Charles VIII and Louis XII, then tried to diminish the extent of venality until the wars in Italy led Louis XII to sell the first financial offices. He again reversed his own stance and revoked venality in 1508. Once more, under financial pressure, Francis I increased the scope of venality by creating offices in all areas of royal justice and financial administration. This expansion found institutional support with the creation of the *bureau des parties casuelles* in 1522, a new branch of royal government devoted to administering the creation and sale of all royal offices not connected to the royal domains.[11]

By the sixteenth century, therefore, the short-term benefits to the crown of using offices as financial instruments, especially in wartime, won out over long-term political concerns regarding the alienation of public power. This would remain the overall trend through the end of Louis XIV's reign in 1715. Lacking complete fiscal sovereignty even during the most absolute of reigns and faced with the high costs of borrowing due to its poor credit reputation, the French crown in the sixteenth and seventeenth centuries saw in the creation of offices a reliable financial expedient.

Changes in the legal status of offices accompanied this quantitative expansion. The notion of life tenure for venal office holders developed over the fourteenth and fifteenth centuries and was guaranteed by an ordinance of October 1467, which Louis XI issued in conjunction with his expansion of venality. Meant to ensure potential investors against the possibility of arbitrary confiscation, this ordinance confirmed the principle that as long as an office existed, its holder could not be deprived of it except by death, resignation, or forfeiture.[12] By the time Louis XIV reconfirmed this ordinance in a declaration of October 1648, life tenure was firmly established and applied to all offices of the *parties casuelles*.[13]

---

[11] Ibid, 2: 15-21. Offices considered part of the royal domain remained under a separate legal status. These included, among others, *greffiers*, notaries and keepers of the seal of royal courts.

[12] Ibid, 2: 15-21; Guyot, *Traité*, 4: 7; Doyle, *Venality*, p. 3. Life tenure, or irremovability, did not, of course, restrict the crown's option of abolishing offices altogether by reimbursing holders their principal.

[13] Guyot, *Traité*, 4: 7.

The granting of life tenure still did not round out the patrimonial possession of offices. Only with the development of succession rights did offices fully enter into the patrimonies of their holders. The trend toward heritability advanced in a piecemeal fashion, most notably during the last decades of the sixteenth century, as rights of succession were sold and attached to particular offices. Such was the case, for example, when an edict of 1572 attached the privilege of succession to the offices of *secrétaires du roi*.[14]

This piecemeal expansion of succession rights culminated uniformly with the establishment of the *paulette* in 1604. Prior to 1604, individuals who held offices of the *parties casuelles* without rights of succession could resign from their offices in favor of a specified third party. For the transfer to be valid, however, the Forty Days Clause required that the resigner live forty days beyond the date when his designated successor received his letters of provision from the office of the Chancellery. Offices whose holders died before resigning or within forty days after effecting the transfer reverted back to the *parties casuelles* where they were considered vacant and available to the crown to resell. The *paulette* offered exemption from the Forty Days Clause to office holders who made an annual payment, the *droit annuel*, equal to one-sixtieth the value of their offices as set by the crown.[15] By refining succession rights in these terms, the crown chose to give up the irregular proceeds of selling vacant offices in exchange for the regular revenues of the *droit annuel*.[16]

The *paulette*, along with the access to the heritability of offices that it conferred, experienced a rough start in the decades after 1604. Despite the overall increase in revenues to the *parties casuelles*, the first three leases for the rights to collect the *droit annuel* ended in net losses for the tax farmers (Paulet, 1604-1606; Saulnier 1606-1612 and Marcel 1612-1618), as they consistently underestimated the extent to which the widely embraced *paulette* would alter the structure of revenues accruing to the crown from offices.[17] More endangering still to these tenuous succession rights, political opposition to the *paulette* surfaced prominently in the Estates General of 1614 and at the Assembly of Notables at Rouen in 1617. This stance was in large part an extension of the opposition to venality in general that had been brewing especially among the nobility and the clergy in the sixteenth century.[18] In the Estates General of 1560, 1576 and 1588, the first two orders had demanded the suppression of venality, especially among higher judicial offices.

---

[14] Mousnier, *Vénalité*, p. 226; Louis-Lucas, 2: 100.
[15] Mousnier, *Vénalité*, pp. 221-226. Again, offices of the royal domain fell under a different legal status. Following the Ordinance of the Domain in 1566, the crown sold these offices with heritability privileges attached, reserving for itself the perpetual option of buying them back. See Louis-Lucas, 2: 80-82.
[16] The establishment of the *paulette* also coincided with a royal bankruptcy and may have been designed as a trade-off to appease disgruntled office holders who were in large measure also holders of royal debt.
[17] Mousnier, *Vénalité*, pp. 267-270.
[18] Smith, *Culture*, pp. 11-18.

They saw in venality the creation of a competing, and base, elite, and they wished instead to restrict these highest offices to themselves. Adding to this opposition to venality in general, the establishment of succession rights in 1604 raised sharp objections from those who felt themselves potentially cut off from access to the highest offices, since those posts might thereafter remain indefinitely in the same families. Lawyers, procurators and notaries, among others, perceived the *paulette* as hindering their chances to attain higher offices.[19] Under this increased pressure, the crown revoked the *droit annuel* and reimposed the Forty Days Clause in 1618. Two and a half years later, this time under political pressure from sovereign courts (staffed largely by venal office holders who benefited from the *paulette*) and under financial pressure, the crown reestablished the *paulette* for a nine year term and thereafter renewed it every nine years, with one exception, until 1709.[20] By the early seventeenth century, therefore, despite recurrent opposition to the private possession of offices and despite numerous policy reversals by the crown, the three elements were in place which provided the legal basis for Guyot's conception of the venality of offices: the contractual exchange of money for public office, life tenure, and heritability.

Yet, though the legal foundations for patrimonial possession were set by the seventeenth century, offices retained their underlying feudal characteristics. At no point did the crown surrender its claims on offices. The King reserved the discretion to abolish offices at any time by reimbursing their holders on his own terms. And since the monarchy was the original source of the public functions embodied in offices, the King held the right to intervene in their transmissions or, more broadly, to rewrite the property rights of office holding. Louis XIV, for example, desired to weaken the influence of entrenched dynasties within law courts, and so he undertook measures in the 1660s to regulate family relations within courts by enforcing age requirements for judges, prohibiting magistrates from marrying the daughters of their colleagues, and prohibiting judges from entering a court where a family member already held an office. Almost as quickly as the crown enunciated these principles it granted dispensations at its discretion.[21] Still, such moves are indicative of the crown's prerogatives to redraw the property rights of office holding, with the prerogative to intervene especially strong at the moment of an office's transmission.

Offices thus never came to be characterized by rights of absolute dominion. As legal constructions, they continued to mirror the conditional possession of and competing claims to real property that remained throughout the Old Regime as a legacy of feudal property division. Relative to landed property, though, the

---

[19] Mousnier, *Vénalité*, pp. 86-87, 275. Indeed, the fears of lawyers, procurators and notaries were justified as families imposed a virtual dynastic hold over the most prominent magistracies over the course of the seventeenth century. See Jonathan Dewald, *The Formation of a Provincial Nobility*, (Princeton: Princeton University Press, 1980), p. 80; and Hamscher, *Parlement*, pp. 3-31.

[20] Mousnier, *Vénalité*, pp. 275-282.

[21] Hamscher, *Parlement*, pp. 25-29 and 190-195.

competing claims to offices were transparent. For each office, it was clear that there were only two claimants, the King and the holder, with precedence always reserved to the King. According to the legal historian Paul Louis-Lucas, this conflict was resolved in the old-regime legal culture by distinguishing between the 'right to the office' held by the office's possessor and the 'right in the office' which only the King, the sovereign creator of offices, held.[22] This distinction between competing rights in and to offices reflects the two distinct elements which together constituted the office: the *titre*, which embodied the extension of royal power granted at the King's will, and the *finance*, the element traded on the market and exchanged against money.[23] When an 'office' was exchanged or inherited, the *finance* passed directly from one holder to the next. The *titre*, however, always returned to the King who then re-granted it by issuing letters of provision to its new grantee.

The language by which the crown drafted letters of provision reflected this duality of property rights. Because the letters granted only *titres*, they never made mention of the price paid for the offices. The language of the letters kept the actual venality of the transaction at a distance from the King's act of delegating public powers. Furthermore, the letters explicitly clarified the King's role in what otherwise would appear as contractual exchanges between private individuals or simple inheritances of family patrimonies. For example, the letters of provision granted to Thomas le Fournier d'Offrenville for the office of treasurer general of finances in Rouen held by his father who had died in office presents in the first person the King's role in granting the office's *titre* to the heir: '...for the full and entire trust that we have in the person of our well beloved Thomas le Fournier sieur d'Offrenville... we have granted and bestowed, grant and bestow, to him by these letters the office of our *conseiller trésorier de France et général de nos finances* in the *généralité* of Rouen...'[24] Similar wording exists in letters granted to those who purchased offices on the secondary market. Thus, in the official language, individuals 'resign[ed] offices in favor of' a second party rather than simply sell them. This distinction preserved the King's role as originator of the power granted in usufruct.

With such prerogatives, the King's rights 'in offices' translated into virtually absolute rights to intervene in their transfers. To possess an office was to do so at the pleasure of the King, despite the money exchanged for that possession and despite the evolution of property rights that culminated with the establishment of heritability. The patrimonial elements that developed over the course of centuries had no independent legal force when confronted with the dual nature of the office and the King's role as grantor of *titres*. Faced with this reality that 'no grantee of a

---

[22] Louis-Lucas borrows this particular formula for distinguishing between the King's rights and the holder's rights from the old-regime jurist Charles Loyseau. See *Étude*, 2: 115-116. Ralph E. Giesey emphasizes this distinction in his article 'Rules of Inheritance and Strategies of Mobility in Prerevolutionary France,' *American Historical Review* 82 (April 1977): 283.
[23] Louis-Lucas, 2: 127.
[24] Archives Départementales de la Seine Maritime (hereafter A.D.S.M.), 2B 149, fol. 30.

title was truly an owner of an office,' Paul Louis-Lucas, writing from a nineteenth-century perspective, argued that despite the King's ultimate rights 'in offices,' his actions remained bound by the contractual agreements that he held with officers.[25] Such contractual limitations, he argued, prevented the King from undermining the patrimonial elements of offices, thus protecting the property interests of the possessors. While true that the granting of a *titre* in exchange for the payment of a *finance* constituted a contractual relationship, Louis-Lucas' argument rests upon an assumption that the King honored all of his contractual obligations all of the time. As the history of financial defaults suggests, however, such was not the case.[26]

Yet, while it is true that external means of contract enforcement lacked as a constraint upon the King, the fundamental political interdependence shared between crown and venal office holders restricted the crown's options. The challenge for the crown was to strike a balance between limiting the alienation of public power and avoiding the crystallization of opposition from a crucial sector of the elite. We can see how the crown arrived at this balance over the course of the seventeenth century if we focus on the string of negotiations over the regular renewal of the *droit annuel*.

Negotiating Succession Rights

Although succession rights had been extended legally with the creation of the *paulette* in 1604, the crown still retained considerable leverage to manipulate those rights. In the pre-Fronde decades of the 1630s and 1640s, the crown had emphasized its interests in preserving political power from any lasting alienation. One path to this objective was to manipulate or threaten to manipulate the property rights of office holders in order to coax political concessions or financial support from them. Inheritance rights were particularly vulnerable to rewriting, since the crown could simply withhold, or threaten to withhold, renewal of the *droit annuel*. The ministries of Richelieu and Mazarin followed precisely this strategy when they used renewal of the *annuel* as a bargaining chip against office holders during three successive rounds of negotiation in 1630, 1639, and 1648. The memory of the revocation in 1618, furthermore, made these threats all the more real. Sovereign courts responded to the crown's demands by taking firmer stances themselves, for example by refusing to register edicts creating new offices. Much of the conflict that surfaced between the crown and the Parlement of Paris in 1648 originated with the crown's hard-line stance against office holders and its reluctance to renew the *paulette* without imposing new financial demands, particularly on the more vulnerable petty officers of lesser courts. The periodic renewals of the *paulette* thus

---

[25] Louis-Lucas, 2: 136.
[26] North and Weingast, pp. 805-808.

had been polarizing episodes in the first half of the century, driving the crown and office holders into increasingly crystallized opposition.[27]

The reestablishment of order following the end of the Fronde in 1653 did little to bring clear direction to royal policy regarding the renewal of the *droit annuel*. Under Fouquet's influence, Mazarin now desired to avoid conflict with office-holding magistrates and so renewed the *droit annuel* in 1657 with the condition only that office holders pay a *prêt*, literally a loan though no mention of repayment by the crown was ever made. Precedent for such a 'surcharge' dated back to the renewal of the lapsed *paulette* in 1620. Office holders in sovereign courts were exempt from the payment of the *prêt*, but instead they were required to 'buy' *augmentations de gages*, or forward a principal sum to the crown in exchange for increased annual payments of their *gages*. These relatively light conditions easily smoothed over any potential conflict arising out of the negotiations of 1657. Yet office holders soon had reason to fear the end of such ease of negotiations with the rise to power of Colbert following Mazarin's death in 1661.[28]

Colbert's antipathy to venality in general was well known. The purchase of offices, he argued, diverted capital away from productive uses, and the private possession of public offices limited the crown's ability to reform crucial areas of government. In a brief memorandum of 1665, he singled out the *droit annuel* as responsible for much of the inflation of office prices that had taken place since the beginning of the century and that had only further placed private interests above the public good in the exercise of office.[29]

Colbert hoped to rein in venality by whatever means possible. He placed formal price caps on judicial offices with the hope of ultimately suppressing them at the official (and reduced) rates, and as early as 1662, he oversaw the compilation of data on the sums paid by all office holders as payment for the *droit annuel*.[30] This information then allowed him to argue against renewing the *annuel* in his memorandum of 1665. Although Louis XIV remained unconvinced to take such a step toward drastically curtailing venality, he did agree to renew the *annuel* for only three years, which surely had the effect of undermining office holders' confidence in their property rights. In the end, however, Louis XIV renewed the *annuel* again in 1668 for a six year term, and thereafter the pattern of nine-year renewals returned until 1709.

---

[27] A. Lloyd Moote, *The Revolt of the Judges: The Parlement of Paris and the Fronde, 1643-1652*, (Princeton: Princeton University Press, 1971), pp. 50, 61, and 125; Bonney, *King's Debts*, p. 179; Mousnier, *Vénalité*, p. 302. In Aix, royal policy toward office holders elicited political opposition within the parlement, but Sharon Kettering considers negotiations over renewing the *paulette* in particular to have had little political impact. See *Judicial Politics*, pp. 182-190, 210-211, and 246-247.

[28] Hamscher, *Parlement*, pp. 7-14.

[29] Colbert, 'Avis sur l'Annuel,' in Pierre Clément, ed., *Lettres, instructions, et mémoires de Colbert*, 7 vols., (Paris: Imprimerie Impériale, 1869), 6: 247-249; Doyle, *Venality*, pp. 21-22; Hamscher, *Parlement*, pp. 11-13.

[30] Bibliothèque Nationale de France (hereafter BnF), Mss. Fr., 18230 and 18231.

The pattern also remained of demanding *augmentations de gages* and *prêts* as a condition for allowing office holders to enter into a new term of the *annuel*. Colbert's oversight of this arrangement allowed for little if any flexibility in the face of potential delays. In 1674, for example, in the midst of the Dutch War, he reminded the First President of the Parlement of Rennes that despite that corps' difficulty in finding money, His Majesty was remaining 'firm' in his decision to require purchase of *augmentations de gages* as the condition for reentry into the *droit annuel*. The Parisian courts, Colbert added, had not experienced difficulty raising their contributions and neither, by implication, should the officers of the Parlement of Rennes.[31]

With the passing of the Colbertian period, Louis XIV adopted a quite distinct approach toward offices. Indeed, by the 1680s, with Louis XIV committing French resources to a policy of political/military expansion that ultimately led to declared war, the crown markedly altered how it handled the periodic renewal of succession rights. It continued to demand *prêts* and *augmentations de gages* from its officer corps every nine years, but threats against office holders disappeared, as did the inflexibility and impatience that Colbert had displayed. Now for the first time the process came to be predictable and transparent. For example, the King's declaration of 30 October 1683 renewed the *paulette* for nine years beginning in 1684 with the usual condition of paying the *prêt* or *augmentation de gages*. The original terms excluded those who had neglected to pay their *droit annuel* during the previous six years. Those who had opted out in the past would not find easy entrance back into the comfortable realm of heritability. But not long thereafter, the crown backed away from that stance. An *arrêt du conseil* of January 1684 reversed the crown's position and opened up access to qualifying for the *droit annuel* to all, the deadline for which was set for the end of the following February.[32] On February 26, expressing the desire to keep officers from falling into exclusion from the *droit annuel* during the next nine years, the King ordered the deadline moved back two months to the end of April, after which time those who had not met the conditions would be excluded for the following nine year period.[33] In the space of four months, the crown had moved from a stance of punishment through exclusion for those who had failed to pay in the past to a position of patience, delaying the deadline for payment in order to ensure access to heritability for all who had opted to fulfill the conditions. Judging from the reaction of provincial officer corps, Louis XIV's flexibility in these negotiations gained a degree of cooperation from venal office holders. The Parlement of Dijon had voted as a corps to borrow the sums needed to finance the *augmentations de gages* required of it, 440,000 livres in all, but was not finding lenders fast enough to meet the deadline imposed by the crown. Nicolas Brûlart, First President of the parlement, lent his own funds to the corps hoping other potential creditors would follow suit. Finally, though, the magistrates

---

[31] Colbert à d'Argouges, 28 December 1674, in Clément, *Lettres*, 2: 369.
[32] Archives Nationales (hereafter A.N.), E 1823, 5 January 1684.
[33] A.N., E 1823, 26 February 1684.

of the parlement were forced to appeal to the crown for further patience. Responding to their request, the King's council stated in an order, or *arrêt*, that the formal offers and submissions made by the corps were sufficient for the time being to gain immediate admission to the *droit annuel*.[34]

Nine years later, the process recurred in a similar fashion, as the King once again demonstrated patience with the delays of officer corps in paying their *prêts* and *augmentation des gages*. On 29 January 1693, almost five months after the initial declaration establishing the conditions for renewal, the King's council extended the deadline until the end of the following March, expressing the wish on behalf of the King to 'accord to all officers who have the intention of preserving their offices for their families the necessary time to find the sums needed.'[35] And in 1701 and 1702, the King's council again granted a two month delay, this time more than five months after the initial action taken to renew the *annuel*.[36] A pattern thus developed in the negotiations for the *paulette* unlike the confrontational stances adopted by both the crown and officer corps prior to the Fronde and unlike the nearly punitive position taken by Colbert. The crown no longer held up renewal as a bargaining chip to press blanket political and financial demands against office holders, and it no longer wavered back and forth between confirming and abolishing succession rights. Louis XIV began to take a negotiating position of patience when faced with the sluggish responses of officer corps, and from the perspective of office holders, uncertainties about property rights diminished considerably.

These periodic negotiations ended with an edict of December 1709 by which the crown abolished the *droit annuel* and adjoined the succession rights of offices to their *titres* in exchange for a one time payment from officers, called the *rachat*, or repurchase, of the *droit annuel*. By the terms of this edict, all those who could finance their repurchase of the *annuel* would be indefinitely exempt from the Forty Days Clause. This shift in royal policy in favor of a one-time lump-sum payment came as negotiations to end the war collapsed and as revenues to the Royal Treasury, already committed to cover obligations from the previous year, were diverted to make emergency purchases of grain following the harvest failures of the *Grand Hiver*. Office holders raised little resistance to this demand, despite facing a number of concurrent extraordinary charges, likely because by then an expectation of stability had set in and they no longer had reason to fear an underhanded attempt to weaken their property rights. In the end, Controller General Desmaretz

---

[34] A.N., E 1819, 31 December 1883; Harlay to Le Peletier, 2 December 1683, in Anette Smedley-Weill, *Correspondance des intendants avec le contrôleur général des finances, 1677-1689*, 3 vols., (Paris: Archives Nationales, 1991), 3: 234.
[35] A.N., E 1874, 29 January 1693.
[36] A.N., E 1919, 31 January 1702.

estimated that the crown was able to raise approximately 24 million livres from this repurchase.[37]

Throughout the latter half of Louis XIV's reign, the crown in its negotiations with officers balanced its need for revenues with a respect for the patrimonial possession of offices. The crown used its legal leverage over the issue of heritability to demand sums from officers, it is true, but it did so in a way that prevented the crystallization of opposition. When faced with delays from officers, intentional or not, the crown extended its time limits and tried to ensure the inclusion of as many officers as possible in the *droit annuel*. Indeed, one could argue that the crown approached these negotiations as if it had an interest in preserving heritability and strengthening overall the property rights of office holding.

Mortgaging Offices

The timing of this shift in attitude suggests that the crown's interest in strengthening the property rights of office holding stemmed from its desire to render offices mortgageable. Jurists of the seventeenth and eighteenth centuries agreed that to pledge an office as collateral, rights of succession needed to be firmly established. Writing as a specialist on customary law in Normandy, Henri Basnage argued that an individual must have firm disposition over goods, including succession rights, in order to borrow against them. On offices in particular, he wrote, 'When offices depended upon the discretion and the liberality of the Prince, pledging the office served no end, since the offices reverted to the Prince who disposed of them as he wished... Finally, the *droit annuel* having rendered the commerce of offices entirely free, they met the conditions to be mortgaged.'[38] For Basnage, succession rights and the free disposition of offices necessarily preceded their use as collateral.

Other jurists echoed this basic tenet. Gabriel Davot, *avocat* in the Parlement of Dijon during the first half of the eighteenth century, formulated the problem as follows:

---

[37] 'Mémoire de M. Desmaretz au Roi,' 1715, in Boislisle, ed., *Correspondance*, 3: 614-619. Some isolated pockets of resistance to the repurchase of the *annuel* did arise, but just as often venal officer corps used the weight of that obligation as an excuse for delaying payment on other charges due to the crown. See Le Peletier to the Contrôleur Général, 3 April 1710, d'Albertas to the Contrôleur Général, 13 January 1711, and d'Argenson to the Contrôleur Général, 23 July 1711, in Boislisle, op. cit., 3: 281-282, 344, and 388-389. The crown reestablished the *droit annuel* in 1723, after which time all offices, both *casuels* and domanial were again subject to the Forty Days Clause, the *annuel* and the *prêt*. A.N. G^7 1325, anonymous memoir.

[38] Henri Basnage, 'Traité des Hipotéques,' in *Les Oeuvres de Maitre H. Basnage*, 3rd edn. (Rouen, 1709), p. 20.

We have said that officers must pay the *droit annuel* to preserve their positions, and that they were subject to creditors' claims. As a result of these two maxims, an officer who has mortgaged his office must pay the *droit annuel* or otherwise reimburse the value of the office or offer a deposit (*'caution'*) to his creditor.[39]

It remained the creditor's responsibility, however, to ensure that an office holder preserve the heritability of the mortgaged office. Failure to do so could lead to his or her financial loss. According to Guyot, an office that reverted back to the *parties casuelles* belonged entirely to the King, and the creditors of the former holder had no recourse. 'Hence,' he states, 'the care that creditors often took to pay in their own name the *droit annuel.*'[40]

Colbert had understood this link between firm succession rights and the ability to pledge offices as collateral. In his memorandum of 1665 in which he argued for the repeal of the *annuel*, he recognized that such an attack against the property rights of office holders as he was proposing would undermine their 'esteem and credit' (*'la considération et le crédit'*), which would have been a positive development, he thought. Colbert found disturbing the idea that office holders owed, in his words, on average 'half the value of their offices' to creditors. Thus despite the rude economic shocks that would have befallen office holders and their creditors alike, Colbert embraced the objective of radically undermining such financial ties by abolishing the heritability of offices.[41]

Louis XIV brought a distinctly different set of views to the table after Colbert's death. As negotiations followed a predictable pattern and as uncertainty diminished, succession rights of office holders became more secure beginning in the 1680s, just as the crown turned increasingly toward corps of venal officers to borrow collectively against their offices to finance *prêts, augmentations de gages,* and the repurchase of newly created offices.[42] As the pressure mounted against office holders to provide financial support for the crown, the crown also enhanced the means for them to garner that support through borrowing. There is indeed little doubt that Louis XIV's government held a strong interest in facilitating mortgages on offices. A February 1683 edict established a public record of mortgaged offices by granting priority claims, in the event of default, to creditors who had lent for the purchase of offices or of *augmentations de gages* and who registered their liens upon the issuance of letters of provision. No other form of property received such attention when it came to fixing procedures for mortgaging and foreclosing.[43] The

---

[39] Gabriel Davot, *Traité sur diverses matières en droit français*, 8 vols., (Dijon, 1751-1765), 3: 438.
[40] Guyot, ed., *Traité*, 4: 72.
[41] Colbert, 'Avis,' in Clément, *Lettres*, 6: 247-249.
[42] Bien, 'Offices,' pp. 89-114; Doyle, *Venality*, pp. 36-42.
[43] François André Isambert, *Recueil général des anciennes lois françaises, depuis l'an 420 jusqu'à la révolution de 1789*, 29 vols., (Paris: Belin-Le-Prieur, 1821-1833), 19: 416-419; Louis-Lucas, 2: 398. The crown tried, and failed, in 1673 to establish a mortgage registry on a larger scale to cover all pledged real property.

financial exigencies faced by the crown and Louis XIV's decision to embrace venality as a financial strategy thus led to a strengthening, rather than to an undermining, of the patrimonial possession of offices.

The Evidence for Strengthened Property Rights

In the years immediately following Colbert's death in 1683, the crown frequently expressed concern about the number of offices that had been lost to families and that were sitting vacant in the *parties casuelles*. Numerous letters written between the Controller General, and officials in the provinces spoke of the abundance of vacant offices for which buyers were needed. At the same time, the crown issued several *arrêts* in order to ease the process of finding candidates to purchase the vacant offices. The crown's concerns were reflected in the preamble to an *arrêt* of December 1684. Shortly after having issued the declaration of October 1683 which extended for office holders 'the option of entering into the *droit annuel*', the King was 'informed that there was a great number of judicial, financial and other types of offices sitting vacant for several years in the *parties casuelles*.' The solutions, as set forth by these different *arrêts*, included lowering the prices of vacant offices, placing responsibility on specific officials for finding buyers, and forbidding any resistance that might be erected against the potential purchasers of vacant offices. These *arrêts* mostly date from 1683 to 1685. Likewise, the extant letters that focused on this problem of vacant offices date mostly from the years immediately following Colbert's death. As the decade progressed, whether because the problem was actually solved or because the crown's attention turned elsewhere, the issue lost its prominence.[44]

At the same time, revenues from the sale of vacant offices also diminished. The venal office system brought the crown revenues in many forms, including mutation fees, payments for the *droit annuel*, sales of new offices, sales of *augmentations de gages*, and sales of vacant offices. In 1686, proceeds from the sale of vacant offices comprised nine per cent of all revenues from offices; this portion diminished to 1.9 per cent in 1690 and then to 1.1 per cent in 1692. In absolute terms revenues from such sales fell from 530,629 livres in 1686 to 220,918 in 1692, and as these proceeds diminished, the sums raised through the sale of *augmentations de gages* and new creations grew from almost 4 million livres in 1686 to 14.5 million and 18.5 million in 1690 and 1692.[45]

The crown in part compelled this shift by requiring that newly created offices, which reached the market in large numbers beginning in 1689, be sold before any

---

[44] De Ris to the Contrôleur Général, 25 August 1684, Miroménil to the Contrôleur Général, 17 November 1684, and Contôleur Général to the procureurs généraux and procureurs du Roi, 1688, in Boislisle, ed., *Correspondance*, 1: 27, 33-34, and 157; A.N., AD IX, 448.
[45] A.N., G^7 1323 and 1325, *États de la recette et depense faitte au bureau des revenues casuels*.

Table 2.1 Transmissions of offices in Burgundy and Rouen, sampling from 1680-1715

	Burgundy		Généralité of Rouen	
Vacant offices	16	5.05%	9	3.05%
New creations	64	20.2	43	14.58
Resignations[a]	108	34.1	105	35.59
Successions[b]	109	34.4	131	44.4
Offices seized[c]	6	1.89	7	2.37
Non-casuels[d]	15	4.73	n/a	0
Total	317	100	295	100

Notes:
[a] Offices resigned in favor of an individual, or traded from one person to another.
[b] Offices inherited which either remained in the family patrimony or were sold by heirs.
[c] Offices seized as collateral by creditors.
[d] Offices not of the *parties casuelles*; in Burgundy these were mostly offices of the *maréchaussées* dependent upon the Prince of Condé.

Source: A.D.C.O., B 53-61; A.D.S.M., 2B 139-153.

others, vacant or otherwise, be put on the market.[46] But while vacant offices might otherwise have sold in greater numbers, the figures still point to an important change in the crown's approach to venality coming between the years 1683 and 1689. Thereafter, the crown moved distinctly away from seeking to undermine succession rights, and the revenues from the sale of vacant offices nearly disappeared. As the crown's financial needs heightened with the outbreak of war in 1689, pressure came to bear on office holders in a different form. Newly created offices hit the market, and office holders themselves came under increased pressure to buy *augmentations de gages*. The two developments fed one another: only with strengthened succession rights could office holders undertake the borrowing necessary to meet these royal exactions.

The turn away from vacant offices as a source of revenues was felt in those towns and cities across France that were centers of government office. According to a sampling of offices that changed hands between 1679 and 1718 in Burgundy and Upper Normandy, very few such transactions, between three and five per cent, were of offices that fell vacant and then found third-party purchasers. (See Table 2.1). Newly created offices, offices traded on the secondary market, and inherited

---

[46] Hurt, *Louis XIV*, pp. 78-81.

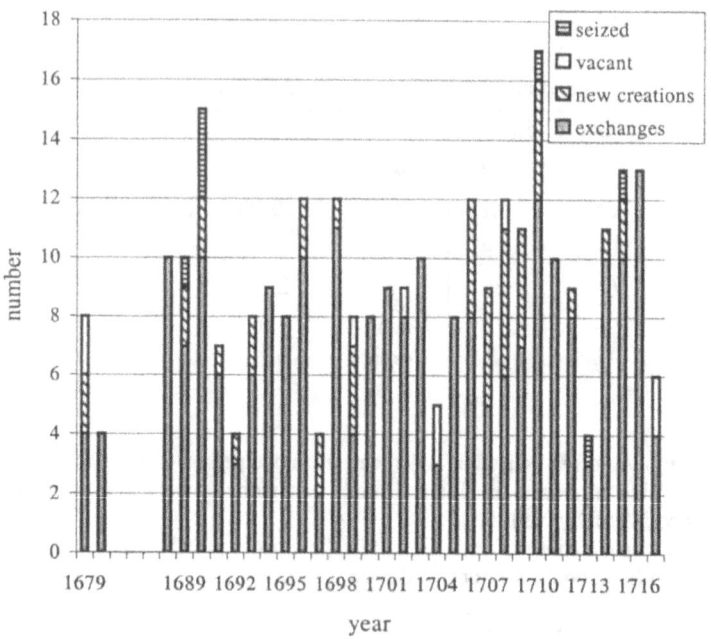

Note: "Exchanges" includes both resignations and successions
Source: A.D.S.M., 2B 139-153.

Figure 2.1 Annual office transmissions, *généralité* of Rouen

offices comprised almost all the remaining exchanges.[47] Our data from Upper Normandy (the *généralité* of Rouen), which include all transmissions of offices under the jurisdiction of the Chamber of Accounts of Rouen, allow us to examine these transactions over time, excluding an unfortunate lacuna in the sources from 1681 to 1687. (See Figure 2.1). At no point, either in peacetime or wartime, did the sporadic sale of vacant offices figure prominently. By contrast, the clusters of newly created offices selling around the years 1690 to 1693 and 1706 to 1710 suggest a royal preference to fund war at least in part by putting new offices on the market for sale.

Of those few offices that were resold as vacant, most were relatively important

---

[47] My sample derives from the letters of provision recorded by the chambers of account in Rouen and Dijon. In all, I examined 317 office transmissions in Burgundy and 295 in the *généralité* of Rouen. Archives Départementales de la Côte d'Or (hereafter A.D.C.O.), B 53 - B 61, *Enregistrements de la chambre des comptes*; A.D.S.M. 2B 139 - 2B 153, *Mémoriaux de la Chambre des Comptes.*

offices from a provincial point of view. In Burgundy, three of the offices were of the Parlement of Dijon, of which one was a procurator and two were counselors. Others were offices of middling courts directly under the superior (formerly sovereign) courts, such as the office of counselor in the bailiwick of Bourg-en-Bresse, held originally by Pierre Michel then sold as a vacant office to the *avocat* Claude Chossal in 1684.[48] One important financial office also found its way back to the *parties casuelles*; the office of *receveur général ancien des finances* of the province of Burgundy, originally held by Nicolas Petit, was sold by the *parties casuelles* to Philibert l'Ardillon in 1684.[49]

Similarly in the *généralité* of Rouen (Upper Normandy), the list of vacant offices resold by the crown includes mostly offices of moderate to high provincial importance. Many were offices of the chamber of accounts in Rouen. These varied from the two offices of *garde livres*, both of which Nicolas François Marc purchased in 1704 for 1650 livres each, to offices of *correcteurs*, such as that sold to Roland Nicolas Goullas in 1679 for 20,000 livres or that sold to Richard Lallemand in 1708 for 10,000 livres.[50] The small number of offices, therefore, that fell vacant and that were subsequently resold by the *parties casuelles* included mostly offices of relative importance, both in terms of status and power conferred on the local level and in terms of their financial value.

Yet we must be careful not to extrapolate from these examples. Not all offices, it turns out, enjoyed the same strengthening of property rights. There is no way to measure the total number and value of offices sitting vacant at any given time. There is indication, though, that as the crown's concern over vacant offices waned over the course of the 1680s, the problem nonetheless persisted, as offices of especially lesser prominence and value sat vacant in large numbers. Pierre le Pesant de Boisguilbert, lieutenant general of the *bailliage* of Rouen and prolific writer of economic and fiscal reform programs, confirmed this view in a proposal he sent to the Controller General's office in 1709.[51] 'Subaltern judicial offices', he argued, were swelling the ranks of the *parties casuelles* due to the disproportionate sums demanded by the King as *prêts* for the renewal of the *droit annuel*. Faced with paying the equivalent of one-sixth the value of one's office every three years merely to meet the conditions for then paying the *droit annuel*, these lesser judicial officers 'often preferred to lose [their offices] after their death than to pay every nine years a sum so disproportionate to the value and revenues of their charges.' Indeed, Boisguilbert continued, the heirs could often repurchase the lost offices for less than what would have been required to preserve the charges. He thus proposed that the King abolish the *prêt*, but only for these lower judicial offices whose holders found themselves disproportionately saddled with financial demands.

---

[48] A.D.C.O., B 54, fol. 76.
[49] A.D.C.O., B 54, fol. 66.
[50] A.D.S.M., 2B 148, fols. 113-115; 2B 139, fol. 162; 2B 149, fol. 162.
[51] A.N., G^7 721, *Mémoire pour faciliter et avancer la levée d'un grand nombre de charges qui sont aux parties casuelles*, accompanied by a letter of 21 August 1709.

Officers such as treasurers general of France and receivers of the *taille*, he argued, could well afford the *prêts* given the value and the fat salaries ('gros gages') of their offices.

Boisguilbert's testimony and a close examination of our evidence, therefore, suggest the need for greater nuance in our assessment of the crown's strategy toward officers and the issue of heritability during the latter half of Louis XIV's reign. Some office holders did fall through the cracks on the issue of heritability. These were predominantly holders of lesser judicial offices of little financial value to the crown, offices that the King evidently did not feel the need to preserve as the patrimonial possessions of his subjects or no longer thought it important to market vigorously once they fell vacant. The crown took a much different approach, though, to those offices that conferred higher social standing and greater political influence in the provinces, those offices whose financial values rose closer to 5000 livres and above, such as the treasurers general and receivers of the *taille* that Boisguilbert mentioned, offices of superior courts and even those of some of the more important *élections, bailliages, sénéchaussée, and présidiaux*. As Boisguilbert suggested, the holders of these offices could afford to pay, or they had the resources to borrow for, the *prêts* or *augmentations de gages* needed to gain readmittance to the *droit annuel*. Further, the officers of superior courts in particular enjoyed the crown's patience and flexibility in meeting the conditions for the *annuel*.

That patience and flexibility, along with the diminished uncertainty surrounding property rights, was thus directed toward holders of relatively valuable offices in the most prominent courts. It was they who were more likely to have the reputations and connections that aided in borrowing significant sums whether as individuals or as corps. Their offices enhanced their reputations, while their reputations facilitated borrowing against those same offices. Thus it remained crucial for Louis XIV's financial strategies to preserve the patrimonial quality of the more valuable offices. To have threatened, directly or indirectly, the heritability of these offices would have undermined more than just the office holders' personal interests. The credit networks on which corps of venal office holders depended for their borrowing, and with them the crown's financial gains from such credit networks, would have been fundamentally undermined by any such rewriting of property rights. Further, considering the feudal aspect of offices and the political alliances forged between the crown and holders of politically constituted forms of property, the holders of relatively valuable offices were potentially important political allies, just as they were financial allies for the crown, and therefore care in coaxing extraordinary financial support from them was all the more important.

The crown therefore faced real extra-legal constraints upon its actions toward office holders, especially toward the more prominent members of the office-holding elite. Property rights and means of contract enforcement did not protect the patrimonial possession of these offices. Yet nor can we say that the crown had a free hand in rewriting property rights and reneging on agreements at will.[52] Rather, the crown's financial use of, or even dependence upon, certain offices protected the holders and preserved the patrimonial qualities of their offices. Unlike his predecessors who leveled blanket threats against the patrimonial possession of offices in order to attain the financial and political submission of the elite, Louis XIV chose a strategy less likely to foment opposition. He met his growing financial needs in large part by shoring up the property rights to offices and then by pressuring office holders to borrow for him.

Squeezing Office Holders

Shoring up the succession rights of venal offices worked in the favor both of officers, able to rest more secure in their hold over their property, and of the crown, with its strategy of war finance that elicited the financial intermediation of privileged corps. By this measure, war finance enhanced the accommodation between the crown and the venal office-holding elite. Of course, this is not the full story. The financial pressure brought to bear against office holders was far from innocuous, and the incomes accruing to offices along with their values suffered. John Hurt, for one, rejects the view of Louis XIV's reign as accommodating and argues that, with regard to financial questions, 'from the administration of Colbert through to that of Pontchartrain, the government steadily encroached upon the vested interests of the magistrates in their venal offices.' Likewise, the 'late reign of Louis XIV indeed subjected the magistrates to a grinding ordeal.'[53] Hurt offers some compelling figures as evidence, detailing the amounts paid by office holders for *augmentations de gages* and the numbers of new sales that drove down the prices of offices. Indeed, it looks, judging from Hurt's work, like office holders under Louis XIV (at least the magistrates in the parlements who were the object of his study), continued to suffer the heavy hand of royal treatment on par with, if not worse than, their predecessors earlier in the century. If this is the case, my argument that Louis XIV acted under historically conditioned constraints, seeking to avoid the political costs of contention borne in the 1630s and 1640s by ushering in an era of accommodation, requires amending, if not discarding. Yet Hurt's focus on 'forced loans,' or the sums demanded of office holders through the purchase of *augmentations de gages*, ignores one telling feature of Louis XIV's approach to venality that indeed sets it apart from that of his predecessors – the widespread tendency of corps to borrow collectively, under royal encouragement, in order to intermediate finances for the crown. Like municipalities and provincial estates,

---

[52] Compare Bonney (*King's Debts*, p. 274) who characterizes the seventeenth-century monarchy as an 'irresponsible political power whose contractual word was not its bond.' While Bonney understands correctly that the crown was not bound by contract, he stops short of considering more pertinent structural constraints on royal action.
[53] Hurt, *Louis XIV*, pp. 83-89 and 95.

corps of venal office holders staved off royal threats to manipulate privileges and property by borrowing for the crown and pledging their offices and the incomes accruing to them as collateral. In Burgundy, judicial corps from the parlement, to the chamber of accounts, to local *bailliage* courts borrowed collectively as intermediaries; in Upper Normandy, there is evidence that a number of courts with financial jurisdiction (the *cour des comptes, aides et finances*, the *bureau des finances*, and various *élections*) along with administrative/financial corps (for example port inspectors) intermediated finances for the crown by borrowing collectively.[54] To be sure, such intermediation brought with it entirely new sets of risk as office holders assumed collective responsibility for debts while remaining dependent on the crown for the ability to service them, and many office holders were left in precarious financial positions when the crown fell behind in its payment of *gages* beginning in 1709. Still, 'forced loans' did not always represent extractions squeezed from the pockets of office holders themselves, and the move toward intermediation by venal office holders, whether they went willingly or not, brought them the unexpected gain of firmer succession rights.

---

[54] A.D.S.M., C 1370-1373, *Bureau des finances, Quittances des finances*. See also Chapter Six. Compare Hurt, *Louis XIV*, p. 74. He acknowledges that parlementary magistrates had the option of borrowing collectively to pay for *augmentations de gages*, but downplays the significance of such arrangements as isolated.

PART II
CROWN AND PROVINCE

Chapter 3

Estates and Ruling Coalitions in Burgundy

Warfare figures prominently in scholarly explanations of the rise of the modern state system. Two groups of scholars, one comprised of Weberian sociologists and the other of theorists of the military revolution, have been particularly instrumental in attributing to warfare its central historical role as a catalyst for political change in the early modern world. Their argument, in its most basic terms, is that warfare propelled the development of the three pillars of 'modern' states: armies, bureaucracies and fiscal systems. To remain militarily competitive on the international stage, states in the seventeenth and eighteenth centuries had no choice but to grow their professional armies by enhancing their authority to tax while strengthening the bureaucratic means of collecting and managing revenues. Those states that did not succeed in sweeping away traditional constraints against taxation placed themselves at jeopardy of being overwhelmed by their more powerful neighbors.[1] For historians of France, it was the crown's ability in the seventeenth century to circumvent estates and rule instead through its own network of intendants that enabled the absolute monarchy to rise out of the considerably weaker Renaissance mold of kingship. Warfare in the first half of the century, including both internal struggles against Huguenots in the 1620s and involvement, first covert and then overt, in the Thirty Years' War, was especially notable for driving these 'modern' developments.[2]

This model of political change, however, fails to hold when viewed against the experiences of France during the final two wars of Louis XIV's reign. Warfare under Louis XIV did not propel the rise of 'modern' structures in the Weberian sense; on the contrary, 'patrimonial' elements of the state were strengthened.[3] Venality, as we have seen, became entrenched *as a result of* the pressures created by warfare. Similarly, as I argue in this and following chapters, provincial estates

---

[1] Theodore K. Rabb, *The Struggle for Stability in Early Modern Europe*, (New York: Oxford University Press, 1975), p. 71; Downing, pp. 74-78; Skocpol, pp. 52-54; Tilly, pp. 67-95.
[2] Major, pp. 261-303; Bonney, *Political Change*; Mousnier, 'Recherches,' pp. 81-113.
[3] Max Weber speaks of a dichotomy between the traditional 'patrimonial state', infused with feudal interests and sensibilities, and the modern 'bureaucratic state' guided by rational thought and professionalism. For a thoughtful critique of Weberian historical sociology, see Lachmann, *Capitalists*.

that survived Louis XIII's attacks in the 1620s and 1630s went on to see their roles expanded and their authority enhanced, likewise *as a result of* the financial demands created by Louis XIV's wars.

How can we understand these divergent outcomes, where warfare at one point in the century engendered attacks on privileges while at another it had the effect of entrenching privilege? One likely explanation is that the crown was never intent on actually abolishing corporate privileges. Louis XIII and Richelieu, it has been argued, never seriously intended to introduce fiscal uniformity across the kingdom, despite the reformist zeal of Marillac; the 'attack' against provincial estates instead ultimately amounted to yet another somewhat clumsy attempt to extort extraordinary levels of financial assistance from privileged provinces.[4] Such was the outcome, in fact, in Burgundy, Languedoc, and Provence where the crown ultimately backed away from its attempts to circumvent those provinces' estates in exchange for lump sum payments. And Louis XIV, for his part, rejected any measures during his personal reign that went so far as to merely call into question the existence of privileged corps, and he found instead that corps served his purposes quite well as long as they remained politically obedient.[5]

While this argument accords well with recent 'revisionist' views of absolutism, it is, nonetheless, incomplete. Local factors too must be part of any understanding of political change in early modern France. Privileged corps were not malleable institutions whose fate the crown enjoyed a free hand to determine. Nor, conversely, were they all equally capable of rebuffing royal attempts to manipulate their privileges and prerogatives. For this reason, outcomes differed when Louis XIII 'attacked', or extorted from, estates in the 1620s and 1630s. Estates in Burgundy, Provence, and Languedoc survived, while those in Dauphiné succumbed and those of Guyenne and Normandy fell victim to attacks that had begun in the previous century. Further, as I argue throughout this and the following chapters, the estates that survived the attacks of the first half of the century did not merely go on to exist in weakened skeletal form. Rather, they underwent a sort of regeneration as they saw their fiscal responsibilities expand and their political authority grow under Louis XIV. Royal determination was certainly the source of much of this later strengthening, yet for such a shift of authority to take place, it required at the very least some resonance with the interests of the local elite. It is this 'social resonance' – estates' ability to promote elites' interests and to garner, in turn, the support of those same elite groups, that this chapter explores.

Indeed, the political effectiveness of the local elite reinforced provincial estates, just as estates in turn helped to shape the political effectiveness of the elite. In those provinces where estates survived, local leaders had offered both active and passive resistance to the royal measures aimed against their provinces. In Burgundy in 1629 and 1630, for example, once the crown created on paper *élections*, or the fiscal circumscriptions that would have made possible lasting circumvention of the

---

[4] Major, pp. 253-260; Collins, *The State*, pp. 52-53.
[5] Major, p. 337.

estates in apportioning and collecting taxes, opposition arose from different quarters throughout the province. Local leaders, aware of the threat directed against the province's fiscal autonomy, planned disturbances in Dijon and Beaune, and rumors that the crown was planning new taxes on wine in particular sparked an uprising of *vignerons* and Dijonnais craftsmen in February 1630.[6] As was so often the case following insurrections in this period, local Dijonnais leaders cast a political shadow upon themselves for not having acted with sufficient zeal in suppressing the disorder.[7] Yet notwithstanding this loss of royal favor, Burgundians resisted long enough for the crown to agree finally to revoke the newly created *élections* in 1631 in exchange for a payment of 1.6 million livres, thus preserving the province's estates.[8]

Why some provinces' elites offered support to their estates while others withheld that support and watched instead as their estates withered in the face of royal attacks has yet to be fully explained.[9] Central to the answer must be the particular estates' 'social resonance' with elites. Only elites had the potential to shape, or in some cases halt altogether, royal initiatives and successfully defend local privileges.[10] Thus their stake in preserving the specific outlines of their province's fiscal autonomy must be considered a prime determinant of the divergent fate of estates. In Burgundy, Provence and Languedoc, for reasons not yet fully explored, elite groups identified their interests with and were more willing to defend their estates when under attack than were such elites in Normany and Dauphiné.[11]

To be sure, attempting to explain definitively why some provinces in the first half of the seventeenth century were able to retain their estates while others were not is beyond the scope of this work. Nonetheless, posing the question helps us to focus on that salient intersection between elite interests and estates. To the extent that we can speak of the political strength of estates, the impulse behind that

---

[6] Major, p. 241; Farr, *Hands*, p. 131; Beik, *Urban Protest*, pp. 126-133.
[7] Farr, *Hands*, pp. 206-207. Mack Holt writes of an 'unofficial alliance' between rioters, artisans and *vignerons*, who were well versed in the pressing political issues, and the town council of Dijon. See 'Culture populaire et culture politique au XVIIe siècle: l'émeute de Lanturelu à Dijon en février 1630,' *Histoire, Économie et Société*, 16 (1997): 597-615.
[8] Major, p. 269.
[9] Some theories emphasize the specific nature of fiscal exemptions to try to understand the level of cohesive support that estates garnered locally. Others correlate the strength of traditional landed classes with the strength of estates. As the authors of these theories are themselves ready to admit, however, empirical exceptions can be raised against both of these proposed explanations, and a fully satisfactory explanation evades us. See Bonney, *Political Change*, pp. 350-360; and James B. Collins, *Classes, Estates and Order in Early Modern Brittany*, (New York: Cambridge University Press, 1994), p. 10.
[10] Beik, *Urban Protest*; Mousnier, 'Recherches;' Porchnev, *Soulèvements*; Lachmann, *Capitalists*.
[11] 'It was true that the inhabitants of Burgundy, Provence, and Languedoc were doing everything legally, and sometimes illegally, in their power to prevent the *élus* from being appointed and from performing their duties once they were': Major, p. 262.

strength must have come from individuals or groups within the ruling elite who benefited from the local political and financial autonomy accorded by estates. I argue here that those estates that survived into the second half of the century were particularly successful in building social resonance and marshalling support for their activities because they provided an arena for coalition building among the local elite. In Burgundy, this coalition of elites benefited from and thus supported both the underlying fiscal functions of the estates and their expanded role as a financial intermediary under Louis XIV. I begin by making a case for the relative success of the Burgundian estates in negotiating taxes under Louis XIV. I then turn to examine the beneficiaries of that success – the ruling coalition of elites, and how the estates promoted their particular interests. Finally, I trace the rise of the estates as an intermediary under Louis XIV and posit their enhanced role as an expression of the ruling coalition's evolving interests.

Estates, Clienteles, and Fiscal Negotiations

As historians have revised our understanding of absolutism over the last two decades, they have looked beyond institutions to explore how power and authority were exercised. As a result, personal ties linking patrons and clients have become central to our understanding of the functioning of government, and Louis XIV in particular has been credited with mastering the personal transmission of authority.[12] Indeed, this argument has been taken to the point where institutions are rendered nearly irrelevant. Provincial estates, for example, appear in some works as nothing more than crossroads for clientele networks where deputies found themselves more concerned with fulfilling their political obligations as defined by their patron/client ties than with protecting a set of interests integral to the prosperous and vigorous functioning of the estates.[13] In Burgundy, the Condé clientele in particular made possible effective governance during Louis' personal reign, especially with regard to managing the estates.[14] To be sure, the Condé clientele was a crucial avenue through which authority was exercised in Burgundy, just as clienteles in general were throughout the kingdom. Yet we must not neglect the impact of institutions in shaping crown/elite relationships. Despite Louis' mastery of patronage and despite the strength of the Condé clientele in Burgundy, the Estates of Burgundy remained a potent political force promoting local interests. Indeed, the ordinary tax levels

---

[12] Kettering, *Patrons*, pp. 213-214; Beik, *Absolutism*, pp. 223-244; Collins, *The State*, pp. 116-119.

[13] 'It was well known that for a nobleman or clergyman to obtain a royal appointment, a more lucrative benefice, or a pension, it was necessary to serve the crown loyally both in the estates and elsewhere, and Louis went far beyond his predecessors in the use of patronage' (Major, p. 340). See also Kettering, *Patrons*, pp. 167-175.

[14] Beth Nachison, 'Absentee Government and Provincial Governors in Early Modern France: The Princes of Condé and Burgundy, 1660-1720,' *French Historical Studies*, 21 (1998): 265-297.

agreed upon between the estates and the crown during the final decades of Louis XIV's reign are entirely consistent with the view that the estates advanced local interests by keeping direct tax levels to a minimum even as the crown's financial needs grew.

The ability to hold regular meetings of estates was a royally granted privilege conferred to Burgundy upon the duchy's entry into the kingdom in 1477.[15] By custom, the estates had three sets of financial and administrative functions. The first, and most important from the crown's point of view, was fiscal. The estates' responsibility was to vote, apportion, and collect taxes. The second, and most important from the provincial inhabitants' point of view, was to protect the privileges of the province. It has traditionally been thought that this responsibility involved first and foremost guarding against heavy fiscal demands from the crown.[16] Additionally, this role as provincial advocate included protecting the province's elite against royal manipulations of their privileged status. This latter role of advocating for the privileged elite had the potential to be at odds with the more traditionally understood role of advocating for the province's tax payers. Because of the estates' strong social resonance with the elite, we can expect the resolution of any such conflict to have favored the elite. Finally, the estates financed and administered projects of local interest, such as road repair work and the construction of canals.

In Burgundy, the crown convened the estates every three years when, for about twenty days, the three chambers representing the clergy, the nobility and the third estate, deliberated both as individual chambers and all together under the presidency of the province's governor and intendant. While convened, the estates fulfilled their fiscal functions by deliberating with the crown's commissioners, voting on the level of the *don gratuit* to be paid the crown over the next three years, and apportioning that obligation between communities. They also tended to various 'public works' projects. In the year following each meeting, a deputation delivered the province's remonstrances to the King during what was termed the *voyage d'honneur*. A smaller 'executive board', the *élus généraux* (hereafter the *élus*), remained in office while the estates were not in session to oversee the collection of taxes and to manage any financial or administrative affairs that arose during the intervening three years. It remained to the *élus* to see that tax revenues flowed smoothly to the royal treasury according to the agreements reached by the estates.[17]

When in session, the Estates of Burgundy appeared as an unwieldy institution, where divergent interests and a concern for protocol within and between the three

---

[15] In this regard, the Burgundian experience paralleled that of most provinces integrated into the kingdom during and after the fifteenth century, whereby specific privileges were granted by the crown and enshrined in charters so as to ease their entry into the kingdom. Bonney, *Political Change*, pp. 344-351.

[16] Major, pp. 40-41.

[17] The *élus* of the Burgundian estates are not to be confused with the *élus* who staffed the tax districts in *pays d'élection*. The latter were mid-level financial officers with a role in apportioning tax obligations, in conjunction with intendants, within their districts.

chambers stifled the expression of a unified voice. In this environment, the clientele of the Condé princes provided a crucial organizing force. As governors of the province, the successive Condé princes, also known as the Dukes of Bourbon, played key roles in the functioning of the estates, including both a formal role presiding over them in conjunction with the intendant and an informal role influencing not only the decisions of the estates, but the composition of the chambers themselves, particularly the chamber of the third estate.[18] This chamber represented the province's towns, and at least until the ascension of Louis Joseph de Bourbon, prince de Condé, in 1740, the successive Condé princes exercised direct personal influence over the designation of town mayors throughout Burgundy. This influence even made itself felt while the offices of mayor were venal and entered into the patrimonies of their individual holders. Thus, in 1713, when the prince of Condé let it be known that he no longer held confidence in sieur de Repas, the mayor of Autun, the *élus* effectively 'bought him out' by reimbursing him the price of his office. The prince then nominated André Canale as successor to whom the *élus* in turn extended the office.[19] Since all of the deputies in the chamber of the third estate were either Burgundian mayors or their subordinates, the Condé princes could rest comfortably knowing that their *créatures*, or loyal agents, filled the ranks of at least one of the three chambers.[20]

The estates regularly recognized the patronage of the Condé princes. At each triennial session, a portion of the budget for local expenditures was set aside to recognize services rendered to the province and to curry favor with important patrons.[21] During the decades under study, the composition of these 'gifts' was nearly unchanging, with the prince himself receiving roughly a quarter and his numerous subordinates another half of what typically amounted to slightly more than 200,000 livres. By comparison, the controller general who advised the King regularly and in person on financial matters received a mere 1.5 per cent, or 3000 livres. Deputies to the estates thus overwhelmingly acknowledged the Condé princes as the most important patrons of Burgundy.

This lopsided strength of the Condé clientele might indeed suggest that the

---

[18] Swann (*Provincial Power*, chapter 3) makes a strong case for the power and reach of the Condé clientele over the operations of the Burgundian estates.

[19] Daniel Ligou, 'Les élus généraux de Bourgogne et les charges municipales de 1692 à 1789,' in *Actes du 90e Congrés National des Sociétés Savantes: Nice, 1965, Section d'histoire moderne et contemporaine* (Paris: Bibliothèque Nationale, 1966), p. 110; Kettering, *Patrons*, p. 94. Following the 1696 agreement to repurchase the offices of mayor, the estates 'united and incorporated' the offices to their institution. Those offices of mayor that had already been purchased, however, remained in the possession of their holders until the estates were able to make full reimbursement.

[20] This influence over delegates extended to the chambers of the first two orders as well, though by less formal means. See François Dumont, *Une Session des États de Bourgogne, la tenue de 1718*, (Dijon: Imprimerie Bernigaud et Privat, 1935), pp. 10-14.

[21] 'Dons, octrois et reconnaissances' in the *Registres des transcriptions des décrets des États*, A.D.C.O., C 3018-3019.

estates acted as a conduit through which the Condé princes realized their political strategies, either acting independently or as brokers for the King. This is the contention of Sharon Kettering when she writes that 'Henri II de Bourbon, prince de Condé, governor of Burgundy from 1631 to 1646, had created an extensive provincial clientele to control the Parlement of Dijon, the Burgundian estates, and the municipal governments.'[22] J. Russell Major offers a similar portrayal of the political ties between the Condé and the estates. He argues that the Estates of Burgundy showed some resistance in negotiations with the 'grand Condé' during the decade of the 1660s. In 1662, after Condé was finally able to reach an agreement with the less than amenable estates over the level of the *don gratuit*, he offered to send a report to the King 'on those who have cooperated best; His Majesty will see if he believes them worthy of some gratification, as this is always done; and he will use it as he pleases.' The following decade, however, was a turning point, Major argues, so that by 1674 the 'will of the estates had been broken, and to Louis' delight, they voted all he requested in a single deliberation. Thereafter, the estates did not seriously oppose his financial requests until near the end of his reign.'[23] It was thus the personal rule of Louis XIV, extending through the clientele of the Condé princes, that reduced the estates to near impotence, according to Major.

To argue his point, Major states that following 1674, the Estates of Burgundy offered little or no resistance to the financial demands made by the crown and readily agreed to the requested levels of *dons gratuits*. Yet while these negotiations may indeed have fallen into a routinized pattern that allowed the parties to avert contention, the amounts agreed upon actually decreased, both nominally and in real terms. Following those contentious negotiations of 1662 to which Major makes reference, the estates had agreed to a *don gratuit* of 1,050,000 livres. By the end of Louis XIV's reign, on the other hand, the typical triennial *don* amounted to between 800,000 livres, as was the case in 1709 and 1712, and 900,000 livres which they agreed to pay in 1715.[24] As shown in Table 3.1, this decrease is made only more significant when calculated in real terms to adjust for the devaluation of the livre under Louis XIV.

The estates raised the sums to meet the obligation of the *dons gratuits* mostly through the levy of the *taille*, which was the principal land tax levied in Burgundy on non-privileged households. There were other regular obligations to the crown

---

[22] Kettering, *Patrons*, pp. 91-94.
[23] Major, p. 344. The statement by Condé is quoted from Georges-Bernard Depping, ed., *Correspondance administrative sous le règne de Louis XIV*, 4 vols., (Paris: Imprimerie Nationale, 1850-55), 1:431. Emphasis added.
[24] A.D.C.O., C 3001-3002, *Registres des décrets originaux des États*. For the formulaic structure of negotiations, see Dumont, pp. 46-53. Julian Swann, 'War Finance in Burgundy in the Reign of Louis XIV, 1661-1715,' in W.M. Ormrod, Margaret Bonney, and Richard Bonney, eds., *Crises, Revolutions, and Self-Sustained Growth*, [Stamford: Shaun Tyas, 1999], p. 301 offers a similar appraisal of Major's contention that the estates 'had been broken.'

Table 3.1 Triennial levels of *dons gratuits* agreed upon by Estates of Burgundy (000 livres)

Triennality beginning	Ordinary Don	Extra-ordinary Don	Total Agreed Upon	Remission Granted by Crown	Total after Remission nominal	real*
1662	—	—	—	—	1050	1050
1676	—	—	—	—	1200	1248
1679	53	1000	1053	0	1053	1095.12
1682	53	1000	1053	0	1053	1095.12
1685	53	1000	1053	150	903	939.12
1688	53	1000	1053	150	903	930.09
1691	53	1000	1053	100	953	886.29
1694	53	1000	1053	153	900	774
1697	53	1000	1053	153	900	756
1700	53	1000	1053	153	900	801
1703	53	900	953	0	953	829.11
1706	53	900	953	0	953	810.05
1709	53	900	953	153	800	616
1712	53	900	953	153	800	552
1715	—	—	—	—	900	828
1718	53	1000	1053	200	853	478

* adjusted to silver value of livre in 1679.

Source: Major, p. 344; Dumont, p. 55; A.D.C.O., C 2998-3002.

as well that the Estates of Burgundy met mostly with revenues from the *taille*, and these included various military contributions, such as the *subsistance*, the *exemption du logement de gens de guerre*, and the *garnison*. In addition, Louis XIV created the capitation, a scaled poll tax, first in 1695 to last through the Nine Years' War and then again in 1702 with the outbreak of war once more. The Estates of Burgundy were able to keep royal tax collectors from entering the province to levy the capitation themselves by agreeing to pay an annual 'subscription' of 1,000,000 livres, of which 584,000 livres was raised as a direct tax and 416,000 livres by borrowing.[25] This annual 'subscription' was then reduced

---

[25] Of this 584,000 livres, the regions of Bresse, Bugey, Valromey and Gex, areas otherwise not under the fiscal jurisdiction of the estates, were to pay 180,000 livres. A.D.C.O., C 2983, fols. 168-171.

Table 3.2 Annual obligations of Estates of Burgundy (000 livres)

Year	Don gratuit	Taillon	Garnison	Exemption du logement	Subsistance	Capitation	Total annual direct taxation Nominal	Real
1679	351	71.55	86	250	345	—	1103.55	1103.55
1682	351	71.55	86	200	300	—	1008.55	1008.55
1685	301	71.55	86	200	300	—	958.55	958.55
1688	301	71.55	86	200	300	—	958.55	948.96
1691	317.66	71.55	86	200	300	—	975.21	867.94
1694	300	71.55	86	200	300	—	957.55	775.62
1697	300	71.55	86	200	300	?*	957.55	775.62
1700	300	71.55	86	200	300	—	957.55	813.92
1703	317.66	71.55	86	200	300	1000	1975.21	1639.42
1706	317.66	71.55	86	200	300	1000	1975.21	1599.92
1709	266.66	71.55	86	200	300	1000	1924.21	1423.92
1712	266.66	71.55	86	200	300	600	1524.21	1005.98
1715	300	71.55	86	200	300	600	1557.55	1370.64
1718	284.33	71.55	86	200	300	600	1557.55	841.08

* The crown levied the capitation directly as a scaled poll tax during its first three years, from 1695 to 1698, and estimates of how much the crown raised remain unknown. See Saint-Jacob, p. 180.

Source: A.D.C.O., C 2982-2983.

to 600,000 livres in 1710 after the estates made an up-front payment of 2.4 million livres called the *rachat de la capitation*.[26]

As Table 3.2 and Figure 3.1 demonstrate, even when these additional charges are included, the real levels of regular annual obligations still did not reflect any royal triumph in squeezing resources out of the estates during the decades of greatest need under Louis XIV. Only with the addition of the capitation did total

---

[26] The estates raised this entire amount for the *rachat de la capitation* by borrowing. I discuss below in this chapter borrowing to meet both regular payments and extraordinary demands. Additionally, the crown created the *dixième*, a tax on individual income, in 1710. This tax was collected by royal agents, however, and the sums were thus not part of the estates' annual obligations to the crown. On the *dixième*, see Kwass, *Privilege*, pp. 33-38; Bonney, 'Secret,' pp. 383-416.

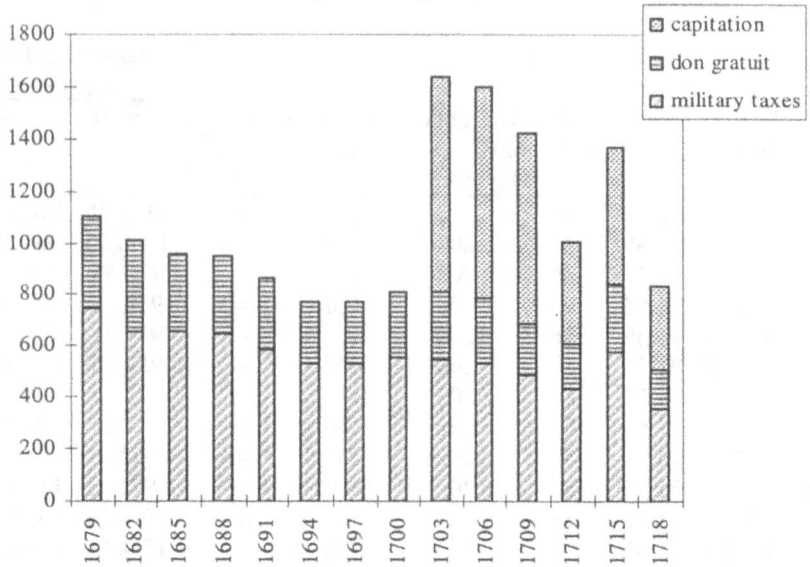

Source: See Table 3.2

Figure 3.1 Direct taxation levels in Burgundy, adjusted to 1679 livre

real obligations increase; this change proved temporary, though, as the diminishing silver content of the livre continued to erode the value of these resource transfers.[27]

These sums should be considered as royal charges, not as the total tax burden carried by the province. Julian Swann offers one measure the burden of these charges upon the *taillables* of Burgundy by examining the *taille* rolls that the *alcades*, a sort of oversight committee, reviewed every three years. He finds that, whereas on the eve of the outbreak of war in 1688 *taille* levels amounted to 1,469,804 livres, by 1712 those tax levels, now including direct tax revenues raised to pay the capitation, totaled 2,660,741 livres. Swann takes this to be a 'striking' increase of 81 per cent, but in real terms it represents a much less impressive increase of 20 per cent, which itself could not be sustained, as the nominal levels fell to an average of 1,822,722 livres per year from 1714 to 1724, or a real increase of only about 10 per cent from 1688 to 1714. Overall, the estates succeeded, thus,

---

[27] Additionally, there were revenues raised directly by royal agents (see note 26) along with revenues collected by the estates to meet local administrative and capital project needs. On local expenditures of *taille* revenues, see William Beik, 'État et société en France au XVIIe siècle: la taille en Languedoc et la question de la redistribution sociale,' *Annales, E.S.C.*, 39 (1984): 1270-1298.

in holding the line against any sharp increases in direct taxation to fund their support of Louis XIV's war effort.[28]

The economic contraction that afflicted most of France during the last decades of the seventeenth century may have contributed to this stagnation in direct taxes, as both the estates and the crown recognized the limited ability of *taillables* to pay. The frequent remissions granted on the *dons gratuits* suggest that the crown was indeed sensitive to these limitations. Still, the premise that the crown bent the estates to its will, as evidenced by the ease of regular negotiations over the *don gratuit*, reflects a one-sided view that ignores the long-term trends whereby negotiations were smoothed over by stagnant or diminishing expectations on the part of the crown.

Furthermore, it is misleading to focus, as Major does, solely on negotiations over the *don gratuits*, since the estates entered into a host of financial relationships with the crown, especially as Louis XIV's financial needs increased following 1689. Thus, the ready acceptance of the crown's requests concerning the *dons gratuits* does not imply by itself that the estates had no power to defend provincial interests, just as the diminution in the level of the *dons gratuits* should not be taken to mean that the financial importance of the estates diminished during this period of warfare and heightened royal need. If instead we view the negotiations over the *dons gratuits* as only one area in the overall financial activity of the estates, we can then consider the outcomes of those negotiations as part of an overall success enjoyed by the provincial elite in protecting its interests.

The Estates and Elite Coalition Building

Provincial estates were particularly well suited to undertake an expanded financial role under Louis XIV because they provided an arena for coalition building among what was both a broad and identifiable section of the elite. The enhanced social resonance of estates that derived from this coalition building made possible their increase in prestige and authority that was needed to expand their financial involvement during the wars of Louis XIV. Coalitions were groupings of individuals and/or interests who shared common political objectives.[29] They were

---

[28] Swann does not account for the changing value of the livre in his calculations. See 'War Finance,' pp. 312-316.

[29] I am inspired in my thinking about coalitions by the work of Marjolein t'Hart on the Dutch Republic. See especially 'Cities and Statemaking in the Dutch Republic, 1580-1680,' *Theory and Society*, 18 (1989): 663-687. Historians of France have mostly ignored coalitions as an organizing force in politics. One exception is James Collins ('Les Conflits des élites locales dans la France moderne: le cas Breton,' *Cahiers d'histoire*, 45 [2000]: 645-674) who has written recently of 'ephemeral coalitions' that arose and fell with 'marvelous rapidity.' His interest in coalitions, though, extends only so far as to understand elite conflict. Likewise, the historical sociologist Richard Lachmann (*Capitalists*) considers coalitions insofar as they shed light on elite conflict.

distinct from other organizing forces that enjoy greater prominence in our understanding of early modern politics and society. They differed, for instance, from patron-client networks in that they were not inherently hierarchical. There could certainly be differences of rank within a coalition, and indeed we would expect such differences in the highly stratified society of seventeenth-century France, but coalitions were by no means strictly vertical relationships of exchange across hierarchical lines of division.[30] Likewise, coalitions differed from the less hierarchical relationships of friendship about which Arlette Jouanna has written, in that they were not posited strictly upon relations of mutual and reciprocal service.[31] Coalitions instead were less explicit groupings, identifiable not by the expressions of loyalty, service, and affection found in correspondences, but in the identification of shared socio-political interests that rallied individuals toward common objectives. Yet we also need to distinguish coalitions from classes, in that they were specific to time and place. Certain coalitions might have been long lasting, but their shape and their strength depended upon the particular institutional and political framework in which they arose.[32] It is to this institutional framework that we now turn, in order to understand why provincial estates in particular were an ideal arena for coalition building.

At the center of the Burgundian ruling coalition were the deputations that gathered at the triennial sessions of the Burgundian estates. These deputations represented a relatively narrow section of the elite, yet despite their restricted make up, the deputies to the estates consistently acted upon an elite agenda that looked beyond narrow corporate interests. Custom, along with an exclusionary stance of the deputies themselves, acted to preserve the strict lines that shaped the deputations. The chamber of the first estate, or clergy, included deputies from the top of the clerical hierarchy down only to the middle ranks of the provincial clergy. At least one, but occasionally all three, of the bishops of Autun, Châlons, and Auxerre, were present; one of these, usually the bishop of Autun, presided over this chamber.[33] Certain privileged cathedral chapters and abbeys sent representatives to make up most of the remainder of this chamber. The majority of the first chamber's deputies thus consisted of the mid to upper ranks of the clergy, with cathedral canons (*chanoines*) and priors of abbeys (*prieurs*) the most numerous.[34] In all, some sixty-five to seventy clerics enjoyed rights of entry into the chamber of the first estate, though as a practical matter fewer actually attended each meeting of the

---

[30] 'Participants [of patron-client relationships] are unequal in status: there is a superior (a patron), and an inferior (a client) in a voluntary, vertical alliance.' Kettering, *Patrons*, p. 13.

[31] Arlette Jouanna, *Le Devoir de révolte*, (Paris: Fayard, 1989), pp. 67-68.

[32] Thus, nor are coalitions necessarily as 'ephemeral' as Collins ('Les Conflits,' p. 646) suggests.

[33] The following information on the composition of the deputation comes from A.D.C.O., C 3018-3019, *Registres des transcriptions des décrets des États*.

[34] Together, these groups numbered 26 out of the 36 deputies in this chamber in 1694, 29 out of the 44 in 1703 and 31 out of the 51 in 1712.

estates.³⁵ The lower clergy with the closest ties to local communities were absent from this delegation. Further, the larger towns of Burgundy, those with cathedrals and abbeys such as Dijon, Autun, Beaune, Châlon and Auxerre, tended to be well represented at the expense of smaller communities.

The chamber of the nobility was similarly exclusive. The right to attend the estates as part of this chamber was strictly limited to holders of fiefs within Burgundy, and landed nobles who only recently acquired their fiefs had difficulty gaining acceptance within this group, for there was a constant struggle on the part of those with access to this chamber to close its doors against newcomers. Those who attained noble status through office holding or from royal letters of ennoblement, therefore, were not welcome within this chamber. Indeed, even those landed nobles of lengthy lineage who then ventured into the profession of the robe lost the privilege of entering this chamber. For this reason, several prominent Burgundian noble families were absent from the chamber of the second estate, including the Chartraire, the Verchère, and the Rigoley.³⁶

The deputies to this chamber attempted as early as 1573 to establish a fixed list of those who could claim the right to attend. They voted to establish committees in each bailiwick that would verify claims and draw up a list of those who could enter their chamber at the next meeting of the estates. Then, toward the end of the seventeenth century, the attempts of the nobility to assure the 'independence of its composition' confronted the rapidly expanding ranks of the newly ennobled within Burgundy. This prompted the nobles of the second estate to draw up yet another list in 1682 to restrict definitively membership in their chamber, this time including only those who held a fief with medium or high justice.³⁷ The 1682 list contained the names of 245 individuals; in general, though, far fewer individuals actually attended each meeting of the estates within the chamber of the nobility. In 1694, 68 members of the province's nobility attended; in 1703 that number fell to 62 and then rose to 75 in 1712. Not all of these deputies were included on the list of 1682. There were six 'newcomers' in 1694, nine in 1703 and twenty three in 1712.³⁸ A succession of further attempts in the eighteenth century to restrict attendance underscores the protracted nature of this struggle.³⁹ The recurrent need to draw up lists and limit membership indicates that this group faced constant pressure throughout the seventeenth and eighteenth centuries from the recently ennobled to join their ranks in the estates and never quite succeeded in cutting them off.

The robe nobility did not find a home in the chamber of the third estate either,

---

³⁵ Swann, *Provincial Power*, chapter 3.
³⁶ Henri Beaune and Jules d'Arbaumont, *La Noblesse aux États de Bourgogne de 1350 à 1789*, (Geneva: Mégariotis Reprints, 1977 [1864]), p. cx.
³⁷ Ibid., pp. lxxxii-lxxxviii.
³⁸ Ibid., pp. 50-59; A.D.C.O., C 3018-3019. We would expect the number of 'newcomers', or those not on the original 1682 list, to have increased over time as new generations inherited fiefs and, thus, the right to attend the estates.
³⁹ Beaune and Arbaumont, *La Noblesse*, p. lxxxix.

where instead a particular 'bourgeois' elite was represented.[40] This chamber brought together representatives of specific, pre-designated, towns. The mayor of Dijon presided over the third estate; a group of towns that made up what was called the large circle, or *la grande roue*, sent two representatives each, usually their mayor along with a lesser town official, to the triennial meetings; and a larger group of towns that made up the small circle alternated amongst themselves the right to send deputations also of two representatives each.[41] The chamber of the third estate thus represented a town-centered elite, where custom and historical chance, not the commercial or demographic importance of a town, determined placement in the *grande roue*, the *petite roue*, or neither.[42] The composition of this chamber was thus actually more tightly sealed against change than was the chamber of the nobility, which, as we have seen, was never able to close itself off completely from newcomers.

In each of the three chambers, therefore, the Estates of Burgundy brought together a relatively restricted deputation resistant to social change. Yet two institutional features of the estates broadened the outlook of the triennial deputations beyond narrow corporate to larger coalition interests. The first of these is the rotation of deputies that occurred within the already restricted groups of individuals who enjoyed the right to attend the estates. For a section of the third estate, this rotation was systematic, with towns of the *petite roue* rotating amongst themselves the right to send delegations. (Each town's delegation was, in turn, determined by local power structures in conjunction with the Condé princes, as noted above). In the first two orders, attendance simply depended upon who, amongst those enjoying the right to attend, decided to join their peers during the reunion of the estates.

Attendance lists from the successive meetings between 1694 and 1703 illustrate the rapid turnover among the 470 individuals who attended at least one of these four meetings. A large majority numbering 341 attended only one of the four meetings. (See Table 3.3). Only eighteen attended all four sessions in a row, ten of whom were deputies in the third estate (nine were venal office holding mayors from towns in the *grande roue*). Measured retrospectively, the rotation rate is equally striking. One hundred fifteen of the 169 deputies in 1697 (68 per cent) had not attended the previous session in 1694. At the 1700 session, 117 of the 184 deputies (64 per cent) had not been present either in 1694 or 1697, and in 1703, 77 of the

---

[40] On occasion, a judicial officer represented a town in the chamber of the third estate. Jean Marc, *conseiller du roy au présidial d'Auxerre*, represented the town of Auxerre at the estates of 1694. Yet nowhere did the important judicial corps of Burgundy, such as the parlement or chamber of accounts, find representation among the three chambers of the estates.

[41] Ligou, 'Les élus,' p. 98.

[42] Henri Beaune and Jules d'Arbaumont offer the example of the small, 'poor', town of Talant, adjacent to Dijon, which at one time had a ducal castle. By virtue of its history, Talant found stronger representation in the chamber of the third estate than five 'large' towns in the county of Auxonne. See Beaune and Arbaumont, *La Noblesse*, p. lxxxvi.

Table 3.3 Attendance rates of deputies to the Estates of Burgundy at four successive meetings, 1694-1703

	one session	%	two sessions	%	three sessions	%	four sessions	%	total
First estate	86	73.50	22	18.80	6	5.13	3	2.56	117
Second estate	123	64.74	40	21.05	22	11.58	5	2.63	190
Third estate	132	80.98	16	9.82	5	3.07	10	6.13	163
All deputies	341	72.55	78	16.60	33	7.02	18	3.83	470

Source: A.D.C.O. C 3018-3019.

156 deputies (49 per cent) had not attended any of the three preceding meetings. There was thus a constant infusion of new individuals whenever the estates met.

To focus upon individuals may overstate the rotation of deputies, since certain families could very well have dominated the proceedings through the presence of different family members over the course of several meetings. Not surprisingly, the lists indicate the recurrence of families especially in the chamber of the nobility. The Foudras family from Châlon, for example, had a regular presence throughout much of the period under study. Louis de Foudras de Demigny partook in the deliberations of the chamber of the nobility in 1694, 1700, and 1703. His son Louis II de Foudras joined him in 1703, and then his son Jacques de Foudras de Rion (later DeMigny) was present in 1712.[43] A number of other families were likewise present at several meetings, including the Joly d'Ecutigny family from Dijon and the Thomassin family from the Charollais, both members of the nobility. And there was some recurrence of family members within the third estate as well, representing especially those towns of the *grande roue*. Claude Charpy represented the town of St. Jean de Losne as its mayor in 1694; the lawyer Jacques Charpy represented the same town in 1703. Jean Pacot represented Talant as its mayor in 1694; André Pacot represented the town, also as its mayor, in 1703.

Certain families, therefore, were indeed present at the meetings of the estates over several generations, yet they amount to only a handful when compared to the total attendance of the estates, and there is no indication that a small number of families dominated the proceedings.[44] This rotation of membership clearly distinguishes the estates from venal officer corps where any changes in membership came about only as offices changed hands either through sale or inheritance. It was the norm in the seventeenth century for venal officer corps to be dominated by a

---

[43] The family relations of the nobility are taken from Beaune and Arbaumont, *La Noblesse*, pp. 109-328.

[44] In this regard, the Estates of Burgundy differed from those of Languedoc where only a handful of bishops and barons dominated the first two chambers of the estates. See Beik, *Absolutism*, pp. 119-130.

handful of prominent families with a dynastic grip on their position.[45] No such dynasticism took hold in the Burgundian estates where 'members' rotated in and out, providing the core of a coalition of interests.

The second, and related, distinguishing feature of estates that promoted the relatively broad outlook of the deputation was the *lack* of direct financial interest that deputies held in 'their' corps. Here, deputies to the estates differed from venal office holders who purchased their offices. Financial negotiations between a venal officer corps and the crown immediately and directly put at risk the investments of the corps' own members.[46] This element of personal property was simply not present in provincial estates. No deputy held a financial stake in the estates as venal officers held in their corps, and though in the second estate possession of a fief conferred the right to attend, the financial negotiations between the estates and the crown did not have a direct and immediate bearing on the value of those fiefs. Lacking a personal financial stake in their corps, deputies to the estates were better positioned to look beyond personal and corporate considerations in defining their interests and in approaching their negotiations with the crown. It is for these reasons that the Estates of Burgundy were an ideal arena for a coalition to form, extending from the deputation outward to include elite interests that spanned the province.

The underlying political objectives that tied together this estates-centered coalition were: 1) the protection of landed revenues, and 2) the defense of the privileged status quo of the province. This was, primarily, a coalition of landed rulers, reflecting the broader Burgundian social structure. The seigneurial system retained a strong hold in Burgundy through the seventeenth and eighteenth centuries, and the province's ruling elite held close ties to the land as both titled seigneurs and non-titled landlords. Some Burgundian land holdings were *allodial* and thus not subject to seigneurial exaction. By far, though, most holdings were *censives* enmeshed in the seigneurial system and subject to a host of dues and jurisdictions. Further, *mainmortable* lands remained numerous in the West of Burgundy. The tenants of these lands were required to gain seigneurial permission before selling their plots; freeing themselves from servile status usually entailed the payment of extraordinary fees.[47] On balance, Burgundy was one of the few French

---

[45] In Burgundy, over the course of the seventeenth century magistrates in the most prominent courts progressively cut their corporations off from new blood, so that by the eighteenth century a handful of families dominated the upper ranks of the robe nobility. Some such families in the parlement were the Espiard, the Thomas and the Pérard. See Gaston Roupnel, *La Ville et la campagne au XVIIe siècle*, (Paris: Armand Colin, 1955), p. 193; and Jules d'Arbaumont, *Armorial de la Chambre des Comptes*, (Dijon, 1881). For similar trends in Normandy, see Dewald, *Formation*.

[46] Bien, 'Offices,' pp. 101-103.

[47] Pierre de Saint-Jacob, *Les Paysans de la Bourgogne du Nord au dernier siècle de l'Ancien Régime*, (Paris: Société des Belles Lettres, 1960), pp. 24-36, 38-40. The costs of freedom from 'la *mainmorte*' were not prohibitive in all cases; throughout western

provinces where the vestiges of feudalism in the countryside remained the strongest through to the end of the Old Regime.

In this context, the possession of large estates, seigneuries, or fiefs constituted a defining characteristic of the provincial ruling elite.[48] Land holding remained both an informal prerequisite for and a symbol of elite status even as Dijon became an important administrative center and as the face of the local elite changed over the course of the sixteenth and seventeenth centuries. Increasingly, members of the Burgundian robe nobility, especially magistrates in the parlement and the chamber of accounts, surpassed much of the older sword nobility in terms of wealth, power, and the possession of rural estates. By the end of the seventeenth century, almost all of the cultivated lands in the Dijonnais region, comprising some fifty villages, were held by Dijonnais robe notables. Similarly, notables in smaller Burgundian towns, particularly those towns like Châtillon-sur-Seine that were local administrative and judicial centers, came to dominate the surrounding countryside as landowners.[49] With the ascendancy of the robe nobility, the ranks of the Burgundian elite underwent significant transformation; still, the possession of landed estates remained one of the primary defining characteristics of elite status, and a primary concern among this elite, as advanced by the estates-centered coalition, was the protection of its landed incomes.

Deputations to the triennial estates, though divided by titled status and rank, shared this underlying interest. Deputies to the chambers of the first and second estates issued from essentially the same families, all of whom we can consider as part of the landed elite.[50] All of the deputies in the second estate, as we have seen, were fiefholders. Some were from military families; others were fiefholding relatives or descendants of robe officials.[51] Thus, while members of the robe nobility were denied direct access to the estates, in many cases their cousins or descendants enjoyed the privilege of attending. Furthermore, the robe elite's interests as landowners and as members of the elite in general certainly overlapped with the interests and concerns of deputies in all three chambers. Put in other terms, the landowning interests promoted in the estates extended beyond the deputations themselves to a broader ruling coalition that included robe officials.

Burgundy pockets of freedom arose in the eighteenth century amidst communities subject to servile condition.

[48] Roupnel, p. 199.

[49] Ibid, pp. 205, 225.

[50] The clerical elite held close ties to both the robe and sword nobilities on several levels. All three groups were major landowners, and the same local families often fed the leading ranks of each group. The abbot Fyot of St. Etienne in Dijon who sat with the leading clerical figures at the estates of 1694 and 1703 was a retired counselor in the Parlement of Dijon. Other clerics from parlementary families included the canons Bouhier and Bretagne and the deans Loppin and Gagne. See Roupnel, pp. 212-213.

[51] At the session of 1718, it is estimated that about one quarter of the deputies in the second estate were descendants or relatives of robe officials, another quarter were sword nobles, and roughly one half were country nobles. See Dumont, p. 31.

Notably absent from both the triennial deputations and the broader ruling coalition, on the other hand, were representatives of commercial interests, despite the increased wealth and prominence of Burgundian merchants after 1650.[52] Even in the chamber of the third estate their presence remained marginal. Occasionally a merchant represented a particular town in this chamber as an *échevin* (alderman).[53] Yet most mayors and *échevins* of Burgundian towns were members of the professions – lawyers, procurators, counselors, or in some cases doctors or surgeons. The municipality of Dijon was typical of Burgundian towns in rarely offering representation within its local government to merchants and mercers.[54] Indeed, its mayors and *échevins* were most often from the same families as were Dijonnais robe officials, families such as the Baudot or the Laloge. The world of commerce was thus effectively kept apart from the landed rulers of the estates-centered coalition.

The *élus*, or the 'executive committee' that oversaw the business of the estates while they were out of session, reflects this estates-centered ruling coalition. Just as the ruling coalition had at its center the deputies to the estates and then extended beyond that core to include privileged and landed interests from throughout the province, so too did the *élus* include representatives from each of the three chambers as well as notables from beyond the estates' deputation. Each of the three chambers designated one member of its deputation to serve as *élu* for the coming three-year term. The clergy chose, alternately, from among bishops, abbots and deans; the third estate chose, alternately, from among the towns of the *grande roue*. In addition, there were *ex-officio* members: the mayor of Dijon (typically an individual drawn from the robe) was always an *élu*, as was the province's treasurer general. Two others were selected from among the officers of the chamber of accounts, and the King designated his *élu du roi*. Including thus a financial official, members of the robe, urban notables, fief-holders and clerics, this executive committee mirrored quite closely the social and professional makeup of the province's ruling coalition. Further, as I demonstrate below, the *élus* took on more and more responsibilities as the estates' role expanded in the latter half of Louis XIV's reign, thus forming a stronger tie between the activities of the estates and the interests of the ruling coalition.

Protecting landed interests and defending the privileged status quo – the political 'program' that united this ruling coalition, meant guarding against both manipulations by the crown and incursions from below. In fiscal matters, the estates supported the interests of large landowners by keeping taxes on their tenants (the non-exempt peasant *taillables*) to a minimum. As noted above, the estates

---

[52] James R. Farr, 'Consumers, Commerce, and the Craftsmen of Dijon,' in *Cities and Social Change in Early Modern France*, ed. Philip Benedict, (London: Unwin Hyman, 1989), pp. 142-153; Roupnel, p. 131.
[53] The merchant Philibert Jan represented Châlon as one of its *échevins* at the estates of 1694.
[54] Roupnel, p. 149.

enjoyed relative success in guarding against wartime increases of those annual charges, such as the *don gratuit*, which were financed mostly by proceeds from the *taille*. The estates could not, however, be tax minimizers in all instances. In order to defend both landed interests and the privileged status quo, the estates had to chart a balance in their negotiations with the crown. On the one hand, they could not erect impassable barriers thwarting the desires of the King at all times, knowing well that if push came to shove, the King could circumvent the estates and impose his fiscal will directly. In other words, the estates needed to remain relevant to the crown's own interests. The experience in Normandy at the beginning of the seventeenth century showed that, as the crown repeatedly circumvented the estates there and collected direct taxes as it wished, the ever increasing obsolescence of that institution enabled its ultimate demise.[55] While Burgundians had successfully rebuffed such measures earlier in the century, it would not at all have been unheard of for the crown to circumvent the estates in an ad hoc manner for the collection of specific revenues.[56] On the other hand, the estates could not grant the King all he wanted, for at that point they would have been of little or no value to local groups.[57]

Furthermore, the mission of the estates to guard peasant tenants (and thus their landlords) against heavy tax burdens could not be pursued at the expense of other concerns. The estates also served to protect the province's privileged standing. To the extent that members of the Burgundian elite benefited from the local financial autonomy conferred by the estates, they also placed a value on preserving the estates' viability into the future. And in addition to protecting the privileges of the province in general, the estates served to shield members of the ruling coalition from both royal manipulations of their status and erosion of their standing from below. Refusal to cooperate with the crown in periods of heightened need would have opened the door not only to royal attacks on the estates' fiscal authority, but to increased sales of newly created offices and privileges as well.

The estates thus balanced a complex web of competing demands in their negotiations with the crown. While the outcomes of specific negotiations differed according to the administrative particularities of the taxes in question, two underlying priorities remained apparent in the estates' approach: to protect their long-term viability and to uphold the interests of the ruling coalition. In adhering to these priorities, the estates continually reiterated which groups belonged to, and which groups were outside of, that coalition. Three examples, or case studies, demonstrate this balance.

---

[55] See Chapter Four.
[56] In Languedoc, for example, where the estates also survived earlier attacks, the crown later succeeded in levying directly (and illegally) 1.1 million livres in 1640 for troop lodgings after those estates refused to provide sufficient funds for a winter quartering. See Beik, *Absolutism*, p. 132.
[57] Ibid., pp. 153-154.

The Taille: Protecting the Tax Base

Integral to the estates' balanced approach to taxation was their opposition to the extension of privileges within the province. Throughout the kingdom, newly created offices and privileges threatened the status and prerogatives of privileged corps. Both venal officer corps and provincial estates made frequent appeals to the crown to halt the sale and extension of privileges, and they were often willing to pay for such a halt. For the Estates of Burgundy, though, such a stance was not always an end in itself. In opposing the extension of privileges throughout the province, including most importantly the proliferation of tax exemptions, the estates were expressing a primary concern for guarding the provinces tax base against erosion and for preserving the integrity of revenues under their control.

Burgundy was a province of *taille personelle*; claims of privileged status in matters of taxation were based upon personal status. Exemption from paying the *taille* could come either from one's status as a nobleman, an office holder or a fief holder.[58] In provinces like Burgundy, claims of privilege were more common than they were in provinces of *taille réelle* where exemptions were attached to specific land holdings. An important and growing gulf thus separated the province's exempt from the mass of Burgundian peasants and 'common' residents of villages and towns. As the number of tax exemptions increased through the sale of offices and titles, the wealthy tended to escape many of the burdens while the remaining *taillables* were left having to support the province's obligations.[59] It was this impoverishment of the tax base that the estates tried to halt, for their timely payments to the crown hinged on their ability to collect sufficient sums.

Usurpation, flight, and social ascension all contributed to the tax base's erosion. At the outbreak of war in 1688 and 1689, the estates at first noted an increased flight of taxpayers from their responsibilities. In several villages, according to the estates' remonstrances, wealthier inhabitants were transferring their residences to neighboring communities where tax burdens were lighter, while retaining a business presence in the original towns. Those who were left residing in the original towns faced heavier burdens from both the *taille* and the lodging of soldiers.[60] The estates had to repeat this complaint in their remonstrances of 1692, and they added to it their observation that the proliferation of privileges and the shifting burden onto the remaining *taillables* was likewise damaging the tax base. The King responded once again, however, that he could do nothing for the moment to address the estates' concerns.

---

[58] Residents of large cities and towns in provinces of *taille personelle* usually enjoyed tax-exempt status. Dijon, however, presented an exception to this rule, and residential status there did not in and of itself confer exemption from the *taille*. See Farr, 'Consumers,' p. 134.

[59] Saint-Jacob, pp. 123-130.

[60] To remedy the distortions caused by flight, the estates asked for the right to impose direct tax obligations based on assessments of individuals at their prior residences for five years following their move. A.D.C.O., C 2982, fols. 202-206.

These concerns did not disappear during the brief interlude of peace following the Nine Years' War. In July 1701, the estates delivered remonstrances pointing to the usurpation of privileged status by the sons of recently ennobled office holders. And in another article of the same set of remonstrances, the estates expressed concern over the growing number of individuals with privileged pretensions who refused to pay the salt tax, a revenue on which the estates depended to service their debts.[61]

Finally, in 1704, the estates asked the King to revoke any tax exemptions the Burgundians may have acquired since 1689 simply by purchasing inexpensive offices, with *finances* of 10,000 livres or less. Their arguments at this point provide a useful summary of their position:

> Your Majesty created during the last war such a great number of offices to which [he] attributed exemptions from the *taille*, from lodging soldiers, and from public charges, that all those who had some wealth, notably in the towns, acquired those offices to an extent that the inhabitants that remain subject to the *taille* are presently not in any state of being able to pay on their own the sums that they were once paying in conjunction with the number of people who have become privileged.[62]

The King addressed the estates' concerns in 1709 and issued a declaration suspending for a period of three years any exemptions from the *taille* attributed to offices created since 1689 for which the original *finances* were under 10,000 livres.[63] The estates responded to this decision with vigor, at times attempting to revoke privileges which had existed long before 1689. Officers of the *cour de la monnoye* in Dijon, for example, had to appeal for protection from the crown against the overly zealous estates who failed to recognize that their offices were 'far from being included in the declarations, [since] the offices which they [held] were created and established several centuries ago, [and] the exemptions attributed to them were confirmed for all time by several edicts, letters patent and *arrêts*.'[64] Office holders from the presidial court of Dijon were also targeted by the estates to be placed back on the *taille* roles, but by order of the Controller General they too were able to preserve their privileges. In the end, office holders in the least prestigious courts, such as the marble table (with jurisdiction over waters and forests) in Dijon or the *grenier à sel* (salt warehouse and tribunal) at Is sur Til, lost their privileges and lacked the patronage necessary to reverse the estates' actions.[65]

Thus, while they had to be reined in, the estates opposed the extension of tax exemptions at virtually all levels of the judiciary below that of superior courts. By taking this stance, deputies were upholding the interests of the elite coalition on two levels. First, they were guarding against rapid social ascension that the sale of

---

[61] A.D.C.O., C 2982, July 1701, fols. 424-427.
[62] A.D.C.O., C 2983, 25 September 1704, fols. 42-48.
[63] A.D.C.O., C 2983, 14 September 1709, fol. 185.
[64] A.N., E 818^b, 8 July 1710, fol. 121.
[65] A.D.C.O., C 5808.

offices and privileges enabled and that threatened to dilute the prestige, authority, and financial interests of provincial rulers. Second, on a level that transcended the personal interests of individual provincial rulers, the deputies of the estates were also rallying around strategies to preserve the long-term viability of the estates along with the benefits accorded by local financial autonomy. The Burgundian leaders were unwilling to allow a shrinking direct tax base in their province since it would leave the estates hobbled and unable to perform their main functions. Such a development could very well have opened the door to the same fate as that suffered by the Norman estates.[66]

The Dixième: *Shifting the Burden Outside of the Coalition*

However, the estates took a different approach to the *dixième* following its establishment in 1710. Collection of this tax was under the control of royal officials. In Burgundy, the *intendant* Trudain oversaw the declarations of wealth and income required of all households in order to assess their liability.[67] The estates, therefore, held no stake in this tax. The *dixième* did not finance any of the annual charges that the estates owed to the royal treasury, and the estates never reached agreement with the crown to assume control over this tax, at least during its first incarnation, in return for regular annual payments.[68] The estates could therefore advocate for scaling back this tax without threatening their own viability, and indeed in their 1712 remonstrances to the King, they appealed for exemptions for any Burgundian already subject to the *taille* and capitation. Delegates to the estates understood the intention behind the *dixième* to be to tax the wealth of 'merchants and others who profit through investing *(faire valoir leur argent)* and especially of those who have not contributed to the war effort.'[69] Hoping thus to spare *taillables* and, in so doing, to protect landed revenues, delegates to the estates did not hesitate to single out merchants, who were distinctly outside the estates-

---

[66] For this reason, the estates in 1708 complained that the receivers from the *greniers et chambres à sel*, those who collected salt tax revenues in Burgundy, were not as forthcoming with their receipts as they should have been. The estates depended upon the revenues from the salt tax for sums that supplemented the *dons gratuits*. Faced with the diminution of these revenues, they requested and attained the rights to inspect the account books of the tax collectors. Here, with the support of the crown, the estates succeeded in expanding their jurisdiction in financial matters and in preserving their role as defenders of local autonomy. A.D.C.O., C 2983, 3 April 1708, fols. 123-125.

[67] *Délaration du Roy pour la levée du Dixième du revenu des biens du royaume*, A.D.C.O., C 361 ter.

[68] According to a report from the intendant de la Briffe, the estates in 1712 rebuffed offers from the crown to hand over to them control over the *dixième* in exchange for 800,000 livres per year. When this tax was revived in 1733, the estates agreed to an annual 'subscription' of 700,000 livres, taking the tax out of the hands of royal officials and placing it under the control of the estates. M. de la Briffe to Controller General, 15 December 1712, A.N. H^1 99, dossier 7; *Arrêt du conseil*, 23 March 1734, A.D.C.O., C 5808.

[69] *Registre des cahiers des remonstrances*, A.D.C.O. 3330, fols. 39-40.

centered ruling coalition, as liable for the tax. However, lacking a direct stake in the *dixième*, the estates also lacked the political leverage necessary to negotiate change, and the *dixième* remained in place without alteration until its revocation in 1718.

The Capitation: Preserving the Privileged Status Quo

While deputies to the estates were willing to step forth in support of *taillables* over payment of the *dixième*, the three orders split over solutions to provide relief from the capitation. The estates, as we have seen, were responsible for making annual payments to the crown under the heading of capitation. They thus had an interest in ensuring its effective collection. The nobility and certain privileged corps were expected to pay fixed amounts toward the annual sum; the non-privileged paid the capitation as a supplement to their annual *taille* obligations. At the 1718 session of the estates, the first two orders refused to entertain a proposal by the third estate to expand the base for this tax by shifting more of the burden to the nobility. In addition to providing relief for *taillables*, greater equity in apportionment would certainly have enhanced this revenue stream, thereby assuring that the estates would meet their yearly obligations. The estates, after all, had acted to reverse the growing inequity in the *taille* roles for this precise reason. Yet the nobility, and along with them the clergy, were unwilling to rewrite the distinctions accorded by privilege when their own standing was at issue. Instead, they rallied to preserve the privileged status quo, including foremost their own privileges and exemptions.[70]

The estates thus defined and upheld their view of the local political hierarchy while negotiating with the crown. The ruling coalition included the landed elite, with an interest in minimizing land taxes, and those at the top of the privileged hierarchy among both the robe (clerical and judicial) and the sword. Merchants, robe officials in courts below the status of superior, and those whose social ascension through the ranks of venality was deemed too rapid, were outside. Protecting the interests of the former was a primary concern for the estates. To do so, however, required a complex juggling act, especially as the estates found themselves under increased pressure to provide extraordinary support to the crown in the decades following the outbreak of war in 1689. Once the estates began borrowing for the crown on a sustained basis, their relevance both to the crown and to the Burgundian ruling coalition was enhanced, as power shifted to the province.

---

[70] Dumont, pp. 63-65.

Intermediation: Shifting the Political Balance

Compelling the Estates to Borrow

The expanded financial role that the Estates of Burgundy undertook as they intermediated for the crown was at once both an expression of the ruling coalition's underlying interests and a force to reshape those interests in light of new circumstances. While the estates never diverged from promoting the ruling coalition's underlying interests in minimizing land taxes and protecting the privileged status quo, they now had to contend with defending their own credit and, with it, the investments of their bondholders.

The crown exercised considerable leverage by which it could compel the estates to borrow for the royal treasury. Louis XIV recognized the value which the ruling coalition placed upon privilege and the preservation of its status quo, and he could use that stance to solicit extraordinary financial support from the estates.[71] The crown typically began its appeals for increased support by issuing edicts that created new privileges for sale. The estates would then typically offer to 'repurchase' the edicts and take the newly created offices and privileges off the market in exchange for a payment to the crown. In 1700, for example, the estates paid the crown 922,000 livres, which they borrowed on credit markets, for the repurchase of twenty-four edicts considered contrary to the province's interests.[72] Of these twenty-four edicts, seven would have created offices such as controllers of marriage proclamations and communal treasurers (*controlleurs des bans de marriage* and *trésoriers des bourses communes*). Three of the edicts were intended to create surtaxes. These included a tax of 10 livres per *arpent* of wood and a surtax payable to the receivers of fines. And two edicts would have created *augmentations de gages* attached to *jurés crieurs* and *premiers huissiers audienciers*.

The bulk of these edicts, then, would have created offices and extended privileges at the lower end of the privileged hierarchy. They did not create offices or dilute privileges among the more powerful venal officer corps of the province, such as the parlement, the chamber of accounts, the *présidiaux*, *élections* or *bailliages*. Rather, they created mostly administrative offices with surtaxes attached, offices of little political import that found favor with Louis XIV as extraordinary financial measures.[73] Few if any of these edicts would therefore have impinged upon the direct personal interests of the deputies of the first two orders of

---

[71] Nora Temple ('The Control and Exploitation of French Towns During the Ancien Régime,' in *State and Society in Seventeenth-Century France*, ed. Raymond Kierstead [New York: New Viewpoints, 1975], pp. 80-81) argues that this actually constituted a disadvantage for provinces with estates, that 'the very existence of this corporate organization [the estates] facilitated the negotiation of irregular subsidies.'

[72] A.D.C.O., C 3019, fol. 69. The estates borrowed the sums to pay these rachats from a wide network of creditors, both Burgundian and non-Burgundian. See Chapter Six.

[73] Louis-Lucas, 2: 27-28.

the estates.[74] Some of the edicts would have altered the governance of towns and thus undermined the interests of the municipal based elite and impinged upon what by then had become the estates' growing role in managing towns.[75] For the most part, though, these edicts would have created those types of offices and extended those levels of privilege which the estates had decried on several occasions in their remonstrances to the crown – those with no crucial function, of little political import but whose proliferation undermined the tax base of the province. Louis XIV and his ministers thus proved adept at identifying and manipulating those sets of privileges that struck at the overall privileged status of the province, and in doing so, they effectively cajoled the estates to offer support.

By arranging for the repurchase of edicts, deputies to the estates were reinforcing the privileged hierarchy within the province, and in some ways they were actually enhancing the social and political standing of certain elite groups. One set of *rachats* in particular demonstrates how the estates promoted the interests of the politically prominent while responding to royal pressures. In 1692, Louis XIV converted into venal offices all of the mayoralties throughout the kingdom, except those of Paris and Lyon. Elsewhere, the customary method of electing the mayor, *capitoul, premier échevin*, or whatever the local designation might be, was to be supplanted by the sale and patrimonial possession of these offices. The crown argued that it was acting to suppress the growing tide of factionalism on the municipal level where favoritism was dispensed with alarming frequency by politically indebted mayors. Of course the financial interests for the crown should not be overlooked either – in Burgundy, the *finances* of these newly created offices amounted to 466,362 livres.[76]

Confronted with this conversion of mayoralties into patrimonial offices, the estates found that their own institution's internal cohesiveness was threatened, since town mayors sat in the chamber of the third estate. Not wanting to see this chamber become one of an entrenched hereditary elite, the estates issued a decree in 1694 offering to purchase all offices of mayor from those who in the last two years had acquired them and then to 'unite' those offices to the corps of the estates.[77] In an edict of January 1696, the King accepted the estates' offer and allowed them to

---

[74] Of the twenty-four edicts repurchased in 1700, one would have impinged directly upon the titled nobility by establishing a province-wide process of verification of noble status to root out usurpers.

[75] Two of the twenty-four edicts would have created the offices of town governors and communal treasurers in each municipality.

[76] A.D.C.O., C 3503, *Registre des maires de la province de Bourgogne*. Not surprisingly, the mayoralty of Dijon was worth the most; its *finance* totaled 100,000 livres. The next most valuable mayoralties were those of Auxonne and Autun which amounted to 32,667 livres and 28,000 livres. The least expensive offices of mayor were those of Fontaine Françoize and Villaine en Duesmois at 1000 and 800 livres respectively. On municipal elections, factionalism, and royal reform, see Hilary J. Bernstein, 'The Benefit of the Ballot? Elections and Influence in Sixteenth-century Poitiers,' *French Historical Studies*, 24 (2001): 621-652.

[77] Temple, pp. 78-79.

purchase the offices from their holders. Those individuals who had already acquired the offices continued to possess them until full reimbursement was made. Thereafter, the estates, and in particular the *élus*, enjoyed the prerogative of designating the mayors and, thus, the deputies to their own chamber of the third estate.

Beyond protecting the internal functioning of the estates from royal intervention, this *rachat* also solidified a hierarchy both within the estates and throughout the province. Within the estates, the repurchase of mayoralties strengthened the first two orders at the expense of the third, since deputies to the chamber of the third estate were thereafter dependent for their positions on the estates as a whole. On a province-wide level, the estates attained an enhanced degree of control and dominance over municipalities with the new-found ability to designate mayors, thus countering at least in part the march toward centralized royal control of towns begun under Colbert.[78] Indeed, thereafter, the estates could count on the province's mayors to act as their agents, or, in the words of Julian Swann, to act as their own set of 'subdelegates' to rival those acting under the authority of the intendant.[79] The municipality of Dijon, however, remained an exception to this development. Before the King issued his edict of January 1696 allowing the estates to purchase the offices of mayor, the Dijon town council had already acted on its own to prevent the conversion of its mayoralty into a venal office. In exchange for 100,000 livres, the crown agreed to unite the office to the municipality itself, thereby preserving the customary method of choosing that city's mayor.[80] The mayor of Dijon, therefore, never became subordinate to the estates, and the individual elected to that post continued to act as both president of the chamber of the third estate and as one of the seven *élus*. Particular elements of the Burgundian elite thus managed to secure an enhanced political and social standing through the actions of the estates. The landed nobility and the clergy strengthened their position over the town-based elite (largely made up of members of the professions), and Dijon, along with its leaders, continued to stand above any other town as an independent political force.

Again, the value placed upon the enhanced standing of the estates, and especially upon the enhanced standing of the first two orders of the privileged elite, rendered them vulnerable to future financial pressure from the crown. In 1706, the crown forced the hand of the estates by creating the venal offices of alternative and triennial mayors. If the estates wished to preserve the changes brought about by the first repurchase for which they had not by then even made full payment, they

---

[78] The Condé princes continued to influence the designation of mayors even after this repurchase. Nonetheless, the union of these offices to the corps of the estates clearly established a hierarchy of provincial authority in which the estates dominated the towns. Julian Swann ('War Finance,' p. 303) states that following this repurchase of mayoralties by the estates, 'any deputy of the third estate who showed signs of independence... risked being called to account by either the governor or the *élus*.'
[79] Swann, *Provincial Power*, chapter 5.
[80] A.M.D., M 24, 26 January 1693.

needed to repurchase this new edict as well. In 1708, therefore, the estates forwarded the crown 950,000 livres, again borrowed on credit markets, for the repurchase of *maires alternatifs* along with twelve other edicts creating offices, *augmentations de gages* and surtaxes.[81]

The estates did not, however, repurchase all edicts which touched upon the composition of municipal government. Occasionally municipalities themselves were pressured into financing repurchases if they wished to preserve the status quo of their governance in the face of royal edicts creating new offices. In 1693, the municipality of Dijon borrowed 66,000 livres to finance a repurchase of two edicts which had created the offices of *procureur* and of *secrétaire et greffier* of the city. With this repurchase, these offices were then joined and united to the municipality which could thereafter choose to fill them or simply leave them vacant.[82] And in 1694, the municipalities of Burgundy together paid 140,900 livres for the repurchase and union to their corps of the offices of colonels, majors, lieutenants and captains of the bourgeois.[83] Although the towns raised these sums on their own through a combination of taxing their residents and borrowing against their municipal revenues, the estates intervened and supervised these extraordinary arrangements. And occasionally in their negotiations with the crown, the estates 'volunteered' the financial intermediation of towns. In 1691, Burgundian towns paid 250,000 livres in *secours extraordinaire* as arranged in negotiations between the crown and the estates, indicating again the Burgundian estates' dominance over the province's towns even prior to the estates' repurchase and union of mayoralties.[84]

On several occasions, therefore, municipalities were left to finance such repurchases on their own if they wanted to prevent the creation of privately held offices and surtaxes. As corps interested in preserving their own privileged status quo, municipalities were as vulnerable as the estates to such royal pressures. As such, it was certainly possible for the Burgundian towns to have repurchased their own offices of mayor and unite them to their municipal corps rather than allowing the estates to step up and finance the repurchase. The municipality of Dijon did just that, and towns throughout the kingdom not under the tutelage of provincial estates reacted to the edict of 1692 in a similar fashion wherever they could afford the *finances*.[85] Why, when the Estates of Burgundy did not feel the need to repurchase all edicts affecting the composition of municipal government, did they come forth to repurchase the offices of mayor? They did so for the simple reason that the introduction of venality specifically among the mayoralties would have adversely

---

[81] A.D.C.O., C 3505 and C 3019, fol. 402.

[82] A.M.D., M 24, 30 August 1693. Between 1693 and 1701, the municipality of Dijon borrowed a total of 511,169 livres for the repurchase of eleven different sets of edicts. Charles Bertucat, *Les Finances municipales de Dijon depuis la liquidation des dettes (1662) jusqu'en 1789*, (Dijon: Nourry, 1910), pp. 140-142.

[83] A.D.C.O., C 327, 5 October 1694.

[84] A.D.C.O., C 3018, fol. 272.

[85] For the example of Rouen repurchasing its office of mayor, see Chapter Four.

affected the internal cohesion of the estates, and by taking the initiative to repurchase these offices, the estates actually increased their prominence and authority in the province. Other creations of municipal offices simply did not have such an impact, and the estates did not feel as compelled to repurchase them.

Just as the estates did not intervene to repurchase all edicts affecting the composition of municipal corps, nor did they act to repurchase edicts altering the privileges of sovereign courts. Rather, members of the Burgundian robe nobility were left to negotiate the protection of their own privileges as they saw fit. Occasionally, the crown created and then sold redundant judicial offices to Burgundians looking for social ascension.[86] At other times, corps of venal officers repurchased those edicts of creation before the offices reached the market. In doing so, the corps prevented the proliferation of privately held offices, and they assumed the *gages* which would have gone to the new officers. These *augmentations de gages* then helped the corps to finance the sums needed for the repurchases, much as David Bien has described.[87] In 1704, the crown announced plans to create 2 presidents, 4 *maîtres des comptes*, 4 *correcteurs*, 4 *audienciers*, 1 keeper of the registers, 2 scribes and 1 receiver in the chamber of accounts. To keep these new offices from falling into private hands, pushing down the value of their original offices and diverting the flow of fees from which the magistrates and accountants profited, the officers of the chamber of accounts negotiated with the King to repurchase the edict of creation and assume the *gages* which would have gone to the new officers. The King's declaration agreeing to this repurchase belies the crown's interests in these negotiations:

> ...and as the number of which the said chamber is composed [totaling] 8 presidents, 28 *conseillers maistres*... suffices to fill all the functions with all the dignity appropriate for a superior court, we have judged most expedient to consider the proposal made to us by the officers of the said chamber to pay us the sum of 300,000 livres to enjoy the sum of 18,000 livres in *gages* to compensate for the emergency aid which we would have attracted from the said new offices which have not been sold yet.[88]

The crown's interests were clearly financial. Creating and selling the offices amounted to an extraordinary means of raising funds. The corps' willingness to acquire for itself the offices along with the attached *gages* only made the crown's search for funds easier. The royal treasury did not have to wait for individual

---

[86] Five offices in the parlement and eight in the chamber of accounts were created by edict in March 1691 and sold by June of that same year, opening a path into the local robe elite to such individuals as Mamet Chevaldin, formerly a controller in the *grenier à sel* at Dijon who purchased the newly created office of *correcteur* in the chamber of accounts for 20,000 livres. A.D.C.O., B 55, fols. 64-109.

[87] Bien, 'Offices.'

[88] A.D.C.O., B 6, *Chambre des comptes*. For a record of the actual payment of this *augmentation de gages*, see A.D.C.O., B 59, 1 September 1705, fol. 18.

Table 3.4 **Principal due for *augmentations de gages* from superior courts, in livres**

Province/Généralité	1701/02	1703	total
Bretagne	1082222	1103000	2185222
Rouen	1063666	1044760	2108426
Dijon	685573	669160	1354733
Montpellier	640000	664400	1304400
Toulouse	571400	566920	1138320
Grenoble	510089	509600	1019689
Bordeaux	506811	503140	1009951
Provence	446794	446106	892900
Metz	248698	260098	508796
Pau	145067	144800	289867
Franche Comté	131243	132090	263333
Clermont	50600	50600	101200
Tournay	—	100000	100000
Montauban	43936	43926	87862
Blois	9600	9600	19200

Source: A.N. G⁷ 1543, *Receptes des augmentations de gages en 1701 et 1702; Bordereau des augmentations des cours des provinces, mars 1703.*

purchasers to come forth; by simply announcing the creation, the crown compelled the members of the chamber of accounts to forward a loan of 300,000 livres.[89]

Because Dijon was such an important administrative center, the Burgundian robe nobility was among the hardest hit in the kingdom by such creations of redundant offices and *augmentations de gages*. Only the sovereign courts in Rouen, Brittany and Languedoc were expected to pay more than the courts of Dijon.[90] This ranking, as detailed in Table 3.4, attests to more than just the high profile of the robe nobility in these few regions. It also suggests that provincial estates, in Languedoc and Brittany as well as in Burgundy, did little to shield the local robe from royal coercion. Among the administrative centers heading this list,

---

[89] There is considerable indication that venal officer corps faced difficulties finding lenders, especially during the decades under consideration. This 1705 *rachat* by the chamber of accounts seems to be an exception, as full payment for the *augmentation de gages* was made within one year. For examples of significant delays as venal officer corps sought lenders, see Chapters Two and Four.

[90] A.N., G⁷ 1543, *Augmentations de gages aux officiers des cours superieures, 1702-1713*. The province of Languedoc is split on both of these lists between Toulouse, where the parlement is located, and Montpellier, home to the chamber of accounts. If these two areas are considered together, the combined total for Languedocian courts tops the list both times.

only Rouen, as part of Normandy, did not enjoy representation through estates, having lost them earlier in the century. The Estates of Burgundy, as we have seen, clearly opposed the extension of privilege throughout the province, and they repurchased scores of edicts to prevent such extensions. Why, then, did they not intervene when the crown threatened to create judicial offices and undermine the privileges of the robe?

Although robe officials were clearly members of the province's ruling coalition whose interests, as both landowners and beneficiaries of the privileged status quo, were upheld by the estates, there seems to have been a calculation on the part of the estates that the particular corps affected were in a position to defend and promote their own interests in such cases by repurchasing the edicts themselves. This was a reasonable calculation since the leading members of the corps had personally vested interests in seeing that new offices did not reach the market.[91] They were likely, then, to react as corps to repurchase the edicts for a sum and acquire the *augmentations des gages* themselves. This was not the case, on the other hand, for the many edicts which the estates did intervene to repurchase. There were no corps bringing together the controllers of marriage proclamations, for example, who could have repurchased newly created offices and joined them along with any surtaxes to their corps. In such cases, the estates stepped forward to prevent a proliferation of privilege. Where sovereign courts were targets of royal financial pressures, on the other hand, the estates could remain confident that there would be no widespread dilution of privilege through the creation of new judicial offices. In their financial dealings with the crown, then, the estates consistently staked out a position that protected above all the province's privileged standing, namely their own financial autonomy and the benefits to the privileged elite that derived from that autonomy.

Meeting both Royal and Provincial Needs

As the remainder of this chapter shows, the estates' promotion of the ruling coalition's interests created a series of arrangements in the latter half of Louis XIV's reign whereby the estates intermediated royal finances to an almost unparalleled extent.[92] The rise of provincial estates as important financial intermediaries then had political implications lasting beyond the Sun King's reign.

---

[91] In fact, members of corps were often divided in how they viewed new creations, with subordinate office holders embracing newly created offices as a means of social ascension. Thus, the estates were effectively leaving judicial corps to negotiate such differences among themselves. Chapter Four explores these internal corporate divisions in Norman judicial corps.

[92] Only the few other prominent provincial estates, those of Languedoc, Provence and Brittany, along with the Assembly of the Clergy, were able to borrow sums of money for the crown on the same order as the Estates of Burgundy. As will be presented in Chapters Four and Six, other privileged corps such as municipalities and venal officer corps borrowed from the public on a much more limited scale and with greater reluctance and difficulty.

As I will argue, successful financial intermediation by the Burgundian estates was made possible only by their political strength. The estates could not have borrowed the sums they did while retaining a reputation as a responsible borrower without effectively being able to assert a will independent of the crown. That 'will' derived locally from the shared interests of the Burgundian ruling coalition.

The extraordinary financial arrangements that developed between the Burgundian estates and the crown proved to be the most flexible element in their overall financial relationship. Regular annual payments by the estates, mostly supported through direct taxation, remained relatively stable during the period of heightened financial need, as detailed above. In contrast, the estates' practice of borrowing against future indirect revenues under their control allowed them to respond to the crown's wartime demands. Indeed, borrowing by the estates served to meet the demands and needs of both the crown and the provincial ruling coalition in two ways.

First, a portion of the regular annual contributions paid to the crown by the estates was raised by borrowing against specific future indirect revenues. The agreement establishing the estates' million-livre annual 'subscription' to the capitation, for example, permitted them to borrow 416,000 livres per year, leaving only 584,000 livres to be raised through direct taxation. Other 'regular' annual obligations, including the *don gratuit*, the *subsistence* and the *exemption du logement de gens de guerre*, were also met at least in part by borrowing against future indirect revenues. As Table 3.5 presents, these portions grew through fits and starts, from around a quarter in the late 1680s to about a third between 1703 and 1710. Their subsequent decrease came about only because, with the 1710 repurchase of the capitation, no longer did the estates have that charge to meet through borrowing. Throughout this period of warfare and heightened demands, then, the Burgundian elite managed to shift some of the province's fiscal burdens away from present direct tax obligations supported with land taxes toward the future indirect tax obligations that backed these loans.

Even more significant in terms of how the estates responded to the King's heightened demands, these same sets of indirect revenues under local control also provided the means by which the estates financed their repurchases of edicts and other extraordinary payments to the crown. Between the years 1680 and 1715, these payments cost the estates a total of 13,389,500 livres for which they borrowed 12,288,030 livres. (See Table 3.6). Without specific revenues under local control that the estates could mortgage, they would not have been able to raise such significant sums for the crown other than by turning to direct taxes on peasant tenants.

Thus, indirect tax revenues under local control accorded a certain flexibility to the estates' financial role. This flexibility did not arise from the nature of the taxes themselves, but by virtue of the particular relationship that evolved between the estates and the crown concerning these taxes. The ensuing negotiations concerning these taxes, then, are crucial for a comprehensive understanding of the financial

Table 3.5 Borrowing by Estates of Burgundy to cover annual direct tax obligations (000 livres)

Year	Don gratuit	for payment of: Subsistence/ exemption	Capitation	Total	Percentage of annual charge
1680	—	432	—	432	39
1681	—	—	—	—	0
1682	—	—	—	—	0
1683	—	—	—	—	0
1684	—	—	—	—	0
1685	130	70	—	200	21
1686	200	—	—	200	21
1687	280	—	—	280	29
1688	—	—	—	—	0
1689	190	—	—	190	20
1690	232	—	—	232	24
1691	260	—	—	260	27
1692	—	—	—	—	0
1693	280	—	—	280	29
1694	—	—	—	—	0
1695	550	—	—	550	57
1696	270	—	—	270	28
1697	270	—	—	270	28
1698	270	—	—	270	28
1699	270	—	—	270	28
1700	270	—	—	270	28
1701	270	—	416	686	72
1702	270	—	416	686	72
1703	270	—	416	686	35
1704	270	—	416	686	35
1705	270	—	416	686	35
1706	270	—	416	686	35
1707	270	—	416	686	35
1708	270	—	416	686	35
1709	270	—	416	686	36
1710	266.66	270	—	536.66	28
1711	266.66	—	—	266.66	14
1712	266.66	—	—	266.66	17
1713	266.66	100	—	366.66	24
1714	266.66	160	—	426.66	28
1715	266.66	260	—	526.66	34

Table 3.5 (Continued)

Year	for payment of:			Total	Percentage of annual charge
	Don gratuit	Subsistence/ exemption	Capitation		
1716	270	—	—	270	17
1717	270	—	—	270	17
1718	270	—	—	270	17

Source: A.D.C.O., C3378-3391, États de l'administration des élus pendant la triennalité.

relationship between the crown and the Estates of Burgundy. The remainder of this chapter will focus on the negotiations between the crown and the estates over the specific indirect tax revenue called the *octrois de la Saône*.

The Octrois de la Saône

The two sets of indirect revenues which the estates pledged in order to meet a growing portion of their annual obligations and to raise their lump-sum payments to the crown were the *crues de sel* and the *octrois de la Saône*. The *crues de sel* were revenues from salt taxes, essentially the Burgundian equivalent of the *gabelle*. The *octrois de la Saône* were tolls on goods shipped along the Saône river. Though the two revenues have slightly different histories, they served the same financial functions during the time period under study, and their mortgaging by the estates had the same long-term political implications.

The *octrois* were initially established as an extraordinary and temporary revenue administered directly by royal commissioners. Though they were nominally temporary, these revenues in fact became permanently entrenched in the fiscal landscape of late-seventeenth and eighteenth-century France, while their administration devolved to the level of the estates. The term *octrois* refers to any revenue accorded to a local government by the crown. By definition, therefore, the revenues from the various *octrois* throughout the kingdom never entered directly into the King's coffers. In the administration of municipal budgets, revenues from *octrois* were typically distinguished from revenues of the *patrimoine*. Towns collectively possessed patrimonial revenues; rights to collect *octrois*, on the other hand, only existed with the express will of the King.[93] Most often the crown granted *octrois* to municipalities; the *octrois de la Saône*, however, were accorded to and administered by the Estates of Burgundy after 1689.[94]

---

[93] Monique Gebhart and Claude Mercadier, *L'Octroi de Toulouse à la veille de la Révolution*, (Paris: Bibliothèque Nationale, 1967), p. 2.
[94] Burgundian municipalities that had their own *octrois* included Dijon, Beaune, Mâcon, Nuits, Semur en Auxois, Chatillon sur Seine and Châlon sur Saône. See Arch. Nat.,

Table 3.6 Borrowing by Estates of Burgundy to cover extraordinary obligations (000 livres)

Year	Purpose of payment	Total obligation to crown	Sums borrowed	Revenues mortgaged
1682	repurchase of edicts	97	97	crues de sel
1689	acquisition of *octrois*	800	800	octrois de la Saône
1691	emergency aid to the crown	700	700	octrois de la Saône
1692	repurchase of edicts	200	200	crues de sel
1693	repurchase of edicts	630	630	octrois de la Saône
1694	emergency aid to the crown	450	450	octrois de la Saône
1696	repurchase of edicts	210	210	octrois de la Saône
1697	repurchase of edicts	307.5	307.5	various
1697	acquisition of *crues de sel*	352	352	crues de sel
1697	emergency aid to the crown	450	450	octrois de la Saône
1700	repurchase of edicts	1020	620	crues de sel
1703	repurchase of edicts	491	416	octrois de la Saône
1706	repurchase of edicts	682	577	octrois de la Saône
1708	repurchase of edicts	950	651.37	—
1710	repurchase of edicts	1000	846.3	octrois de la Saône
1710	repurchase of *capitation*	2400	2400	octrois de la Saône
1712	repurchase of edicts	200	200	—
1714	repurchase of edicts	2000	2000	—
1715	repurchase of edicts	450	380.86	octrois de la Saône
Total:		13389.5	12288.03	

Source: A.D.C.O., B 55; C 3018-3019, 3499, 3524.

The crown first established the *octrois de la Saône* in 1668 as a means of financing Colbert's program to verify and then amortize municipal debt in Burgundy.[95] At this point, the estates as yet held no control over or stake in these revenues. The intendant and the commissioners deputized for the verification of municipal debt, oversaw the leasing of the rights to collect the *octrois* and administered the receipts and expenditures of the revenues.[96] Throughout this process of municipal debt amortization, towns lost much of their financial

---

H¹*140ᵇ. For a brief history of the *octroi de Dijon* under the Old Regime, see the first chapter in Robert Laurent, *L'Octroi de Dijon au XIXe siècle*, (Paris: SEVPEN, 1960).

[95] Charles Arbassier, *L'Absolutisme en Bourgogne: l'intendant Bouchu et son action financièr*, (Dijon: Thorey, 1919), pp. 143-151.

[96] A.N., E 1820, 27 March 1683, fol. 86. As with practically all indirect taxes, the collection of the *octrois de la Saône* was farmed out to the highest bidding company.

independence to the crown's commissioners who, even after reducing the level of municipal debt to manageable levels, retained strict control over towns' revenues and expenses in an attempt to assure continued solvency.[97] At the outset, therefore, the establishment of the *octrois de la Saône* coincided with a strengthening of royal control over local financial matters.

The *octrois* were collected at eight points along the Saône between Pontallier in the north and Mâcon in the south.[98] At each point, established tariffs determined the items to be taxed and the rates of taxation. The items taxed included consumption goods, such as wine, fish, and animal skins, semi-finished products and raw materials such as grain, iron, wood cut for wine barrels and charcoal. As an internal toll, this was the type of indirect tax which observers both then and now condemn for creating market distortions, not only regressively taxing items of mass consumption, but hindering the integration of France's domestic market by adding to transport costs. The *octrois de la Saône* only represented one set of many tolls scattered throughout France, with goods often subjected to internal customs, municipal *octrois* and private tolls (*péages*) as well.[99] This host of tolls often proved prohibitive to long distance commerce within France, thereby favoring local

---

[97] A.N., E 1838, *Minutes d'arrêts relatifs à la liquidation des dettes des villes de Bourgogne, Charolais, Mâconnais et Auxerrois*. Hilton L. Root (*Peasants and Kings in Burgundy: Agrarian Foundations of French Absolutism*, [Berkeley and Los Angeles: University of California Press, 1987], pp. 35-40) argues that the crown held a strong interest in ensuring the solvency of towns, since those towns on a strong financial footing could best meet the crown's financial exigencies. For the same reason, following Colbert's campaign to eradicate municipal debt, towns were forbidden to ever again mortgage their patrimonial revenues or common holdings. This explains why municipal *octrois* remained in existence after the amortization of municipal debt, despite repeated stipulations on the part of the crown that such *octrois* were only for debt servicing and would be abolished upon amortization. Thereafter, the crown could circumvent its own restrictions against towns mortgaging their patrimonial revenues by pressuring them instead to borrow against their *octrois*, with the resulting sums going to the crown. Thus the crown granted a 6 year continuation of the municipal *octrois* 'that had been raised for the amortization of their debts' to Burgundian towns in 1696 in exchange for a payment of 146,444 livres, against which revenues the towns borrowed the sums demanded by the crown. See A.N., $H^{1}*140^b$, 26 May 1696.

[98] The eight points of collection along the Saône were at Pontallier, Auxonne, St. Jean de Losne, Seurre, Verdun, Châlon sur Saône, Tournus, and Mâcon.

[99] Items principally taxed by municipal *octrois* in Burgundy were wine, livestock, wood and iron. Altogether, the numerous tolls on the transport of goods within France could multiply prices many fold. Ernest Labrousse offers the example of a barrel of wine valued at 36 livres traveling from Languedoc to Paris. Altogether, the tolls and internal customs would add 225 livres 16 sous to the cost, bringing the sale price in Paris up to 500 livres after adding the costs of transport. See *Esquisse du mouvement des prix et des revenus en France au XVIIIe siècle*, 2 vols., (Paris, 1933), 1:272.

consumption of products at the expense of long distance transport and an integration of internal markets.

Despite such distortions within Burgundy, the Saône proved indispensable to regional commercial activity. While not a main trade route linking the economies of northern and southern Europe, the Saône represented a vital outlet for the export of wines, grain, iron and wood both south toward Languedoc and Provence and north toward Paris. More locally, the Saône linked numerous Burgundian communities along the river valley.[100] Dependent upon the river as they were, it was largely the inhabitants of the Saône valley, whether as consumers, producers or exporters of goods, rather than long distance merchants traveling through the region, who bore the costs of the *octrois de la Saône*.

Contemporaries testified to these costs borne by both the mass of consumers and the region's merchants. In two letters to the office of the Controller General in June 1681, Claude Bouchu, intendant of Burgundy, underscored the damage to commerce caused by the *octrois*. The first letter singled out the numerous municipal *octrois* as harmful to trade in the region. These *octrois* proved effective in reimbursing municipal debts, yet they also hindered long-distance trade from entering the region as merchants from Franche Comté and Germany shifted to alternate routes, leaving local traders and consumers the burden of supporting these levies. In his second letter that month, Bouchu specifically addressed the *octrois de la Saône*. Despite the large debt of over half a million livres still owed by Burgundian municipalities, Bouchu urged the Controller General to abolish the *octrois de la Saône* and finance the payments instead with a surtax on salt or even a direct tax imposed upon the communities. To preserve the *octrois*, he argued, would be 'the most unjust, for it only strikes merchants and the inhabitants along the river [*riverains*] and destroys commerce.'[101]

The crown actually heeded Bouchu's concern and abolished the *octrois de la Saône* the following month. The remaining level of municipal debt was deemed manageable with the revenues from the *crues de sel* and from direct taxes levied on the towns' inhabitants.[102] Then, seven years later, in an *arrêt du conseil* of July 1689, the crown reversed its position and reestablished the *octrois de la Saône*, clearly in response to wartime financial exigencies. Finding itself in need of quick and responsive supplies of money, the crown first granted the revenues of the

---

[100] Jean Richard, ed., *Histoire de la Bourgogne*, (Toulouse: Privat, 1978), p. 231; René Durand, 'Le Commerce en Bourgogne à la veille de la Révolution Française,' *Annales de Bourgogne*, 2 (1930): 224, 330-333.

[101] Bouchu to Colbert, 4 June 1681 and 21 June 1681, in Smedley-Weill, *Correspondance*, 3: 217. According to Lionel Rothkrug, there was widespread recognition under Louis XIV that the proliferation of tolls and duties throughout the kingdom had negative political and economic consequences. See *Opposition to Louis XIV: The Political and Social Origins of the French Enlightenment*, (Princeton: Princeton University Press, 1965), pp. 123-124 and 141-144.

[102] A.N., E 1810, 12 July 1681, fol. 13; E 1820, 27 March 1683, fol. 86; and E 1821, 14 August 1683, fol. 29.

octrois for a period of seven and a half years to the Estates of Burgundy in return for a payment of 800,000 livres, after which time 'the said *octrois* [would] remain abolished and suppressed.'[103] This post-1689 arrangement over the *octrois de la Saône* differed significantly from that prior to 1681, however. No longer were the crown's commissioners controlling the administration and spending of these revenues; such matters became the domain of the estates. At the same time, the estates saw their budget grow dramatically, their financial responsibilities to the crown increase, and their role as protector of provincial interests evolve.

Although the legislation granting the *octrois* always stipulated their temporary nature, the crown continued to renew the estates' rights to collect them in exchange for further payments made to the Royal Treasury. Thus, beginning in 1689, the *octrois de la Saône* provided the Estates of Burgundy a stable and slowly increasing addition to their revenues. (See Table 3.7 and Figure 3.2). The initial lease to a company of tax farmers in 1689 was set at 105,000 livres per year. This amount was quickly raised in 1691 to 175,000 livres, reflecting an across the board increase of fifty per cent in the *octrois'* tariffs. Thereafter, the amount earned annually by the estates through their leases of these revenues to tax farmers tended to hover around 200,000 livres until 1709 when it increased to 270,000 livres.[104] In real terms, this represents more than a doubling of annual revenues from the *octrois* between 1689 and 1715.

This steady rise in revenues from the *octrois* funded several timely extraordinary payments to the crown. Indeed, the acquisition of the *octrois* did not come to the estates without a price. In exchange, they borrowed against the future receipts of these revenues to finance emergency wartime payments to the crown, to repurchase edicts, and to contribute to the annual payments of the province's *capitation*.[105] As Table 3.7 presents, while the receipts accruing directly from the *octrois'* revenues between 1689 and 1715 totaled 5,570,000 livres, the sums borrowed during the same period against future *octrois* totaled 11,311,135 livres. All of the principal borrowed against the *octrois* went to the crown in lump sum

---

[103] A.D.C.O., C 5366, *Arrêt du 13 septembre 1689*. By the *arrêt* of 5 July 1689, the tariffs for this newly reestablished *octrois* stood at half of what they levied against each product when they were abolished in 1681.
[104] A.D.C.O., C 5366-5367. It is true that the price of the leases did not necessarily reflect the precise amount received by the estates for any particular year, given the possibility of shortfalls. Farmers were held responsible, however, for meeting the yearly payments agreed upon between themselves and the estates. The estates, for their part, used all legal means available to ensure full payment by the tax farming companies. Thus the leases seem to be relatively accurate gauges of the sums earned by the estates.
[105] A.D.C.O., C 3018-3019.

Table 3.7 **Annual revenues collected from and sums borrowed against** *octrois de la Saône* **(000 livres)**

Year	Annual revenues collected		Sums borrowed	
	Nominal	Real*	Nominal	Real*
1689	105	105	800	800
1690	105	94.5	0	0
1691	175	157.5	450	405
1692	175	159.25	0	0
1693	175	159.25	630	573.3
1694	175	143.5	450	369
1695	175	143.5	0	0
1696	175	143.5	210	172.2
1697	199	163.18	450	369
1698	199	163.18	0	0
1699	199	163.18	0	0
1700	199	171.14	522	448.92
1701	159	138.33	400	348
1702	220	176	416	332.8
1703	220	184.8	1248	1048.32
1704	205	159.9	0	0
1705	205	157.85	832	640.64
1706	205	168.1	577	473.14
1707	205	174.25	0	0
1708	205	176.3	699	601.14
1709	270	202.5	0	0
1710	270	180.9	3246.3	2175.02
1711	270	180.9	0	0
1712	270	180.9	0	0
1713	270	180.9	0	0
1714	270	202.5	0	0
1715	270	240.3	380.835	338.94
totals:	5570	4471.11	11311.135	9095.42

* adjusted to 1689 livre.

Source: A.D.C.O., C 3018, 3019, 3498, 3499, 5366, and 5367.

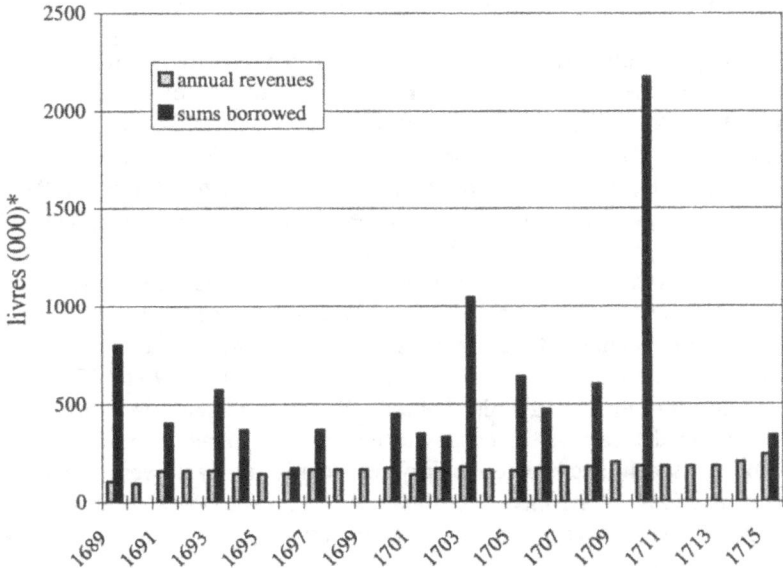

* adjusted to 1689 livre

Source: See Table 3.7.

Figure 3.2 Annual revenues and sums borrowed against the *octrois de la Saône*

payments, less a percentage of handling costs retained by the estates' treasurer.[106] The crown thus benefited from a ready and flexible supply of funds to finance its war efforts. The total amounts borrowed against the *octrois* as they appear in Figure 3.2 demonstrate the flexibility of this relationship as the estates raised significant sums for the crown during the periods 1689 to 1697 and 1700 to 1710, roughly coinciding with the Nine Years' War and the War of the Spanish Succession (1689-1697 and 1701-1713).

The estates thus saw their relationship both with the crown and with the

---

[106] In 1705, of the 217,862 livres collected from the *octrois de la Saône*, 213,333 livres were used to pay creditors, while 4,529 livres, or 2.1 per cent, covered expenses. These included the handling fees of the estates' treasurer (2,030 livres) and his procurator (200 livres), *épices* paid to the chamber of accounts (2,244 livres) and miscellaneous expenses (55 livres). A.D.C.O., C 3386.

province change after 1689. From the crown's point of view, the estates became a valuable intermediary that contributed to emergency wartime financing. Financially, this came at a relatively low cost to the crown, the simple granting of the *octrois de la Saône* over a definite period of time. Yet this arrangement had real limits, and its effectiveness for the crown was clearly finite. As Table 3.8 demonstrates, the *octrois* were accorded to and mortgaged by the estates further and further into the future. Throughout the period of the Nine Years' War, revenues tended to be mortgaged at a regular rate of around five to seven years into the future. By 1700, for example, the revenues of the *octrois* through 1707 had been mortgaged. This differential quickly increased in the years following, so that by 1710 revenues were mortgaged through 1748, or 38 years hence. This mortgaging of revenues further and further into the future could not continue indefinitely at the pace to which both the crown and the estates had become accustomed. Indeed, after 1715, no new revenues of the *octrois de la Saône* were granted and mortgaged until 1727 when the estates borrowed against the revenues of 1749 and 1750.[107]

In addition to having finite bounds, this arrangement also required a certain vigilance on the part of the estates to ensure repayment of bonds and their own credibility as a financial intermediary, especially as loans were secured on more distant revenues. While their importance to the crown increased as an intermediary securing sources of credit, so too did their importance to the Burgundian elite as a guarantor of both bonds in a narrow sense and property and privilege in a broader sense. Thus, while the crown faced limited financial costs, it bore definite political costs as the estates undertook with vigor their new role as guarantor of bonds, asserting the financial independence necessary to ensure the safety of their subscribers' investments. After establishing this arrangement on an almost adhoc basis to finance war in the short term, the crown found itself faced with the political opposition of the estates whenever it attempted to redirect or diminish the revenues of the *octrois*.

In order to protect investors and (not unrelated) provincial privileges, the estates placed a high value on their hold over these revenues, and this position at times caused their negotiating positions to appear outwardly contradictory. On more than one occasion, for example, they decried the creation and sale of offices of commissioner brokers of wine and spirits (*courtiers commissionaires de vins et autres liqueurs*) and the damage that these offices would do to the local wine trade, given the surtax on wines to which the new officers would have had rights. Such concerns led the estates to repurchase these offices both in 1692 and in 1705. Yet at the same time, they willingly accepted and vigorously defended their hold over the *octrois de la Saône* which levied duties on wine at all eight points of collection.[108] Control over revenues was clearly the main concern of the estates, and for this reason a surtax on wines collected by venal officers was deemed

---

[107] A.D.C.O., C 5366.
[108] A.N., E 1872, 22 April 1692, fol. 43; A.D.C.O., C 3353, 19 March 1705.

Table 3.8 *Octrois* accorded to and mortgaged by the Estates of Burgundy

Year accorded	Mortgaged from	Mortgaged to	Differential (yrs.)*
1689	1689	1696	7
1690	—	—	—
1691	1691	1696	5
1692	—	—	—
1693	1697	1698	5
1694	1699	1700	6
1695	—	—	—
1696	1701	1701	5
1697	1702	1704	7
1698	—	—	—
1699	—	—	—
1700	1705	1707	7
1701	1708	1709	8
1702	1710	1711	9
1703	1712	1717	14
1704	—	—	—
1705	1718	1721	16
1706	1722	1726	20
1707	—	—	—
1708	1727	1730	22
1709	—	—	—
1710	1732	1748	38
1711	—	—	—
1712	—	—	—
1713	—	—	—
1714	—	—	—
1715	1731	1731	16

* 'Differential' represents the time between the year accorded and the upper limit of the revenues mortgaged.

Source: A.D.C.O., C 5366-67.

insidious, while the *octrois de la Saône* found a fierce defender in the very institution that controlled them. Five episodes during this period in which the estates actively defended their independence as a financial intermediary together demonstrate how they viewed their role and defined their interests.

Merchant passports Nine years after having originally granted the *octrois de la Saône* to the Estates of Burgundy, the crown began issuing passports to merchants who supplied the army, by which privileges they remained exempt from any internal tolls other than royal customs duties. According to Edmé Lamy, farmer of the *octrois de la Saône* from 1704 to 1716, this issuance of passports contributed to abuse on the part of merchants trying to avoid payment of the tolls and thus undermined his financial interests, responsible as he was for the fixed annual payment of 205,000 livres per year to the estates as stipulated in his lease. The estates took the matter up with the crown in a request to the King's council. As a result, an accord was reached among the three parties by which the crown revoked all passports granted to merchants for the transport of military supplies along the Saône, excepting artillery and arms, in return for 18,000 livres paid yearly by Lamy to the royal treasury for as long as the present war was to last.[109] In the same *arrêt* the crown added to the *octrois* a ten per cent, or 2 sous-per-livre, surtax, over the next 23 years, further increasing Lamy's lease by 47,000 livres annually, which the estates mortgaged to raise a further 699,000 livres in loans agreed upon as the price for the ten per cent increase. In the case of the merchant passports, the estates had seen their tax farmer's interests undermined, and they supported Lamy's position against the merchants, thereby 'rendering the product [of the *octrois*] more advantageous to the province.' While Lamy was thereafter able to tax such merchants, this change came at his cost of 18,000 livres per year. The merchants who had had passports issued to them, on the other hand, witnessed their privileged positions stripped from them.

Harvest failure In 1709, France witnessed the beginning of one of the worst subsistence crises of Louis XIV's reign as freezing temperatures and heavy rains destroyed the grain harvests in several regions. In response, the crown ordered, by a declaration of April 27, that no taxes would be raised on the transport of grains within the kingdom in an attempt to provide some price relief to consumers. The Estates of Burgundy, however, saw this declaration as endangering both their interests and those of Burgundian towns who themselves depended upon municipal *octrois* to meet their budget requirements. In a request to the crown, the estates argued that this prohibition would again undermine the ability of their tax farmers to meet their obligations, which would in turn cause a 'great delay in payments that we [the estates] are beholden to make and would seriously alter the credit of the said estates and towns.' The crown agreed with the estates, recognizing that this was a time when 'we need help for extraordinary expenses,' and thus, on November 5, 1709, the crown issued another declaration exempting both the Estates of Burgundy and towns of the province from the prohibition on grain tolls. Thereafter, the estates could once again collect taxes on grains and bread transported along the

---

[109] A.D.C.O., C 5367, *Arrêt du Conseil*, 13 April 1708. This issue of passport proliferation was taken up once more by the estates in 1731 after the crown again began issuing them to merchants transporting troop supplies. See A.N., H^{1}105.

Saône for consumption by the region's inhabitants.[110] In this case, the estates clearly did not identify their mission as protecting the inhabitants of Burgundy from onerous tax burdens. Rather, they conceived their interests as protecting both their own credit rating and the financial solvency of the province's towns, interests that coincided for the time being with those of the crown.

Royal suppression of surtaxes Following the close of the War of Spanish Succession and the death of Louis XIV, the Regency government undertook a campaign to bring order to the crown's finances by suppressing both offices and surtaxes and reimbursing their holders. As part of this program, the crown abolished all of the 2 sous-per-livre surtaxes on tolls and customs duties, including the surtax on the *octrois de la Saône* accorded in 1705 which, as stated above, had increased Edmé Lamy's lease by 47,000 livres per year. Faced with the prospect of losing this surtax, the estates argued that in fact it had never brought in more than 20,000 livres per year, or much less than the annual interest payments made against the principal borrowed to acquire the surtax. Again, claiming that repayment of sums borrowed necessitated the continued levy of this surtax and that without such revenues they would be 'exposed to [legal] pursuits by [their] creditors whose loans would no longer be guaranteed', the estates asked for clarification from the crown, arguing that the intention of the declaration was to suppress the surtaxes only on royal tax farms.[111] The estates hoped for a favorable decision sooner rather than later, as merchants, citing the crown's declaration, were already refusing to pay the surtax. This time, the crown's response did not exactly correspond to what the estates had hoped. Sticking true to its campaign to suppress surtaxes, the Regency confirmed the abolition of the 2 sous-per-livre surtax on the *octrois de la Saône* and promised to lessen the estates' future obligations by 20,000 livres per year until full reimbursement of the sums borrowed to finance the surtax was achieved. In this instance, the estates continued to equate their interests with the protection of their credit and argued for the continuation of the surtax. The crown, on the other hand, no longer finding itself at war, actually insisted on suppressing the surtax, even at its own expense.

Tax farmers' requests for relief The estates' role as guarantor of bonds also brought them into occasional conflict with tax farmers who were unable to make their payments or who sought decreases in their leases. In the last years of the seventeenth century, while France was momentarily at peace, the province of Burgundy suffered a local food shortage, at which time the intendant Ferrand ceased all exports of grain from the region between October 14, 1698 and the following July 20. Seeing the receipts from his farm of the *octrois* decrease, Claude Mielle sought a diminution of his lease as compensation for Ferrand's actions. The estates vehemently opposed any such relief, arguing that by the terms of their

---

[110] A.D.C.O., C 5366, *Déclaration du Roi*, 5 November 1709.
[111] A.D.C.O., C 5366, *Arrêt du Conseil*, 12 June 1717.

contract, Mielle could not claim any such compensation, 'even under pretext of the said [export] prohibitions, having renounced in his contract any indemnity, even for reasons of plague, war and famine and any other cause foreseen or unforeseen.'[112] The crown's decision favored Mielle, and his lease was lowered by 40,000 livres for the year which remained in his contract.[113] Mielle's Parisian connections may have helped his case. The company of financiers that he represented was comprised exclusively of Parisians, the only case between 1689 and 1728 of a company leasing the rights of the *octrois de la Saône* that did not have some Burgundian representation. Furthermore, during the bidding in 1696 which led up to his contract, a highest bidder had already been chosen by the estates when Mielle presented his company's offer. Mielle's bid had presented no increase over the previous high bid, but his proposal benefited from the support of the Prince de Condé, and the estates reluctantly granted him the contract despite fears that the originally high bidding company might sue. Faced with this company's subsequent default, the estates lost their case outright, and as a result they bore the costs of the momentarily faltering *octrois* revenues. As for the crown, finding itself for the time being at peace, it likely did not feel as compelled as it had during wartime to protect the credit of the estates.

Tax farmers' defaults Following the Mielle lease, Jean Cabrol of Châlon sur Saône gathered four Parisians and the Dijonnais Pierre Cazotte in a company to farm the *octrois* for 220,000 livres per year beginning on January 1, 1702. Within the first year of their lease, this company fell behind in payments because, as Cabrol claimed before the estates of 1703, troop movements along the Saône were displacing taxable merchandise from boats to overland roads where they avoided the *octrois*.[114] The two Burgundians of this company, however, were unable to procure the crown's support as Mielle had, and they found themselves in debtor's prison with their debts to the estates amounting to 240,000 livres. After spending two weeks in prison, Cabrol and Cazotte gained their freedom after the Parisians of the company paid 20,000 livres owed from 1702 and promised to pay another 60,000 livres presently owed for 1703.[115] Then, the following year, the Estates of Burgundy sought and received permission from the crown to break the contract with Cabrol and associates and install a commissioner to manage the collection of the *octrois* until a new bidding process could take place. The Burgundian Edmé Lamy, with whom the estates already had a 20 year history of conducting business, took over collection of the *octrois* and then negotiated his own lease to farm these revenues through 1716. When given free reign, therefore, the Estates of Burgundy used all means necessary to ensure regular and predictable payment of revenues

---

[112] A.D.C.O., C 5366, *Arrêt du Conseil*, 28 June 1701.
[113] A.D.C.O., C 5366, *Extrait des registres du conseil d'état*, 3 November 1696.
[114] A.D.C.O., C 5366, 5 December 1702; *Décret des États*, C 3019, fol. 173.
[115] A.D.C.O., C 5367, 7 April 1703 and 24 March 1703.

from the *octrois*. From the estates' perspective, all risk and responsibility assumed with the collection of indirect taxes lay with the tax farmers.

Conclusion

After 1689, both the crown and the estates increasingly turned their attention to extraordinary affairs and debt management. Instructions for the intendant and governor presented to them on the eve of the estates' opening sessions mention negotiations over the *don gratuits* as a matter of routine, essentially urging the crown's representatives to dispense with the formalities of ordinary business and turn to extraordinary affairs. The instruction for the 1712 session, for example, urge the governor to:

> bring the estates around to deliberating on the level of the *don gratuit*, which [His Majesty] desires of them, as soon as they are assembled, and to this end, (the duke) is to demand of the said estates the sum of one million livres, payable in three equal yearly payments. His Majesty will allow, nonetheless, Monseigneur le Duc to accept 900,000 livres if the estates are willing to grant it in one single deliberation and on the same day the request is made.[116]

Indeed, since 1674 the estates as a matter of routine granted on its first vote the increasingly customary *don gratuit* of 1 million livres, which the governor, as agent of the king, accepted with his own gift to the estates of a remission, usually of 100,000 livres.[117] By 1712, however, matters of much greater importance awaited the estates' attention once such routine matters, along with ensuring the upkeep of roads, bridges, and stables, were handled. At that point, the King's representatives would be able to address the estates' debt which, the King feared, was growing too large and presenting Burgundian tax payers with too great a burden in interest payments. The crown's attention was understandably shifting from the customary contributions to the extraordinary support that the estates mobilized through their borrowing.

A similar reordering occurred within the estates as well. In negotiating the province's financial obligations to the crown, deputies to the estates succeeded in shifting attention away from ordinary obligations, met with current direct tax revenues, to extraordinary contributions which could be met with future indirect revenues. An administrative shift took place also, whereby the *élus* took on greater responsibility for financial management on a year-round basis. They negotiated the leases with tax farmers to collect the *octrois de la Saône*, they negotiated loan contracts, they retained copious records that ensured timely interest payments and reimbursement of principal, and when they had the latitude to do so, they actively

---

[116] A.N., H^1 99, dossier 7.
[117] Swann, 'War Finance,' p. 300.

determined the order of reimbursement.[118] In short, the *élus* oversaw what was clearly becoming the most important aspect of the estates' activities.[119]

Such a shift, both from the perspective of the crown and from within the estates, accords well with that broader political trend of the seventeenth century that saw provincial corps transformed from governing bodies to administrative bodies. Since Tocqueville wrote of the loss of political liberty under the Old Regime, historians have equated this transformation of corps with increased centralization.[120] The case of the Estates of Burgundy, as they assumed the role of financial intermediary under Louis XIV, should caution us against seeing only greater centralization in what is otherwise a useful way of understanding local political change.

Indeed, as the above examples concerning protection of the *octrois* revenues show, the estates' priorities evolved after 1689, and their increased emphasis on administration did not mean that they simply enforced dictates from above. Fundamentally, the estates continued to balance the demands of both the crown and the province's privileged elite. To meet the crown's heightened needs while protecting landed incomes from heavy direct tax burdens, the estates assumed their new role as a major borrower for the crown. Future indirect taxes, detrimental especially to groups outside of the ruling coalition, namely merchants and local consumers, replaced land taxes as the means of supporting the crown's extraordinary needs. Control over those revenues thereafter became a driving issue for the estates. In order to carry out their expanded role as a financial intermediary, the estates adopted positions in defense of their bondholders and, more broadly, the ruling coalition.

All too often, provincial estates are taken to be tax minimizers in all instances. Where historians see them succeed in preventing the crown from enforcing rapacious demands, they speak of the 'fiscal limits of absolutism.' Where, on the other hand, estates are seen to fail in keeping taxes to a minimum, historians speak

---

[118] Most records refer to agreements made between 'the estates' and tax farmers. It is clear, however, that it was the *élus* in particular who were undertaking those negotiations in the name of the estates. See, for example, A.D.C.O., C 5366, *Extrait des registres du conseil d'état*, 3 November 1696. For the *élus*' involvement in loan negotiations, see A.D.C.O., C 3378-3390, *États de l'administration des Élus pendant la triennalité*. For their active management of reimbursement schedules, see A.D.C.O., C 4562, *Déliberations concernant toutes les subrogations de créanciers faites en l'année 1713*.

[119] Swann, *Provincial Power*, chapter 3.

[120] Alexis de Tocqueville, *L'Ancien Régime et la Révolution*, (Paris: Gallimard, 1967), pp. 98-109; Roland Mousnier, *La plume, la faucille et le marteau*, (Paris: Presses Universitaires de France, 1970), pp. 231-252; Jean-François Dubost, 'Absolutisme et centralisation en Languedoc au XVIIe siècle, 1620-1690,' *Revue d'histoire moderne et contemporaine*, 37 (1990): 372-374; Michael Breen, 'Legal Culture, Municipal Politics and Royal Absolutism in Seventeenth-Century France: The Avocats of Dijon, 1595-1715,' Ph.D. diss., Brown University, 2000, pp. 322-323.

of the triumph of absolutism.[121] The Estates of Burgundy, however, clearly did not look at all times to minimize the tax burden of Burgundians. They charted instead a much more balanced, even sophisticated, approach to financial negotiations that sought to promote the interests of the ruling coalition. Indeed, given the right conjuncture, namely peace, the crown was more willing than were the estates to decrease or suppress outright the burden of the *octrois de la Saône*. Outright, if temporary, suppression came in 1681 after the crown's representative in the province condemned the damaging social and economic effects of the tolls. In contrast, following the War of the Spanish Succession, the Regency found that it could only decrease the levies by abolishing the ten per cent surtax, and then only at its own cost and against the wishes of the estates. As these two episodes demonstrate, circumstances had changed dramatically between 1681 and 1717 as the crown witnessed an erosion of its options regarding the *octrois de la Saône*. By 1717, any suppression of the *octrois* without granting other sources of funds to the estates would have been tantamount to forcing a default on the estates, and it was against this eventuality that the estates consistently defended themselves from 1689 on, for the most part successfully.

There was no concrete mechanism by which the estates were able to constrain the crown against a forced default. The arguments presented in this chapter suggest that confrontation and intransigence on the part of the estates could never have been considered as a serious long-term strategy to defend Burgundy's liberties and privileges, let alone the estates' credit reputation. Instead, cooperation between the crown and estates was key, and the shift in power that enabled the estates to borrow such extraordinary sums and protect their credit originated in both the monarchy and in the provincial ruling coalition. Both parties recognized the necessity of cooperation when, for example, in 1692 the estates asked the crown for a strengthening of their borrowing ability. They were experiencing trouble borrowing money in Paris, unable to convince potential lenders that they had 'sufficient authority to take out the said loans and mortgage the said revenues, without which however they could not have found any sums [to borrow].' The King responded to the estates' request by confirming and then publicizing their legal authority to mortgage the revenues.[122]

It would thus be mistaken to think of provincial estates, with the support of the local ruling coalition, as the last bulwark defending the province against royal coercion. Louis XIV certainly had nothing to gain by consistently and permanently undermining privileges for short term financial gain as long as he could strike arrangements with privileged corps that provided him with the type of financial support that he received from the Estates of Burgundy. As such, other corps too, like the Parlement of Dijon or the municipalities throughout the province, intervened to protect privileges just as the estates did. In this regard, Louis XIV's strategy mirrored very much his approach toward office holders. As seen in

---

[121] See, respectively, Collins, *Fiscal Limits*; Major, *From Renaissance Monarchy*.
[122] A.N., E 1872, 15 April 1692, fol. 37.

Chapter Two, despite his legal prerogative to undermine and rewrite at will the rules for the patrimonial possession of offices, Louis XIV chose to strengthen the private hold over public charges and, thereby, to strengthen the ability of holders to mortgage their offices. Similarly, the crown, as grantor of the *octrois* along with numerous other revenues, could legally dispense with and redirect them at will. Though he tried on occasion to do just that, Louis XIV generally allowed the estates to tighten their hold over these revenues so as to strengthen as well their ability to mortgage them.

Yet this is not the whole story. In addition, there must have been some provincial source of strength that empowered the estates to protect the province's privileges. As demonstrated above, the Estates of Burgundy, more that any other privileged corporation within the province, provided an arena for coalition building among the province's elite. Their rotating membership and the lack of a direct financial stake that their 'members' had in the corps directed the estates away from a strategy of intervening only to protect the specific interests of the deputies and led them instead to defend property and privileges that benefited an entire coalition of provincial leaders. Thus, a broad and reasonably well defined elite, including those who shared in the exercise of local authority, namely members of the robe, the landed elite, both noble and non-noble, and those enjoying prestige and privilege on the provincial level, stood to gain from the estates' activities. They in particular benefited from the protection of the privileged status quo, from the intervention of the estates that effectively slowed the proliferation of individual and collective privileges, from the protection of investments in the estates' bonds[123] and, more broadly, from the protection of property and provincial liberties. The broader 'social resonance' that the estates thus cultivated lent that institution the strength needed to borrow reliably for the crown. In comparison with sovereign representative institutions on the European stage, this would have been nothing new or unique; in the context of old-regime France, where privilege determined access to power and where those privileges could be revoked by the King, in a context of political particularism where the crown could and did dominate by dividing corps along their individual interests, provincial estates were indeed unique for providing such an arena for coalition building.

The long term political costs of this 'coerced cooperation', then, lay in the devolution of public power away from the crown to both individuals (office holders with strengthened property rights) and privileged corps, a devolution that would severely limit the crown's financial options in the eighteenth century. The immediate gains for the crown, on the other hand, lay in the political consolidation and accommodation which kept provincial elite groups loyal while allowing the crown to mobilize resources for the war effort. These are the developments that have drawn the recent attention of such historians as Beik, Kettering and Major.

---

[123] Here, a much broader network of individuals and interests benefited from the estates' activities, especially throughout the eighteenth century as the clientele of lenders to the estates expanded dramatically. See Chapter Six.

The strategies that made possible this political consolidation, however, involved more than extending Louis' personal ties through powerful brokers such as the Condé. Institutions, too, made the accommodation possible, and in provinces with differing institutional ties to the monarchy we see how the precise contours of that accommodation varied.

Chapter 4

Royal Strategies and Elite Responses in Normandy

Introduction: The Politics of Taxation in a *Pays d'Élection*

This chapter examines the evolving financial relationships between the crown and local elite groups in the *généralité* of Rouen in Upper Normandy during the latter half of Louis XIV's reign with a view to comparing the royal strategies and provincial responses in the Rouennais example to those found in Burgundy. In the Burgundian case, an estates-centered coalition of rulers arose, and the estates themselves were integrally involved in both the financial interaction and the political accommodation between the crown and the provincial elite. This study of royal finances in the *généralité* of Rouen will examine whether or not similar interaction and accommodation were possible where estates did not exist.

Socio-economic distinctions between the Rouennais and Burgundian elites existed alongside the institutional differences that separated the two provinces. There was, to be sure, much overlap. Even more so than Dijon, Rouen was an important administrative city; under Louis XIV it was home to the Parlement of Normandy, a chamber of accounts, a *cour des aides*, and a *bureau des finances* for the *généralité*.[1] Lower courts and financial jurisdictions, such as bailiwicks, *élections*, and *greniers à sel* were also present throughout the *généralité*. The robe nobility thus held a strong presence in Rouen just as it did in Dijon. Yet unlike in Dijon, the Rouennais robe elite shared space at the top of the local hierarchy with a prominent commercial elite.

The port of Rouen, situated near the mouth of the Seine, was an ideal transfer point for the shipment of goods, connecting Paris and the surrounding regions of Picardie, Lower Normandy and Brittany to the growing Atlantic and Baltic-based trades.[2] A vibrant merchant community thus formed in the city. As was the case

---

[1] The oldest of these sovereign courts was the *cour des aides*. In 1499, just prior to the Parlement's founding, Rouen was home to only nine royal judges of any significant standing – eight from the *cour des aides* and the lieutenant general of the bailiwick. By 1600, in addition to the parlement with eighty-three officers, the crown had also created two new sovereign courts, the chamber of accounts with 64 members and the *bureau des finances* with 12 treasurers-general. See Dewald, *Formation*, p. 69.

[2] Jean-Pierre Bardet, *Rouen aux XVIIe et XVIIIe siècles: les mutations d'un espace social* (Paris: SEDES, 1983), p. 192.

with the less prominent Burgundian merchants, Rouennais merchants formed a group largely distinct from the local robe and sword nobilities in terms of their professional, political and family ties.[3] Yet unlike in Dijon, Rouennais merchants exercised power on the local level through, among other avenues, their control of the municipality of Rouen. Upper Normandy was thus home to two distinct elite groups with separate provincial bases of authority: a robe elite with close professional and familial ties to the Norman sword nobility, and the commercial elite.

The face of the ruling Rouennais elite thus differed in important ways from that of the ruling Burgundian elite. In addition, and perhaps not unrelated, the institutions that in large part determined the financial ties between local elite groups and the crown differed in the Rouennais and Burgundian cases. The *généralité* of Rouen was a territory which, along with the other two Norman *généralités* of Caen and Alençon, had lost the privilege of representing its financial interests in the Estates of Normandy. The year 1655 marked the last time the crown convened the Estates of Normandy, and that meeting came after a period of seventeen years when they had met only twice. Indeed, the Estates of Normandy were already well on their way to obsolescence by the beginning of the seventeenth century. Though a *pays d'État*, Normandy also had *élections*, or royal tax districts, established throughout the province, and as early as the 1560s, the estates found themselves excluded from the task of apportioning the *taille*.[4] Thereafter, the crown could levy and collect what it wanted in direct taxes whether the estates consented or not, and indeed, in the first half of the seventeenth century when the estates continued to exist on paper, they tended to approve only a fraction of what the crown demanded, but the full amount was collected by royal officers anyway.[5] Already obsolete, the estates ceased meeting by the beginning of Louis XIV's personal reign, and Normandy was divided into three *généralités*, all *pays d'élection*.

The absence of estates affected the financial relationships between crown and province on at least four distinct levels. To begin with, there was no single deliberative body to bring together a coalition of provincial rulers in negotiation with the crown and to manage the province's finances. As it concerns the historian's task, the absence of any such central institution that gave cohesive voice to provincial rulers in financial matters is reflected in the scarce documentation available to the researcher. The documentation that does exist is much more

---

[3] The portion of magistrates in the Parlement of Normandy who were the sons of bourgeois diminished over the sixteenth and seventeenth centuries from about 15 per cent from 1539-1558 to about 6 per cent from 1619-1638. As the financial returns to office holding diminished in the seventeenth century, parlementary offices tended to remain longer in the same families over generations. With the resultant development of dynasticism in parlementary office holding, the familial ties between robe and commercial elites diminished over the seventeenth century. See Dewald, *Formation*, pp. 77-79, 160.

[4] Bonney, *Political Change*, p. 356; Collins, *Fiscal Limits*, pp. 39-40.

[5] Major, p. 286.

dispersed than in a *pays d'États* such as Burgundy, and the researcher must rely on sources from judicial corps and municipalities and on administrative records left by intendants. While these dispersed sources do not always offer a continuity of perspective on the evolving relationships between the crown and members of the provincial elite, they do at least reflect the distinct bases of power around which the separate elite groups of Rouen gathered.

Secondly, where estates were absent, intendants played a much greater role in the administration of finances. A stark contrast exists between the intendants of Burgundy and those in the three *généralités* that comprised the province of Normandy. In a letter to the *Contrôle Général* in 1683, Nicolas Harlay, intendant of Burgundy, complained that his range of responsibilities remained limited, since collection of the *taille*, reimbursement of the *étapes*, or local troop quartering costs, and management of public works were all in the hands of the estates.[6] Indeed, intendants in *pays d'États* acted much as advisers and assistants to the provincial governors, especially where governors took an active political role, such as in Burgundy.[7]

In the *généralité* of Rouen, on the other hand, the intendant oversaw both the apportionment and collection of the *taille*. Following the reforms of the late 1630s and 1640s, intendants in *pays d'élection* asserted control over the division of *taille* obligations both among *élections* within their *généralités* and among the parishes that made up the *élections*, duties which before had resided within the jurisdiction of the *trésoriers généraux* and of the *élus*.[8] And while the collection of taxes in *pays d'élection* still remained in the hands of venal officers, intendants were responsible for ensuring the smooth operation of their activities, and they could replace receivers at will with persons of their own choosing to collect taxes by commission.[9] In addition, the intendant of Rouen closely supervised municipal finances and managed the upkeep of the region's ports and fortifications.[10]

Additionally, there was a greater role accorded to *traitants* in the *généralité* of Rouen. These were the financiers who contracted with the crown to sell newly created offices and privileges. Again, we can look to the case of Burgundy to demonstrate the contrast with a *pays d'États*. In 1709, the Estates of Burgundy

---

[6] Harlay to Le Peletier, 20 September 1683, in Smedley-Weill, *Correspondance*, 3: 233.

[7] Major, p. 284. See also the discussion in Chapter Three comparing the *dons et octrois* granted by the Estates of Burgundy to the governor and his clients to those offered the intendant and his assistant.

[8] Esmonin, *La Taille*, pp. 38-194; Bonney, *Political Change*, pp. 163-190.

[9] Esmonin, *La Taille*, pp. 428-446. This authority predates the systematic establishment of intendants and was exercised by the crown as early as the reign of Francis I. See Hamon, pp. 47-48.

[10] The *échevins*, or town councilors, of le Havre from 1671 were fined 130 livres for not having fully accounted for municipal expenditures. The *arrêts* from the King's council that had called for investigation into their activities stated repeatedly that direct oversight of municipal finances and of ports and fortifications remained the domain of the intendant. A.N., E 1819, 11 September 1683; E 1830, 14 August 1685.

entered into a dispute with the Chamber of Accounts of Dijon, having rejected the chamber's claim that it held the jurisdiction to examine the account books of the estates' treasurer in all instances. The estates countered that much of their treasurer's responsibilities involved extraordinary activities such as collecting funds for *rachats* of edicts. In such instances, the estates argued, they were substituting for and acting 'in place of *traitants*, who themselves would be under no compulsion to submit to the accounting of the said chamber...'[11] The estates thus perceived their own intervention in extraordinary financial matters as largely displacing *traitants*, whose presence and activity in Burgundy were thereby greatly reduced.

In the *généralité* of Rouen, on the other hand, *traitants* intervened on a more regular basis in extraordinary financial affairs. Individual financiers, or more often companies of financiers, advanced sums to the King in exchange for the right to sell certain offices, surtaxes or *augmentations de gages*.[12] There was no province-wide institution to prevent the arrival of *traitants* as the Estates of Burgundy did through their numerous repurchases of edicts, and the result in Upper Normandy, all else equal, was a greater proliferation of privilege. As with all other extraordinary financial measures, though, the crown faced limits on its use of *traitants*, as will be explored below.

Finally, under no obligation to negotiate fiscal issues with a representative body, the crown was able to establish unilaterally the level of direct taxation in the *généralité* of Rouen. As demonstrated in Chapter Three, the levels of direct taxation in Burgundy were rather inflexible and increased only moderately in real terms, and then only with the introduction of the capitation. We might reasonably expect greater latitude on the part of the crown to raise taxes in times of need where estates were absent. In the Rouennais case, however, the absence of formal institutional constraints (i.e. estates) appears not to have given Louis XIV free rein to raise direct tax levels as a source of war financing.

To determine *taille* levels throughout the Kingdom's *pays d'élection*, Louis XIV and his ministers in the *conseil des finances* first calculated the total revenues needed to meet the anticipated expenses of the forthcoming year. They then apportioned this sum among the *généralités*, drawing up what was called the *brevet de la taille*.[13] Each intendant then received his own *brevet* that contained only the figure that applied to his *généralité*. The intendants next sent back detailed reports to the *conseil des finances* advising whether their *généralités* could pay the full amounts and how the obligations should be divided among *élections*. Finally, the *conseil* sent commissions back to the intendants with the final *taille* amounts to be

---

[11] A.N., G⁷ 1763.

[12] A comprehensive examination of the activities and provincial connections of the *traitants* will follow in Chapter Five.

[13] Esmonin, *La Taille*, pp. 22-35. There were eighteen *généralités* under Louis XIV which, as *pays d'élection*, he could tax directly: Paris, Soissons, Amiens, Châlons, Orléans, Tours, Bourges, Moulins, Lyon, Riom, Poitiers, Limoges, Bordeaux, Montauban, Rouen, Caen and Alençon.

collected along with the apportionment among the *élections*. Intendants, with the help of *élus*, then turned to the task of dividing the burden of each *élection* among parishes, at which point receivers were ready to gather the revenues from parish collectors.[14]

The crown thus had the unilateral ability to set *taille* levels as it saw necessary in the Kingdom's *pays d'élection*. Furthermore, whenever the crown faced unforeseen expenses, it could simply add surtaxes to the tax levels already set down in the *brevets de la taille*.[15] This was a system that in theory accorded to the crown the flexibility that it needed to raise the levels of taxation whenever its needs increased. In practice, however, such flexibility is not apparent as the figures of *taille* receipts demonstrate.

The movement of *taille* receipts from the *généralité* of Rouen, detailed in Figure 4.1, suggests that the crown faced informal constraints against raising direct tax levels in this *pays d'élection*. In nominal terms, *taille* receipts from this *généralité* had barely recovered in 1719 the levels attained under Colbert's ministry.[16] They had begun to diminish toward the end of the 1680s, continued to fall through the end of the century, and recovered only slowly and haltingly over the next fifteen years. This decline and gradual recovery coincided with Louis' two major wars, periods when we would expect the crown to have raised taxes wherever it had the authority to do so. The 'stickiness' of *taille* receipts is even more striking when the devaluation of the livre during the period under study is considered. The steady drop of the silver content of the livre during the 1690s and the first decades of the eighteenth century quickly eroded the already stagnating, or at times diminishing, nominal receipts. The war years thus actually marked a decline in *taille* receipts from the *généralité* of Rouen when calculated in real terms.

But, as elsewhere, the *taille* was not the only direct tax levied in Normandy. There, as in Burgundy, the crown established the capitation in 1695, abolished it with the close of war in 1698 and reestablished it again in 1702. Yet unlike in Burgundy, the crown levied the capitation directly as a poll tax, and its receipts

---

[14] Ibid., pp. 22-102.

[15] For example, the crown added 28,000 livres to the *taille* levels of 1688 in the *généralité* of Rouen to finance repairs on the port of Tréport, and it levied 50,000 livres each year between 1695 and 1698 on all three *généralités* of Normandy for 'work done to fortifications.' A.N., E 1845, 13 July 1688; E 1889, 18 January 1695.

[16] The levels of *taille* receipts are from the *État sommaire de la province de Normandie*, published in Gerard Hurpin, *L'Intendance de Rouen en 1698*, (Paris: C.T.H.S., 1984), pp. 302-304. The figures from this *État sommaire* are very close to those offered by Esmonin for the years where the two sets overlap (1663-1681). Esmonin's figures are from the *commissions de la taille* sent to the intendants. They thus represent reasonable projections of receipts, based in part on the intendants' reports, and not the precise amounts collected. The *taille* levels indicated here are indicative of movement over time and should not be taken as accurate figures of revenues collected from the taxpayer. See Esmonin, *La Taille*, p. 545.

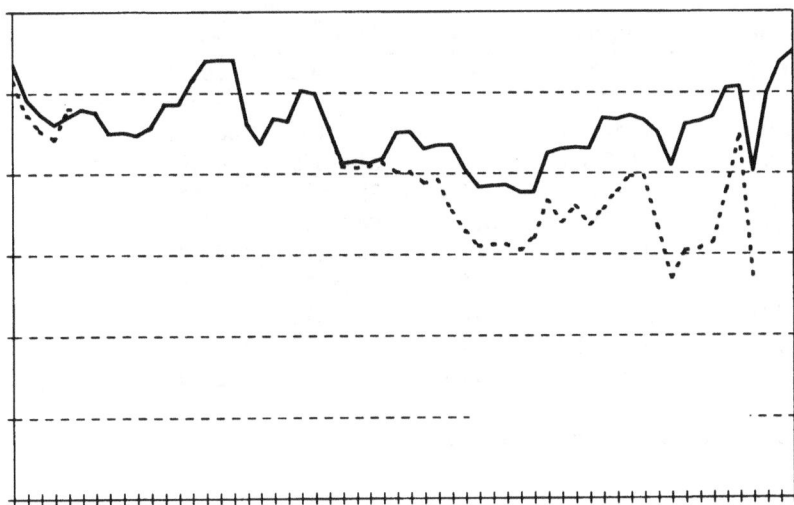

Source: Hurpin, pp. 302-304.

Figure 4.1 *Taille* levels, *généralité* of Rouen

depended on the population, how it was divided into the twenty-two designated classes, and which groups, if any, were able to negotiate exemptions or reductions.[17] Because there was not a set amount paid annually by the *généralité*, and because there was no single deliberative body managing the collection of the tax, documents indicating the total amounts paid are scarce, and figures should be taken as estimations. Approximately 500,000 to 600,000 livres were raised each year between 1695 and 1698.[18] Then the amounts increased slightly when the tax was reestablished during the War of Spanish Succession, as the figures in Table 4.1 indicate.

The capitation, therefore, succeeded in raising real direct tax levels in the late

---

[17] This is in contrast to Burgundy where the estates negotiated a 'subscription' to the capitation, whereby they paid the crown 1,000,000 livres per year to keep royal tax collectors from entering the province and collecting the capitation as a poll tax. See Chapter Three.
[18] Hurpin, pp. 99, 222.

Table 4.1 Levels of *taille* and Capitation in *généralité* of Rouen, selected years, in livres

Year	Taille	Capitation	Total Nominal	Total Real*
1680	2186666	—	2186666	2186666
1685	2287398	—	2287398	2287398
1690	2254105	—	2254105	2006153
1694	2179885	—	2179885	1765707
1697	1925111	627586	2552697	2067684
1698	1928819	500000	2428819	1967343
1700	1885307	—	1885307	1602511
1703	2161538	757015	2918553	2422399
1705	2343001	834671	3177672	2415031
1706	2336519	719413	3055932	2475305
1707	2358182	857793	3215975	2701419

* Real values are adjusted to 1679 livre.

Source:
Taille: Hurpin, pp. 302-304.
Capitation, 1697-1698: Hurpin, p. 99. The figure for 1698 is an estimate offered by the intendant la Bourdonnaye.
Capitation, 1703-1707: A.N. H¹ 1588/44, *État du produit par année des fermes et deniers imposes dans la généralité de Rouen.*

1690s and in the first decades of the 1700s slightly beyond the levels reached by the *taille* alone under Colbert. To this, the crown added the *dixième* in the final quarter of 1710, which brought in annual sums of 1.3 to 1.4 million livres from the *généralité* of Rouen.[19] (See table 4.2). The overall trend in Upper Normandy thus corresponds closely to the situation in Burgundy where the *don gratuit* and specific military taxes decreased, both nominally and in real terms, until the capitation and later the *dixième* were established, raising direct tax receipts beyond the 1679 level.[20] Immediately following the reestablishment of the capitation in Burgundy, the estates' regular annual obligations to the crown that were met mostly with direct tax revenues were 49 per cent higher than they had been in 1679, though, as noted in the previous chapter, that increase was quickly eroded by the successive devaluations of the livre. In the *généralité* of Rouen, on the other hand, real direct tax levels in 1703 stood at just 11 per cent beyond their 1679 levels, though it is

---

[19] AN G⁷ 1138-1139, *Bordereaux généraux du dixième jusqu'au 6e décembre 1713; Estat montant des rolles du dixième des années 1715, 1716, et 1717.*
[20] See Chapter Three, Table 3.3 and Figure 3.1.

Table 4.2 *Dixième* revenues from the *généralité* of Rouen, in livres

Year	Amount listed in tax roles	Remission granted	Amount received
1711[a]	1433934	—	1367809
1712	1436336	—	1319956
1713[b]	1433955	—	722890
1714	—	—	—
1715	1437009	—	—
1716	1350078	1931	—
1717	1433018	2060	—

[a] Annualized from figures granted for the five quarters from October 1, 1710 through December 31, 1711.
[b] Amount received for 1713 listed as of 6 December 1713.

Source: A.N. G⁷ 1138-1139, *Bordereaux general du dixième jusqu'au 6 decembre 1713; Estat du montant des rolles du dixième des années 1715, 1716, 1717, et des diminutions accordées...*

also the case that these tax levels continued to increase after 1703 both nominally and in real terms before being eroded by the diminishing value of the livre during the 1710s. Overall, the flexibility to increase taxes in times of war appears to be absent. Was there indeed any meaningful advantage conferred to the crown by the absence of estates in Normandy?

This apparent inability on the part of royal officials to significantly raise direct taxes in the short term in this *pays d'élection* must be understood within its context. To begin with, the *taille* levels attained under Colbert in this *généralité* were already quite high; indeed the entire province of Normandy had historically been taxed at levels higher than most of the rest of France. Indeed, the heaviest burden in Normandy predated the disappearance of estates, pointing to the financial rewards reaped by Henry IV and Louis XIII for having been able to circumvent provincial autonomy and impose their financial will long before the estates' *de jure* demise.[21] And while it is true that the direct tax burden in the *généralité* of Rouen diminished as a percentage of total crown receipts over the course of the seventeenth century, at around the turn of the eighteenth century the per capita burden there was still

---

[21] 'The estates in provinces where there were royal tax collectors were in a weaker position to resist the fiscal demands of the crown than those in regions where agents of the estates performed this duty. Nowhere was this truer than in Normandy, which had long contributed more to the crown than any other region of comparable size.' Major, p. 158.

Table 4.3 Comparison of direct tax levels in Burgundy and *généralité* of Rouen, nominal (000 livres) and per capita

Year	Total direct taxation		Per-capita direct taxation[b]		
	Rouen	Burgundy	Rouen	Burgundy	R/B
1680	2186.67	1103.5	2.95	1.37	2.16
1685	2287.4	958.55	3.09	1.19	2.60
1690	2254.1	958.55	3.05	1.19	2.56
1694	2179.99	957.55	2.95	1.19	2.48
1700	1885.3	957	2.55	1.19	2.15
1703[a]	2918.5	1559.21	3.94	1.93	2.04
1705[a]	3177.6	1559.21	4.29	1.93	2.22
1706[a]	3055.9	1559.21	4.13	1.93	2.13
1707[a]	3215.9	1559.21	4.35	1.93	2.25

[a] Figures for these years include the capitation receipts, adjusted in the Burgundian case to include only that portion paid from direct taxes.
[b] Per-capita tax levels are calculated based upon population estimates by Vauban at the turn of the eighteenth century. See Dupâquier, 2: 75-77.

Source: See Tables 3.2 and 4.1.

significantly higher than it was in the province of Burgundy.[22] As the figures in Table 4.3 indicate, the per capita direct tax levels in the *généralité* of Rouen averaged more than double those in Burgundy both before and after the establishment of the capitation.[23]

The decline in direct tax levels at the end of the century, corrected only by the introduction of the capitation, must therefore be considered within this broader

---

[22] In the early seventeenth century, the *généralité* of Rouen paid about 11-13 per cent of total direct taxation among *pays d'élection*; that proportion dropped to about 6 per cent by the beginning of the eighteenth century. While the total nominal receipts of the *taille* from all *pays d'élection* in the 1700s stood roughly where they did in the 1630s and 1640s (39.2 million livres in 1640; 38.5 million in 1707), the levels in Upper Normandy actually decreased (4.98 million in 1640; 2.34 million in 1705). See Collins, *Fiscal Limits*, p. 162; Boislisle, *Correspondance*, 2: 588-597. Vauban estimated the populations of Burgundy and the *généralité* of Rouen at the turn of the eighteenth century to be 806,000 and 740,000 respectively. See Jacques Dupâquier, ed., *Histoire de la population Française*, 4 vols., (Paris: Presses Universitaires de France, 1988), 2: 75-77.

[23] The 1710 establishment of the *dixième*, collected by royal agents in both Burgundy and Normandy, did little to change the relative per-capita tax burdens, with inhabitants of the *généralité* of Rouen paying on average 1.76 livres/year and those of Burgundy paying .87 (based on total rounded estimates of 700,000 livres/year in Burgundy and 1.3 million in the *généralité* of Rouen).

context that saw inhabitants of Normandy taxed at relatively greater rates than those of Burgundy. Furthermore, part of the decline following the Colbert ministry can be attributed to the economic and demographic crises of the late century. While the nominal receipts of the *taille* in the *généralité* fell by about 28 per cent between 1662 and 1698, the population decreased about a quarter during the same period, and the proportion of wastelands to cultivated lands increased.[24] Another possible constraint might have come from the crown's own intendants. They found favor with their superiors in Paris, particularly with the Controller General, when tax revenues flowed into the hands of treasurers smoothly and completely. Excessive *non-valeurs* (taxes gone unpaid), or any disturbance touched off by tax collection amounted to failure on the part of the intendants. While advising the *conseil des finances* on the proposed tax levels, they thus had an interest in exaggerating the financial hardship of their *généralités* and keeping the final figures manageable.

The advantages to the crown of taxing unilaterally were thus at least partially offset by other constraints. The necessity to negotiate taxes with estates in Burgundy clearly kept levels there low, while the ability to circumvent obsolete estates and then simply not convene them after 1655 provided the crown, all else equal, greater flexibility to levy higher tax levels in Normandy. But non-institutional factors influenced tax levels as well, as the proportional decrease of the tax burden in Upper Normandy over the course of the seventeenth century suggests. Furthermore, unmediated royal control over setting and collecting direct taxes rendered receipts in Normandy more susceptible to the vagaries of harvests and land rents. Whenever *taillables* were unable to pay their obligations, the crown had to absorb those losses directly. Negotiations with estates in Burgundy, on the other hand, carried at least the advantage of predictability for the crown, since the estates remained responsible for making full payment of agreed upon amounts, and since, as demonstrated in Chapter Three, they vigilantly guarded their tax base in order to protect their relevance and viability. Overall, though, whether in *pays d'États* or *pays d'élection* it is clear that Louis XIV could not rely on direct taxation as a significant source of war financing. After all, general receipts from all of the *pays d'élection* stood in the early 1700s at roughly the same nominal level as they had seventy years earlier.

Over the course of the seventeenth century, indirect tax receipts, especially from the General Farms, constituted an increasing share of ordinary receipts, from about 20-25 per cent of total revenues in the 1640s to 45-55 per cent by the end of the century. One might argue that direct tax levels in *pays d'élection* languished in the face of increased needs between 1689 and 1715 simply because the crown could turn to indirect tax revenues as a more flexible source of ordinary receipts. Certain indicators, though, suggest that indirect tax revenues did *not* respond to increased royal needs as a substitute for direct tax revenues. The indirect revenues that made up the General Farms reached a plateau in the 1680s at around 60 million livres per year after increasing steadily during the ministry of Colbert. The

---

[24] Hurpin, p. 221.

returns then began to drop from a high of 63 million livres in 1690.[25] There is no reason to think that the returns in the *généralité* of Rouen strayed from these trends. Nor was there a move on the local level to substitute direct with indirect tax obligations as the Burgundian ruling coalition engineered through the intermediation of the estates. As I demonstrate below, the Rouennais commercial elite clearly opposed any such increases in indirect taxes, although it ultimately failed in preventing the crown from creating and extending new duties and tolls during the period under study. It seems, therefore, that ordinary fiscal measures did not constitute the financial frontier of Louis XIV's reign. Extraordinary measures, on the other hand, proved key to financing the Sun King's wars in *pays d'élection* just as they did in *pays d'États*.

The Politics of Venality and Privilege

In Burgundy, as detailed in the previous chapter, the crown was able to forge a relationship with the estates whereby they acted as a major financial intermediary, providing the crown access to credit while protecting the privileged status and financial autonomy of the province. Privilege pervaded the Norman political landscape as well. While no estates existed there, the crown still had opportunities to engage corps as financial intermediaries. The results for the crown, however, were mixed. Louis XIV was able to divide the Norman elite along lines of privilege and access to power and resources, since the local leaders lacked the institutional arena to form a broad and tenable coalition. Yet while the crown was able to single out privileged corporations and engage them as financial intermediaries, the smaller and more particular privileged corps that populated Upper Normandy were unable to respond to the crown's extraordinary needs with the speed and with the sums of money that were mobilized in Burgundy by the estates. Such mixed results were evident, for example, as the crown sought extraordinary financial support from judicial officer corps, from *traitants* responsible for selling offices and *augmentations de gages*, and from municipalities and merchants.

Judicial Corps

In the *généralité* of Rouen, as elsewhere throughout the Kingdom, judicial officer corps acted as financial intermediaries, forwarding funds to the crown that they borrowed on credit markets and receiving, in exchange, interest payments from the crown in the form of *augmentations de gages*. As we have already observed, the crown enjoyed considerable leverage over officer corps. The King reserved the prerogative to create offices and extend privileges, and such moves typically elicited preemptive moves by privileged corps to 'buy off' the crown.

The Parlement of Normandy, as the province's principal sovereign court and,

---

[25] Dessert, *Argent*, pp. 161-162; Bonney and Bonney, *Malet*, pp. 38, 288.

thus, the most notable embodiment of local privilege, provided the greatest potential among the Rouennais courts for the crown to engage as a financial intermediary. Magistracies within the parlement – the offices of president and *conseiller* – were among those that the crown approached with great care in order to protect their heritability while eliciting the services of their holders as intermediaries.[26] Thus, in 1689, the parlement decided in its deliberations to borrow 250,000 livres to offer the crown as emergency assistance for the war effort in exchange for *augmentations de gages*. Recognizing that the Parlement of Paris and other sovereign companies of the Kingdom had offered 'considerable sums' to the crown, the Parlement of Normandy felt it needed to offer a sum 'in proportion to the dignity of the company.'[27] In this instance, coming as it did in the first year of war, the crown did not use any direct pressure to obtain this support; all that was necessary was for the First President of the parlement to raise the specter in corporate deliberations of the King 'being obliged to support several armies and engage the common enemies of the state who want to invade and usurp the Kingdom.'

On other occasions, the parlement paid to preserve the traditional functioning of the institution and to protect the value of members' privileges. In 1698, the court borrowed funds to reimburse each of its procurator substitutes (*substituts de M. le procureur du roi*) 10,800 livres that they had personally paid the crown two years earlier for the acquisition of new functions. Moving to reverse the disruptive changes that these new functions brought with them and to 'preserve the established practices of the said parlement,' the magistrates voted to finance the reimbursement as a corps.[28] The crown was thus able to retain the original *finances* it had received in 1696 from the procurator substitutes, while the parlement as a corps paid to suppress the new functions and restore the internal status quo of the institution. As a final example, the parlement paid 33,000 livres in 1707 and another 42,900 livres in 1708 to acquire *augmentations de gages*. The second sum was to restore the magistrates of the chamber of requests 'to the same condition as before the edict of April 1706,' or before the crown had created redundant offices in that chamber.[29] Again, the court was acting as a single unified corps to preserve its traditional functions and privileges.

Other courts, too, borrowed money to pay the crown for *rachats* of edicts, the suppression of offices or the preservation of the status quo in their internal functioning. The *bureau des finances* borrowed 36,000 livres in 1700 and then 82,600 livres in 1704. The first sum went to the crown to unite the newly created office of treasurer general of France to the corps, the second payment financed the suppression of two offices of treasurer general, thereby actually diminishing the

---

[26] See Chapter Two.
[27] A.D.S.M., 1 B 212, fol. 404.
[28] A.D.S.M., 1 B 217, fol. 39.
[29] A.D.S.M., 1 B 226, fol. 5; 1 B 227, fol. 19.

number of offices in the bureau.[30] And, in addition to financing such repurchases and suppressions, officer corps also forwarded sums to the crown for readmission to the *droit annuel* which extended the heritability of their offices.[31] The total amounts paid by Rouennais courts were thus quite significant. Over the two-year period 1701-1702, the sovereign courts of Rouen pledged the crown a total of 1,063,666 livres for *augmentations de gages*. In comparison, the Dijonnais courts promised 685,573 livres – significantly less than their Rouennais counterparts but still more than what the courts of any other province pledged except those of Brittany and Languedoc.[32] Such figures testify to the importance of Rouen as a center of judicial office holding, and they suggest on the surface that the crown succeeded in its strategy of erecting privilege as a bargaining chip against Rouennais office holders. Yet at the same time, the crown faced certain difficulties engaging judicial officer corps as financial intermediaries, difficulties masked by the total borrowing figures but apparent in the deliberations and correspondences of the corps.

Two interrelated factors, the limited ability of corps to borrow and the varying market value of offices, affected the crown's ability to secure extraordinary financial support from officer corps. Venal officer corps frequently proclaimed their inability to borrow sufficient funds to meet the crown's needs. In March 1703, magistrates in the Parlement of Normandy received a letter from Controller General Chamillart expressing the King's displeasure at the court's delay in forwarding 400,000 livres in principal for *augmentations de gages*. The letter questioned the parlement's zeal in supporting the King and suggested not so subtly that the 'delay could very well lead [the King] to create new offices which would be very damaging to the present office holders...'[33] The magistrates explained their delay as due less to a lack of zeal than of ability, as they had done 'everything they could to find money.' The court's agents could not find lenders, and the office holders themselves had difficulty borrowing as individuals, as they had already borrowed heavily the previous year to gain readmittance to the *droit annuel*.

In another exchange of correspondence that same month, the parlement reported that it might have found a lender for part of the amount, but feared that he or she might have a change of heart: 'We have found a sum of nearly 50,000 livres which we will borrow immediately if the creditor does not choose to lend to the

---

[30] A.D.S.M., C 2297, fols. 8 & 17. The suppression of two offices in 1704 only momentarily slowed the expansion of this court, this despite Colbert's pledge in 1661 that he would work hard to suppress all of the *trésoriers de France*. Reduced to ten in 1672, the number of such offices in Rouen rose to 24 by 1707. Not all of these offices found purchasers; in some cases the corps purchased the offices and held them until buyers came forth. This, at the very least, left the members of the corps with the discretion to determine whether or with whom to fill these offices. See Jean Vannier, *Essai sur le bureau des Finances de la Généralité de Rouen 1551-1790*, (Rouen, Lestringant, 1927), pp. 15-17.
[31] See Chapter Two.
[32] A.N., G^7 1543. See Chapter Three, Table 3.4.
[33] A.D.S.M., 1 B 222, fol. 29.

chamber of accounts rather than to the parlement, which we are worried about.'[34] Four months later, the Parlement was still claiming that it could not find funds 'in this province to pay the crown for the *augmentations de gages*,' and in August of that year, the first president committed himself to doing what he could to find the necessary sums on the Parisian credit market.[35]

Other judicial corps faced similar difficulties. In 1689, Chamillart wrote to the president of the *bureau des finances* to express the King's dissatisfaction with the court's offer of 34,200 livres in emergency assistance to the crown. The president answered Chamillart by invoking the personal financial difficulties of the members and the impossibility of borrowing on the credit markets.[36]

The testimonies and claims of the courts therefore suggest that they faced serious barriers to finding funds on the local credit markets. This was indeed a common refrain of venal officer corps throughout the Kingdom when, for example, they sought to make the payments necessary for periodic readmission to the *droit annuel*.[37] Such claims may well have represented delay tactics on the part of office holders reluctant to place themselves in the risky position of acting as financial intermediaries, since such services entailed mortgaging personal property in order to back royal loans. Yet if these claims were mere delay tactics, the crown ultimately retained the upper hand to coax money from the corps; office holders clearly understood that the crown could always raise funds by creating offices. Indeed, as noted above, Chamillart explicitly threatened to do just that with the parlement in 1703. While stalling may have offered office holders a means of registering their opposition to royal financial strategies, and while such delay tactics may have represented understandable reluctance on the part of office holders, they did not represent viable long term strategies for the corps. On the other hand, it is quite possible that officer corps did face real constraints in finding lenders as they claimed. Private capital markets languished during these last decades of Louis XIV's reign largely as a result of frequent monetary manipulation. Also, offices were being leveraged to greater degrees, and their market values faced downward pressure as the crown continued to create offices and strip many courts of their revenue raising functions.[38]

Marketing Judicial Offices

The market for offices and the ability of the crown to find buyers for newly created offices thus influenced the calculations of both the crown and corps. If buyers of

---

[34] A.N., G^7 1543.
[35] A.D.S.M., 1 B 222, 18 July 1703, fol. 67; 20 August 1703, fol. 86.
[36] Chamillart to the Bureau des Finances of Rouen, 21 December 1689, in Smedley-Weill, *Correspondance*, 3: 354.
[37] See Chapter Two.
[38] Philip T. Hoffman, Gilles Postel-Vinay, and Jean-Laurent Rosenthal, 'Redistribution and Long-Term Private Debt in Paris, 1660-1726,' *Journal of Economic History* 55 (June 1995): 256-284; Idem, *Priceless Markets*, pp. 50-68; Hurt, 'Les Offices,' pp. 3-31.

new offices were to be found, corps could not reasonably afford lengthy delays, legitimate or not, in raising the sums needed to keep offices off the market.[39]

Different categories of offices, though, attracted different levels of demand. We can divide newly created offices into several categories, including judicial offices in superior (or formerly sovereign) courts, offices in lower royal courts, financial offices whose holders were responsible for collecting revenues, and administrative offices, such as inspectors, registrars and clerks of the court (*greffiers*).[40] A detailed evaluation of the markets for these different offices is beyond the present scope, but some indirect indications exist for certain of these categories of offices in Upper Normandy. Records exist, for example, for the sale of offices in the chamber of accounts. While not as prestigious or powerful as the parlement, the chamber of accounts was a superior court, and it provided important avenues for social advancement among the local robe.[41]

These records from the chamber of accounts suggest that newly created robe offices tended to sell within two to five years after their arrival on the market. A steady demand for these offices arose especially from the ranks of both Parisian and Rouennais lawyers seeking social advancement. A royal edict of April 1704, for example, created several offices in Rouen's chamber of accounts, including two presidents and six *conseillers maîtres des comptes*, the accountant/magistrates responsible for verifying receivers' accounts.[42] The crown sold both offices of president in 1706, and one office of *conseiller maître* found a buyer that same year for 30,000 livres.[43] Of the remaining offices of *conseiller maître des comptes*, four were sold in 1708 for 25,000 livres each, and the one remaining office sold for that same amount in 1709.[44] In addition to these eight offices, the crown also sold three offices of *auditeur* and two offices of *correcteurs*, all of which were created by the

---

[39] The bourgeois desire for ennoblement constituted the greatest motivation to purchase offices, along with the potential for profit and the prestige of office. The extent to which each of these considerations motivated potential buyers depended on the specific type of office. See William Doyle, 'The Price of Offices in Pre-Revolutionary France,' *The Historical Journal*, 27 (1984): 831-860.

[40] Another useful way of categorizing the myriad offices would be by their degree of ennoblement conferred to the purchaser. See ibid.

[41] According to Doyle (Ibid., p. 839) non-parlementary superior courts, such as the chamber of accounts in Rouen, provided the ideal arena for bourgeois ennoblement. Such courts 'gave only second-degree nobility, but they had light or non-existant duties, and a family could ennoble itself over two privileged, unexacting generations.' On the Parlement of Normandy and social advancement through holding offices in that court, see Dewald, *Formation*.

[42] A.D.S.M., 2 B 149, fols. 11 & 53. Similar legislation had created several offices in the Chamber of Accounts of Dijon in 1691, of which eight had found buyers that same year. See Chapter Three.

[43] A.D.S.M., 2 B 149.

[44] A.D.S.M., 2 B 149-150.

same legislation of April 1704.⁴⁵ Thus, all of the offices of president and *maître des comptes* sold within five years, though the crown was forced to lower the price of the latter office by 16 per cent after 1706 to sell the five remaining. While they were not taken up instantly, this rate of purchase nevertheless suggests that the crown could reasonably expect to find buyers for judicial offices after only modest delays and price reductions.

Who were the buyers of these offices? Were they indeed aspiring elites waiting on the sidelines for the opportunity to invest in their own social advancement? In many cases they were, though at this particular juncture, not all of the purchasers of offices in the chamber of accounts were newcomers, since the chamber itself was undergoing significant institutional realignment just as the newly created offices reached the market. By a royal edict of October 1705, the crown united the Norman chamber of accounts with that province's *cour des aides*, creating out of the two courts one single *cour des comptes aides et finances*. As corporate mergers today create employment redundancies, so too did the merger of these two courts necessitate the reimbursement and suppression of some offices and the change in function of many others. Following the merger, for example, only one office of procurator general was necessary in the new court, whereas there had been one in each of the two original courts. The crown offered the procurator general with seniority, Sr. Pauyot, the remaining post of procurator general in the new court, while extending to the other, Sr. de la Rivière Lesdo, the option of exchanging his old office of procurator general for one of the two newly created offices of president.⁴⁶

Similarly, there were two first presidents vying for the one remaining office of first president in the newly united court. Sr. d'Hocqueville, first president of the *cour des aides* eventually opted to be reimbursed the value of his office and leave the post of first president in the new court to Sr. Bonnetot of the chamber of accounts. Bonnetot personally reimbursed d'Hocqueville 60,000 livres. The remaining 70,000 livres needed to fully compensate d'Hocqueville was granted him in the form of the second office of president created in April 1704. He quickly turned around and sold that office for its full price to Adrien de Rouen de Bermonville, a former *conseiller* in the *cour des aides*, thus receiving full payment for his suppressed office of first president.⁴⁷

Most of the offices sold, though, went to individuals from outside the chamber and the *cour des aides*. (See Table 4.4). In addition to the two offices of president, the edict of April 1704 created fourteen offices for which I have found letters of provision recorded in the chamber's registers.⁴⁸ Of these fourteen letters, nine

---

⁴⁵ Of the three offices of *auditeur*, one sold in 1706 for 14,000 livres, one in 1707 for 14,000 livres, and the last in 1709 for 13,000 livres. The two offices of *correcteur* sold in 1707 for 16,000 livres. A.D.S.M., 2 B 149-150.
⁴⁶ A.D.S.M., 2 B 149, fol. 11.
⁴⁷ A.D.S.M., 2 B 149, fol. 14.
⁴⁸ A.D.S.M., 2 B 149-150. The fourteen offices under consideration here include all 6 offices of *conseiller maître*, 5 of *auditeur*, and 3 of *correcteur*.

116   *Corps and Clienteles*

Table 4.4 Purchasers of new offices in Chamber of Accounts of Rouen

Purchase date	Office	Purchaser	Previous occupation
1706	auditeur	Robert du Hamel	unknown
1706	maître	Louis Henri Vauchelle	avocat, Parlement de Paris
1707	auditeur	J.-B. François Pellerin	avocat, Parlement de Rouen
1707	correcteur	Nicollas Le Page	unknown
1707	correcteur	Henri Anth. Piquet de Baignanpins	unknown
1708	correcteur	Ambroise d'Aubanton de Villebois	unknown
1708	maître	Claude Laurens	unknown
1708	maître	Alexandre Hamel des Moulins	avocat, Parlement de Paris
1708	maître	Charles le Coq	auditeur, Ch. des Comptes
1708	maître	J.-B. François Pellerin	auditeur, Ch. des Comptes
1709	auditeur	François Pesnelle	receveur payeur, Ch. des C^{tes}
1709	auditeur	Louis de St.-Ouen	avocat, Parlement de Paris
1709	maître	Ayme Laurens de Paul	correcteur, Ch. des Comptes
1710	auditeur	Guillaume Charles Jourdain	avocat, Parlement de Paris

Note: All offices created by edict in 1704.

Source: A.D.S.M., 2B 139-153.

indicate the buyers' professional backgrounds. Four of the individuals purchasing new offices were lawyers in the Parlement of Paris (*avocats au Parlement de Paris*). Two of these *avocats* bought offices of *conseiller maître*, and two bought offices of *auditeur*. In addition, an *avocat* from the Parlement of Rouen, Jean Baptiste François Pellerin, purchased an office of *auditeur* in the Chamber in 1707. He then purchased the newly created office of *maître* in 1708 and sold his old *auditeur* office the following year to another *avocat*, Jean Pierre Pouchin.[49]

Four of the buyers already held offices in the chamber when they purchased the newly created posts. These include the above mentioned Pellerin who switched offices after one year in the Chamber, along with Ayme Laurens de Paul, *correcteur*, who purchased an office of *maître* in 1709, Francois Pesnelle who held the office of *receveur payeur des gages de la chambre des comptes* from 1691

---

[49] A.D.S.M., 2 B 150, fol. 50.

until he purchased one of the offices of *auditeur* in 1709, and Charles le Coq, *auditeur* and purchaser of one of the offices of *maître* in 1708.[50]

Slightly more than half of the individuals who purchased the newly created offices, therefore, were from outside the chamber. Five of the nine for whom we have clear information had served as *avocats* at other courts prior to joining the chamber.[51] In addition, of those five whose letters of provision do not mention their professional background, only one seems to have had close family ties to the court.[52] These new creations, therefore, while expanding the ranks within the chamber of accounts, provided opportunities for families trying to build careers in the robe and ascend the social ladder. Most came from outside the institution, but members of the chamber, too, found opportunity to move up in the court and purchase offices of greater prestige and power.[53]

The local elite, therefore, stopped well short of uniformly opposing new creations of offices. Indeed, some members of the targeted corps themselves actually benefited from such creations to advance their careers. Each creation both undermined some office holders' interests and benefited others'. The crown could, therefore, rest assured of its ability to attract buyers for its newly created judicial offices in sovereign courts, and while the corps searched for lenders to finance *augmentations de gages*, they recognized that the crown's option of creating and selling redundant offices remained viable. Indeed, these same opportunities existed for the crown in Burgundy, too, since the estates typically did not intervene to repurchase newly created offices in sovereign courts. At some levels, therefore, the crown enjoyed the same leverage in both *pays d'États* and *pays d'élection* to use privilege as a divisive tool in coaxing extraordinary support. On the other hand, the marketing of non-judicial offices, in particular those administrative offices upon which Louis XIV came increasingly to depend as financial expedients, took a turn in Upper Normandy quite distinct from the Burgundian case.

---

[50] A.D.S.M., 2 B 142, fol. 163.

[51] Serving as an *avocat* after completing law studies was a common path to building a career in the robe. Indeed, working at least one or two years as an *avocat* was a necessary qualification for becoming a magistrate in the Parlement of Rouen. Dewald, *Formation*, pp. 22-31.

[52] I surveyed the letters of provision from 1679 through 1717 (records for the years 1681-1687 are missing) in search of matching family names and found that Robert du Hamel likely had relatives on the court when he purchased one of the offices of *auditeurs* in 1706. Jacques du Hamel, previously *maître des comptes*, purchased the office of president in 1698, and Charles du Hamel held the office of *receveur payeur des gages* until 1712. A.D.S.M., 2 B 145, fol. 84; 2 B 151, fol. 6.

[53] In such cases, their old offices provided paths for others to move into the Chamber as well. As mentioned above, Pellerin, who as *auditeur* bought the office of *maître* in 1708, sold his *auditeur* office to an *avocat*; Pesnelle sold his office of *receveur payeur des gages* to an officer in the *grenier à sel* of Bernay in 1709 when he bought the office of *auditeur*. A.D.S.M., 2 B 150, fols. 50 & 53.

Marketing Administrative Offices and Privileges

Again, the sources available are scarce and offer only indirect appraisals of the market. Occasionally, as the crown came to depend more and more upon the sale of offices and *augmentations de gages* as extraordinary financial means, the office of the controller general instructed its intendants to report on the status of *traités*. These were the contracts drawn between the crown and financiers (*traitants*) whereby for an agreed upon sum paid to the crown in regular installments the *traitants* received the right to sell certain offices, *augmentations de gages* or surtaxes and retain a profit on their sale. In their reports, the intendants listed all outstanding *traités*, the amounts already collected against them by the *traitants*, the amounts still due to be collected and paid to the crown, and, at times, the intendants' assessment of whether the *traitants* would likely be able to fulfill the obligations set forth in the *traités*.[54]

One such report was drawn up by the intendant of Rouen, Nicolas Étienne Roujault, in 1713. It listed *traités*, both outstanding and fully paid, dating back as far as 1703. These included, for example, a *traité* from 1708 for the sale of offices of *avocats du roy* in the *élections*, *greniers à sel* and other jurisdictions for a total of 203,700 livres, another from that same year for the sale of monopolies to liquor merchants for 444,000 livres, and a *traité* from 1710 for the sale of *augmentations de gages* to presidents in the *présidiaux*, or lower courts, of the *généralité* of Rouen valued at 18,000 livres.[55]

These *traités*, then, were for the sale of lower judicial offices, commercial privileges, surtaxes, and *augmentations de gages*. In short, they extended privilege at the same level and brought newly created offices to the market of the same sort which in Burgundy the estates intervened to keep from reaching the market by repurchasing their edicts of creation. In the *généralité* of Rouen, by contrast, *traitants* stepped in to find buyers for the newly created offices. Yet, while there were no estates in Normandy to halt the arrival of these offices and privileges, market forces there did significantly slow the process.

Along with a potential for large profits, *traitants* assumed risks that they might not find buyers for their offices and privileges at profitable prices. These risks were especially high during the last years of the War of the Spanish Succession following the economic and financial crises of 1709. The 1713 report from Roujault, summarized in Table 4.5, reflects these changing conditions. Several of the *traités* met with such a lackluster response that the crown had to reduce the amounts owed by *traitants* so that they, in turn, could lower the prices of the offices

---

[54] Regardless of their degree of success in selling their offices or *augmentations de gages*, *traitants* were legally responsible for full payment to the crown of the sums originally agreed upon. However, the crown had no interest in bankrupting *traitants*, as it had a stake in their continued solvency. It thus tended to reduce the amounts of the *traités*, often by significant amounts, if the *traitants* could not find buyers. See Dessert, *Argent*, p. 162.
[55] A.D.S.M., C 1071.

Table 4.5 Status of *traités* in Rouen in 1713, grouped by years of origin of contracts

Year	Number of contracts in report	Original amounts	Moderated amounts	Amounts recovered	Percentage recovered
1703	1	18700	18700	3000	16.04
1704	2	177927	70346	60203	85.58
1705	—	—	—	—	—
1706	1	415481	415481	64330	15.48
1707	4	869311	573756	176775	30.81
1708	9	2106568	1157944	300106	25.92
1709	6	1113728	781180	185513	23.75
1710	2	47239	47239	5877	12.44
1711	2	115400	115400	15133	13.11
1712	3	163767	163767	0	0.00
totals	30	5028121	3343813	810937	24.25

Source: A.D.S.M., C 1071.

or privileges for sale. The two *traités* that dated from 1704 were reduced the most, by slightly more than sixty per cent, after the *traitants* simply could not sell the offices at the rates originally projected.[56] The *traités* for the three years between 1707 and 1709 were reduced on average by between thirty per cent and one-half. But even after these reductions, *traitants* still could not recover and pay what was due. Only twenty five to thirty per cent of the reduced sums due on the *traités* from 1707-1709 had been recovered by 1713.

One of the thirty *traités* included in this report had been completely realized by 1713 with the original amount fully paid by the *traitant*. This was the *traité* for the sale of alternative and triennial municipal offices, contracted in 1709 for the sum of 18,591 livres. Several *traités*, on the other hand, had brought in absolutely nothing by 1713. Those that dated from 1712 are understandable, as their offices or privileges had been on the market for only about a year by the time the report was drawn up. But there were also *traités* dating back to 1708 against which nothing had been collected.[57]

The totals of these *traités* provide a useful indication of the effectiveness of the

---

[56] These two *traités* were for the sale of offices of *scindics des procureurs et des huissiers audienciers* and of *greffiers des experts*, united to the offices of *greffiers des juridictions royalles* in 1708.

[57] These included the 1708 *traité* for the sale of offices of *avocat du roy de police* for a total of 43,500 livres, a 1710 *traité* for the sale of 18,000 livres in *augmentations de gages* in the *présidiaux*, and a 1711 *traité* for the sale of offices of *greffiers des juridictions* for 29,000 livres.

crown's financial strategy. The thirty *traités* in this report were originally contracted for a total of 5,028,121 livres.[58] As *traitants* faced difficulties finding buyers and paying the amounts owed to the crown, this total was reduced to 3,343,813 livres. This sum is actually quite close to the amount which the Estates of Burgundy paid the crown during the same eleven-year period for its various *rachats* of edicts. Five different *rachats* negotiated by the Estates of Burgundy between 1703 and 1712 totaled 3,323,000 livres.[59] The sharp distinction between the two cases, however, lies in how much of these sums was actually paid the crown. Every last livre committed by the Estates of Burgundy to finance their *rachats* was transferred to the crown; they were able to raise the sums through their effective borrowing arrangement where specific crown-granted revenues were mortgaged to guarantee the loans. In the *généralité* of Rouen, on the other hand, only 810,937 livres, or about one-quarter of the reduced sums had been paid against these thirty *traités* by 1713.

The King and his ministers were aware of the difficulties that they faced in *pays d'élection*. On a similar report sent to the *Contrôle Général* by Lambert d'Herbigny, intendant of Rouen in 1703, the King's ministers recorded their reactions and instructions to the intendant. Where the intendant had made an entry for the *traité* of *offices de controlleurs des espices* and noted that the *traitant's* 'agent has neither sold nor received anything' for the *traité*, the ministers wrote in the margin:

> Yet it has been more than one year since this *traité* was negotiated; you (the intendant) need to familiarize yourself with the details right away to judge how much we can make and in how much time, while avoiding costs.[60]

And regarding the *traité des offices de lieutenant de maires et assesseurs* of May 1702 totaling 110,175 livres and for which only 19,375 livres had been raised by 1703, the intendant explained the delay by invoking all of the extraordinary charges faced by towns. The ministers responded:

> It is unfortunate that the state of affairs forces us to use all of these extraordinary

---

[58] The total of all *traités* during this same period 1703-1712 throughout the entire Kingdom was 372,197,973 livres. As one of the wealthier *généralités* of the Kingdom, Rouen was certainly the object of more than 1.35 per cent of all the *traités* negotiated. The numerical totals from this 1713 report, then, should not be taken as absolutes, but rather as indicators of the effectiveness of securing finances through *traitants*. See Dessert, *Argent*, p. 167.

[59] See Chapter Three, Table 3.6. This total does not include the 2,400,000 livres paid by the estates in 1710 for the repurchase of the capitation.

[60] 'Il y a cependant plus d'un an que ce traitté est fait, il vous faudroit entrer dans le destail des rolles dès à présent pour connaistre ce que l'on en poura tirer en quel temps, et éviter les frais.' A.N., G^7 1494; H^1 1588/44.

means, but now is the time when the intendant's attention is most needed to propose the necessary ways to secure the financial assistance that we have planned.[61]

Given the state of the market, then, the *traitants'* profit motive, strong though it was, was not a sufficient mechanism to keep the extraordinary funds flowing to the crown at the rate it expected.

To remedy this, as the above quotes suggest, the crown drafted the assistance of its commissioners in the provinces, the intendants. In several letters to the intendant of Rouen, the Controller General exhorted him to do all he could to help particular *traitants* find buyers. Thus, one letter instructed the intendant '...to facilitate the sale of these new offices and to give the *traitant* the protection (i.e. political support) that he will need.'[62] In another letter, the Controller General wrote:

> ...since the *finance* that should come from the sale of these offices was designated by His Majesty to be used for the pressing expenses of war, I ask you to do all in your power to find buyers and to give to the agent responsible for recovering the funds in your *généralité* the protection that he will need.[63]

In its search for extraordinary finances, the crown thus instructed its intendants to help the *traitants* by all means possible and even to act as salesmen themselves and find potential buyers for the new offices. This support from intendants was crucial – if offices were not sold at anticipated rates, the receipts from extraordinary financial strategies suffered, and, more gravely, the *traitants* themselves risked bankruptcy for 'remaining for too long in debt' to their creditors. An insolvent group of *traitants*, the crown figured, was of little use to it in times of financial need.[64]

The crown, therefore, did face serious limits to the extent to which it could secure extraordinary finances simply by creating and selling offices, *augmentations de gages* and surtaxes. Judicial offices, particularly at the level of superior courts, found buyers on a consistent basis, though strong elements within the affected

---

[61] 'C'est avec regret que la conjoncture des affaires oblige d'avoir recours à tous ces moyens extraordinaires,... mais c'est dans cette occasion où l'attention de M. l'Intendant est plus nécessaire pour proposer les moyens nécessaires, pour en tirer le secours que l'on s'est proposé.'
[62] '...faciliter le débit de ces nouvelles charges et de donner au traitant la protection dont il aura besoin.' A.D.S.M., C 1071, 24 May 1709.
[63] '...comme la finance qui doit provenir de la vente de ces offices a esté destinné par Sa Majesté pour être employée aux despenses pressantes de la guerre, je vous prie de faire tout ce qui sera en vous pour trouver des acquereurs et de donner au commis qui sera chargé de ce recouvrement dans votre généralité toute la protection dont il aura besoin.' A.D.S.M., C 1071, 9 June 1707.
[64] A.D.S.M., C 1071, 28 August 1706. Instructions such as these surely fueled the long-standing complaint leveled by judicial office holders that intendants were allied with *traitants* against their interests. See Beik, *Absolutism*, p. 164.

corps together with the crown often showed a preference for keeping those offices off the market whenever possible in exchange for lump-sum payments, or *rachats*. This disposition required patience on the part of the crown as judicial corps tried to piece together the lending clienteles needed to finance their *rachats*. On the other hand, the sale of lower judicial and administrative offices along with *augmentations de gages*, commercial privileges and surtaxes – in other words the offices and privileges least likely to be kept off the market through *rachats* – proved barely responsive to the crown's needs. Still, two sources of extraordinary financial support remained for the crown in the *généralité* of Rouen: municipalities and, particular to the commercial economy of the region, merchants.

The Rouennais Commercial Elite

The municipality of Rouen Like the municipalities in Burgundy, those of Upper Normandy faced a crown whose financial plans included converting elective municipal offices into venal offices, creating redundant offices thereafter, and using privilege as a bargaining chip to engage them as financial intermediaries. Unlike the case in Burgundy, however, there were no provincial estates to step in and finance the occasional *rachat* of edicts. Thus, municipalities such as Rouen were left to devise their own financial contingencies when, in 1692, Louis XIV created venal mayoralties throughout most of the Kingdom.

Rouen had not had a mayor since 1382.[65] Over the course of the sixteenth and seventeenth centuries, a tight-knit group of merchants and bourgeois secured an oligarchic hold over the town's governance, much as oligarchies were able to do through their control of electoral procedures in towns and cities throughout France.[66] Prior to the King's creation of a venal mayoralty in 1692, this commercial elite managed the town's financial and administrative matters through its control of the council of six *échevins*. The indirect method of choosing this council every three years assured that only residents of bourgeois status influenced the selection and that only the most prominent and politically connected were chosen. The specific criteria for bourgeois status and the privileges conferred to those who held it differed from municipality to municipality, but in general this designation was reserved for the most stable and well-off non-noble urban population. In Rouen, bourgeois status was attained after ten years as a resident and after having paid specific taxes, namely the *taxe des pauvres* and the *taxe des boues*.[67] Those with bourgeois status, then, chose an electoral corps of forty notables (increased from

---

[65] Following a local revolt, Charles VI suppressed the office of mayor in Rouen and transferred the judicial and military powers once enjoyed by the municipality to the royal bailiwick. Provincial governors then assumed these powers in the mid-sixteenth century. Philip Benedict, *Rouen during the Wars of Religion* (Cambridge: Cambridge University Press, 1981), pp. 34-35.
[66] Bernstein, 'Benefit,' pp. 634-36.
[67] Gérard d'Arandel de Condé, *Les Bourgeois de statut à Rouen, 1664-1790*, (Rouen, 1971), p. 2.

twenty-four in 1665), which in turn elected the six *échevins* along with four *quarteniers*. Outgoing *quarteniers* were regularly elected as *échevins* (four of the six) the following term. The restricted and indirect fashion of selecting the town council assured that a narrow and exclusive group remained in control of municipal power. Pierre Bardet refers, for example, to the 'political domination by the urban elite' and asserts that 'the same closed group controlled local offices.'[68] Appendix 1 contains biographical information on some of the members of this urban commercial elite.

When confronted with the prospect of a hereditary mayoralty and, thus, the establishment of dynastic rule over the municipality, the town council sought as early as 1692 to repurchase and unite the office of mayor and thereby preserve the bourgeois and merchant community's oligarchic control over the municipality. In 1695, since a buyer for the office still had not come forth, the King agreed to accept 60,000 livres from the town to unite the office to the municipal corps and thus take it off the market.[69] Thereafter, the electoral corps of forty notables nominated suitable candidates to serve as mayor every three years. The King still retained a hand in filling the post of mayor; nonetheless the merchant elite succeeded in forestalling any entrenchment of a hereditary, dynastic, and possibly competing elite at the pinnacle of local government.[70]

Intent on preserving the commercial hold over municipal power structures, the town council continued to repurchase other edicts that would have converted municipal posts into venal offices. In 1704, the town paid the crown 75,000 livres to repurchase offices of lieutenant mayor, assessor and concierge of the town hall; and in 1707 it paid another 28,000 livres for the repurchase of alternate offices of mayor and deputy mayor.[71] The municipality also financed additional *rachats* that protected the status of the local bourgeoisie. In 1692, the municipality paid 330,000 livres that served both as emergency assistance to the crown and as payment to preserve the right of *franc fief* for the bourgeois of Rouen, and in 1706 a payment of 226,000 livres was made in exchange for the royal confirmation of the privileges of the town's bourgeoisie.[72] As indicated in Table 4.6, the total of all

---

[68] Bardet, *Rouen*, p. 100. The translation is mine.

[69] During the intervening three years, Jacques Brunel du Quesnay, *conseiller procureur du roi au présidial de Rouen* had been appointed by the King as acting mayor.

[70] Prior to each term the electoral corps submitted a list of three nominees for mayor from which the King made the final selection. To rotate power among different orders, the nominees were to be chosen in alternance from the sword nobility, the robe, and the bourgeoisie and merchants of the town. In 1695, it was the turn of the robe, thus the King was presented with a list that included Marc Antoine Hellouin de Menibus, *avocat général au parlement*, M. de Guibray, *conseiller au parlement* and M. Bigot de Montville, also a *conseiller au parlement*. The King selected Hellouin de Menibus to serve the three year term. A.M.R., A 29, 15 July 1695, fol 51.

[71] A.M.R., A 29, 27 May 1704, fol. 246; 28 June 1707, fol. 283.

[72] Exemption from the *franc fief* was very valuable to the Rouennais bourgeoisie. With its preservation, the non-nobles of the city who owned noble fiefs in the countryside were not required to pay the heavy royal tax levied specifically on just such landlords. The privileges

Table 4.6 Total extraordinary obligations of municipality of Rouen

Year	Amount, livres	Purpose
1689	300000	emergency aid to crown
1690	3240	repurchase of municipal office
1692	330000	emergency aid and confirmation of *franc fief*
1695	60000	repurchase of municipal offices
1704	75000	repurchase of municipal offices
1704	25000	repurchase of municipal offices
1704	8000	repurchase of municipal offices
1704	20000	repurchase of municipal offices
1704	240000	acquisition of surtax on butchers
1706	226000	confirmation of privileges of Rouennais bourgeoisie
1707	28000	repurchase of municipal offices
1713	105000	repurchase of municipal offices
1715	141343	suppression of surtax on butchers
total:	1561583	

Source: A.M.R., A 28-30.

rachats and emergency assistance payments to support the war effort between 1689 and 1715 amounted to 1,561,583 livres.

These *rachats* are similar in some respects to those financed by the Estates of Burgundy, though the total sums involved are significantly less. The groups that dominated both corps, or the broader ruling coalition in the Burgundian case, were motivated to preserve the privileged standing of the local elite along with a degree of local autonomy in the face of Louis XIV's penchant for creating and selling new offices. Yet there were also important differences separating these two cases of territorial corps acting as financial intermediaries. To begin with, the municipality of Rouen faced the same constraints as did local judicial corps in finding lenders on the credit market. This explains the three-year delay in financing the *rachat* of the office of mayor created as venal in 1692. In 1693, the town council voted to offer the crown 100,000 livres for the office of mayor, but recognized at the same time that the offer was largely symbolic, since money was scarce and they could raise 100,000 livres only in the event of 'finding the money in loans which seems impossible at present.'[73] When in 1695 the crown agreed to accept the council's

---

of the bourgeoisie of Rouen, in addition to the exemption from the *franc fief*, included the exemption from the military *ban et arrière-ban*, exemption from the *taille*, and the privilege of free fairs. A.M.R., A 28, 30 June 1692, fol. 431; A 29, 4 December 1706, fol. 274. See also Arandel de Condé, p. 29.

[73] A.M.R., A 28, fol. 412, 19 January 1693.

offer of 60,000 livres, the money was still not available, and the town council was able to offer only a promise to pay. And again, when the crown created alternate municipal offices in 1703, the council stated that the 'town has no funds and is entirely incapable of paying anything for the reunion of the said offices to the town's corps...'[74]

When the municipality did borrow to finance *rachats* or to make other extraordinary payments, it borrowed against specific indirect revenues, or *octrois*, granted by the crown. Rouen had at its disposal three different sets of revenues to mortgage, an *octroi sur boissons* levied on wine, cider and other alcoholic beverages, an *octroi* on firewood, butter and cheese, and, following the reunion of the offices of *inspecteurs aux boucheries* to the town's corps, a surtax levied on butchers.

The *échevins*, however, were reluctant to accept control over and then mortgage these revenues. In 1706, the town council opposed the establishment of the *octrois* on firewood, butter and cheese to finance the confirmation of bourgeois privileges, recognizing that the taxes would 'weigh heavily on the public.'[75] The *échevins* voted to send a delegation to Paris to appeal for a 'considerable diminution' of this tax which, to the council's disappointment, it did not receive. Again, in 1714, the municipality argued that these same *octrois* were responsible for keeping merchants from doing business in Rouen because of the high costs they imposed on goods transported through the town gates. The council voted to ask the King for a decrease by one-half of the *octrois*, and this time, the King granted the reduction.[76]

This reluctant disposition contrasts with that of the Estates of Burgundy, which willingly accepted control over the *octrois de la Saône* despite their recognized damaging effects on commerce in the province and which then vigorously protected their hold over those revenues. The commercial interests that dominated the municipality of Rouen, on the other hand, seemed ambivalent at best about fulfilling such a role as financial intermediary. It opposed the levying of indirect taxes even when offered the prospect of controlling the collection and administration of the revenues.

A further distinction lies in the method by which the municipality raised funds. At no point during the period under study did the municipality of Rouen float bonds as the Estates of Burgundy did. Rather, the leaseholders of the town's *octrois*, the professional financiers who contracted to collect the taxes, agreed to forward the *rachat* sums to the Royal Treasury and then reimburse their own principal and interest by collecting the *octrois* for an agreed upon number of

---

[74] A.M.R., A 29, 12 July 1695, fol. 51; 8 March 1703, fol. 222.
[75] A.M.R., A 29, 4 December 1706, fol. 274.
[76] A.M.R., A 30, 24 August 1714, fol. 443.

years.[77] Then, in 1710, local elements from within the merchant community moved to take control over these financial transactions. Rather than taking competitive bids from prospective leaseholders, the town began conducting business with a single financial company that began to manage all of the town's extraordinary financial affairs. This company of seven individuals, all described as Rouennais merchants, advanced the sums due to the crown from the municipality for various *rachats* and took over the leases of the *octrois* to reimburse themselves and their creditors, much as the individual leaseholders did prior to 1710.[78] Yet this company was not a collection of professional financial interests providing services to the town on a competitive and contractual basis. Rather, the individuals who comprised the company had direct ties to the town council and used those personal connections to end the competitive bidding and to monopolize control over extraordinary financial affairs. All seven members of the company served at least once as town *échevin*, either prior to or during their activity in the company.[79] And among the six *échevins* and four *quarteniers* elected to the town council in 1710, three members of the financial company were chosen, two as *échevins* and one as a *quartenier*. The elder brother of another member, Nicolas Marye, was elected *échevin* as well. This financial company originated from the depths of the town's bourgeois elite that made up its governing class.

Coalition building in the face of Louis' divide-and-rule strategies thus faltered. The commercial and merchant interests that dominated the municipality were surely behind the reluctance of the council to offer the town's services as a financial intermediary. Such financial engagement necessarily entailed the establishment or continuation of *octrois*, which were rightly seen as harmful to local commerce. The core group of merchants in control of the municipality was thus caught in a bind. It needed to finance *rachats* to protect the privileges of the town's bourgeoisie and the independence of local governance under its oligarchic control, but it was not interested in accepting control over *octrois* detrimental to its

---

[77] Thus in 1689, when the municipality agreed to pay the crown 300,000 livres for emergency assistance, the lease holder of the *octroi sur les boissons* was instructed to pay the Royal Treasury 150,000 livres by the end of May 1689 and another 150,000 livres by the following November 15. A.M.R., A 28, 10 May 1689, fol. 318. The experience in Dieppe was quite similar. In April 1689 the town council began searching for lenders to help finance 120,000 livres in *secours extraordinaires*. By June of that same year, the mayor and *échevins* realized that creditors were simply not to be found, and they decided instead to solicit advances from the lease holders of the town's *octrois*. A.N., E 1853, 12 April 1689, fol. 45; 7 June 1689, fol. 75.

[78] A.M.R., A 30, 7 July 1710, fol. 328. The seven members of the financial company in 1710 were Philippe le Baillif, Nicolas Marye, Nicolas Cabeuil, Louis Judde, François Planterose, and Meslon Cécille. A.M.R., A 30, 13 June 1710, fol. 327.

[79] Philippe le Bailiff, for example, was first elected *échevin* in 1698; Nicolas Marye was elected *échevin* in 1677, 1692 and 1695 and was *prieur des consuls*, or head of the regional commercial jurisdiction, in 1667. See Charles le Picard, *Catalogue des maires et échevins de la ville de Rouen et des Prieurs des Consuls depuis leur institution jusqu'en 1790*, (Louviers, 1895).

strongly held commercial interests. The best that the council could do was to finance the *rachats* while urging the King to reduce the weight of the *octrois*.[80] Meanwhile, as long as the municipal *octrois* were going to be collected, a small group of the town's core elite positioned themselves to benefit by gaining control over the *octrois*, thereby preventing any outside financiers from profiting from these already detrimental taxes.

In the end, the municipality itself never technically assumed the role of financial intermediary in the way that the Estates of Burgundy did. It remained the legal recipient of various *octrois* granted by the crown, but the *de facto* intermediaries were the private individuals, either the professional financier/lease holders or, after 1710, the local company of merchants who forwarded sums to the crown, which they had most likely borrowed from their own personal clienteles of lenders, and who then reimbursed themselves with revenues from the *octrois*. Control over revenues was thus an important issue for Rouen's merchant elite. As long as the municipality was unable or unwilling to act as a financial intermediary in the way that the Estates of Burgundy did, and as long as that role was deferred to private individuals, a group of leading merchants opted to step in, assume a direct role in handling these finances, and displace the intervention of professional financiers. Merchants reacted very similarly to another set of *octrois* created by the crown and granted not to the municipality, but rather to the town's chamber of commerce.

The Rouen chamber of commerce With the temporary outbreak of peace at the turn of the eighteenth century, the crown created the council of commerce to facilitate consultations between royal ministers and merchants.[81] This council, composed of two *conseillers d'État*, the Controller General of finances, two masters of requests who prepared reports, and twelve deputies each representing a designated commercial town, was to meet at least weekly to shape royal policy on commerce. Shortly afterward, the crown established institutional uniformity among twelve designated merchant communities by creating chambers of commerce in their towns.[82] In the *arrêts* creating these chambers, the crown stated that their purpose was to establish a forum where merchants could bring forth their complaints about policies detrimental to commerce along with their suggestions for enhancing trade. The chambers were then to deliberate on the matters raised by the merchants and send reports reflecting their points of view to the council of commerce in Paris.[83]

---

[80] As the deputies of the Burgundian estates understood, these two positions were contradictory. They suggest the true ambivalence that the municipal elite felt toward controlling and mortgaging indirect revenues.
[81] Thomas J. Schaeper, 'The Creation of the French Council of Commerce in 1700,' *European Studies Review* 9 (1979): 313-329.
[82] Henri Wallon, *La Chambre de Commerce de la Province de Normandie, 1703-1791*, (Rouen: Imprimerie Cagniard, 1903), pp. 12-13. Besides Rouen, the crown created chambers of commerce in Lyon, Bordeaux, Toulouse, Montpellier, La Rochelle, Nantes, St. Malo, Lille and Bayonne.
[83] A.N., E 1830, 19 June 1703, fol. 375.

Thus, beginning with the creation of the council of commerce in 1700 and culminating with the creations of the various provincial chambers the following years, the crown established an institutional network through which it could receive the suggestions, grievances and opinions of merchants and form policy accordingly. There is some question about the crown's motivation for these creations. Lionel Rothkrug has argued that the crown, weakened by years of war and economic depression, conceded to the Kingdom's disgruntled merchants a voice in policymaking. Thomas Schaeper, on the other hand, perceives the creations as a function solely of the crown's initiative, not out of a position of weakness, but from a desire to institutionalize its governing strategy that had for long emphasized consultation with the elite.[84] Overlooked by both Rothkrug and Schaeper, and as the case of the Rouen chamber demonstrates, the crown also had financial motives, as it was essentially creating new corps which it could then engage as financial intermediaries.

The establishment of a chamber of commerce in Rouen signified continuity with existing bodies more than it did innovation. In 1556, Henry II had created the jurisdiction of the *prieurs* and of the *juges consuls*, or the *juridiction consulaire*, and until 1703 this body oversaw and arbitrated any dispute concerning trade agreements, bills of exchange, or business transactions undertaken at trade fairs.[85] This organization then became the chamber of commerce, headed by the same offices of *prieur du conseil* and of *juges consuls*, joined by five *syndics*, or legal advocates. To hold these elective offices, individuals had to have conducted business as merchants in Normandy for at least fifteen years. The merchants who comprised the chamber, or before that the *juridiction consulaire*, were very close to, and indeed overlapped with, the municipal elite that dominated the town council. Indeed, several members of this tight-knit merchant elite served as both *échevin* on the town council and as either *prieur du conseil* or *syndic* in the chamber.[86]

In addition to 'creating' the chamber of commerce and integrating the local merchant elite into a broader consultative network, the crown earmarked revenues from *octrois* to provide for the costs incurred by this chamber. These were intended to offset primarily the costs of sending a deputy to the council of commerce in Paris. Initially, the chamber was to have collected the revenues from a temporary set of dues on merchandise entering Rouen called the *octrois des marchands*. Then, after financing the initial costs of establishing the chamber, these *octrois des marchands* were to be abolished and replaced on January 1, 1705 by the more modest *octrois* of 15 sous for each hundred pounds of soda ash and of wooden

---

[84] Schaeper, pp. 313-319.
[85] Picard; Hurpin, *Intendance de Rouen*, p. 88.
[86] For example, Jacques Asselin was elected *échevin* in 1671, 1680 and 1686 and served a one-year term as *prieur* in 1677. Likewise, Nicolas Marye served a term as *prieur* in 1667 and was then elected *échevin* in 1677, 1692 and 1695. In addition, five of the six merchants who comprised the municipal financial company in 1710 served at least one term as syndic in the Chamber of Commerce, the exception being Louis Judde. See Wallon, pp. 375-389.

barrels entering the province, considered sufficient to cover the 8000 livres in annual deputation costs.[87]

Contrary to these plans, however, while the chamber did gain control over the more modest *octrois* to cover its deputation costs beginning in January 1705, the *octrois des marchands* were never abolished. Rather, the crown extended them at first for nine years to finance the suppression of the newly created offices of controllers of weights and measures, then followed this first extension up with repeated moves to renew and earmark the revenues further into the future.[88] In January 1711, the crown extended the *octrois des marchands* nine years to finance a 220,000 livres *rachat* by the merchant community of '*rentes provincialles*', or forced loans that would have been collected from individual merchants.[89] A further renewal in 1712 financed a 150,000 livres payment intended to keep the crown from doubling the rates at which the *octrois* were collected; a six-year extension in 1713 financed a 150,000 livres *rachat* of a surtax called the *dixième d'industrie*; and as a final example, a six-year extension in 1715 financed a 115,508 livres suppression of a surtax of 2 sous/livre on the sale of cloths.[90]

Like the merchants sitting on the Rouennais town council, the members of the chamber of commerce did not welcome the establishment of these *octrois*, and they accepted only with reluctance their chamber's role as a financial intermediary. Contrary to Rothkrug's argument that the crown established the council and the twelve chambers of commerce to appease disgruntled merchants, the particular framework in which the chamber at Rouen was created actually met with vocal opposition from the local merchant community. Focusing their opposition primarily on the *octrois*, the merchants recruited the *cour des aides* of Rouen to support their stance, and when this court registered the royal legislation creating the chamber, it did so with the stipulation that there would be no new *octrois* created. The merchants were willing, the court argued, to serve in the chamber and finance their deputations to Paris with funds pooled from the community. After all, such had been the practice of the former *juridiction consulaire*. The King was not swayed however, and he ordered the *cour des aides* to register the legislation as he originally presented it.[91]

Once again, however, the merchant community showed itself flexible and adaptable to the circumstances dealt to it by the crown. After the crown's first extension in 1705, as the merchants realized that they were not going to succeed in suppressing the *octrois des marchands*, they did what they could to secure their own control over these revenues. The 1705 legislation that had initially extended the *octrois* for nine years had not granted control over them to the chamber; instead the tax was to be 'continued and raised for His Majesty's profit' by a group of

---

[87] A.D.S.M., C 222.
[88] A.N., E 1932, 13 June 1705, fol. 290.
[89] A.N., E 824^b-825^a, 27 January 1711, fol. 76.
[90] Wallon, pp. 190-192.
[91] Ibid., p. 28; A.N., E 1924, 18 September 1703, fol. 247.

professional financiers.[92] The merchant community perceived this arrangement as damaging twice over to its interests. Not only were the *octrois* going to remain in place and harm local commercial activity, but a professional financial company from outside the community was set to profit from the merchants' misfortunes. Once the chamber's appeal to suppress the *octrois des marchands* failed, the merchants decided at least to fight for control over the revenues. This required the payment of a 'considerable sum' to the *adjudicataire* who had already leased the rights to collect the *octrois*, but the merchants found such a cost worth the benefit of controlling taxes essentially levied against their own economic activities.[93]

For this same reason, after the chamber regained control over the *octrois*, the merchant community preferred at least to use further extensions of these revenues to finance the *rachats* of other indirect taxes which the crown proposed to create and which outsiders or professional financiers would likely have had a hand in collecting. Thus, they repurchased with the revenues under their control the forced *rentes*, the *dixième d'industrie*, and the surtax on cloths.[94] Unable to prevent the creation and repeated extension of the *octrois*, the merchants valued at least the ability to control them.

It would be a stretch to argue, however, that the Rouennais merchants were fortunate to be able to use the *octrois* for causes beneficial to their community.[95] While the *octrois* did indeed finance the *rachat* of taxes harmful to merchant interests, this arrangement certainly represented the lesser of two evils from the merchants' perspective. Just as the crown altered privileges in such a way as to pressure the Estates of Burgundy to repurchase edicts, so too did it create commercial taxes and threaten further to undermine merchants' interests in order to coax them into financing *rachats*. This was a much more bitter pill for the Rouennais merchants to swallow, however, as they felt the damaging effects of the *octrois* more heavily than did the ruling coalition of Burgundy. The Rouennais merchants, whether convened in the chamber of commerce or in control of the town's municipality, were reluctant accomplices to the crown's strategy of using privilege to engage corps as financial intermediaries.

Conclusion

Can we speak, then, of an accommodation in this *pays d'élection* similar to that

---

[92] A.N., E 1932, 13 June 1705, fol. 290.
[93] Wallon, pp. 102-104.
[94] Ibid., p. 190.
[95] This is the view of Henri Wallon (Ibid., p. 189): 'This is perhaps the only example of a royal tax, of which the control was granted to a community of merchants who, without having the free disposition over the revenues, still saw to it as much as possible that they were used to service the interests that they (the merchants) represented.' The translation is mine.

which developed between the crown and the Burgundian elite during Louis XIV's war years? While Louis XIV remained committed in broad terms to protecting the privilege and property of the Kingdom's politically endowed elite, the comparative view of the preceding chapters suggests that this accommodation took a rather distinct form in provinces of differing privileged standing.

Few historians of the early modern French state have adopted explicitly comparative approaches in order to weigh the significance of particular institutional distinctions for the political consolidation of the Kingdom in the seventeenth century. Nora Temple's study of the increasing royal control over towns is one exception that merits some attention. Temple argues that provincial estates carried with them a mixed bag of benefits and costs to inhabitants of *pays d'États*. The estates' ability to bargain with the crown to secure favorable terms for regular taxation was clearly a benefit. Yet, Temple argues, the disadvantage of estates 'was that the very existence of this corporate organization facilitated the negotiation of irregular subsidies. The provincial estates' ardor for preserving local independence and privileges made them vulnerable to government pressure and extortion.'[96] As this study of elite groups in both Burgundy and Upper Normandy suggests, the broad outlines of Temple's arguments are correct: ordinary taxation on a per-capita basis was higher in Upper Normandy, whereas the ruling elite in Burgundy seemed ever so willing to forward the crown sums in order to preserve the province's privileged status. Further, the extent to which and the efficiency with which the Estates of Burgundy mediated finances for the crown while repurchasing edicts contrasts sharply with the difficulties the crown faced marketing offices and privileges in Upper Normandy through the intermediation of *traitants*. Yet Temple's focus on the royal exploitation of privilege ignores the motivation of the privileged elite groups themselves who were the targets of this supposed exploitation.

The crown clearly took advantage of the value that local elite groups in Burgundy placed upon the province's privileged status, as Temple suggests. Yet Louis XIV was able to follow much the same strategy in Upper Normandy where a commercial elite likewise valued its control over local power structures and the preservation of local autonomy.[97] In both cases, to preserve local control and

---

[96] Temple, pp. 80-81.
[97] Temple's argument hinges upon an empirical comparison between the municipality of Auxerre, in Burgundy, and Moulins, capital of the Bourbonnais, a *pays d'élection*. Because Auxerre was under the tutelage of the Burgundian estates and local privileges were thus all the more prominent, she argues, its residents faced a series of costly *rachats* under Louis XIV. The residents of Moulins, on the other hand, only had to finance two sets of *rachats* during the same period. The comparison may not be representative, however. The municipality of Rouen appears to have faced extraordinary demands on the same order as, if not heavier than, the municipality of Dijon during the period under study. While Dijon financed 11 sets of *rachats* from 1692 to 1701 for 511,169 livres, Rouen financed 4 extraordinary payments from 1689 to 1695 for 693,240 livres. As the case of Rouen

autonomy, the respective ruling elite groups agreed to repurchase edicts and raise money for the crown. To be sure, the Estates of Burgundy proved more adept at raising extraordinary sums for the royal treasury, but this was not so much a function of Burgundy's privileged status as it was the institutional strengths and particularities of the estates themselves.

Further, in Burgundy, the extraordinary payments agreed upon by the estates entailed a shift toward what was already the preferred fiscal balance for the ruling coalition – an emphasis on indirect taxes (better still, *future* indirect taxes) as substitutes for direct taxes in the present. Those among the ruling coalition who valued the local financial autonomy accorded by the Burgundian estates were surely not exploited by their 'willingness to act as a broker for *rachats des offices*,' as they retained their privileged standing and their dominant status as large landowners while shifting fiscal burdens toward commercial activity and the rather regressive practice of taxing consumption.[98]

Those who valued local control over municipal structures in Rouen, on the other hand, preserved their positions by going along with a program of taxing their own economic activities. It is no wonder, then, that the town council of Rouen intervened for the repurchase of municipal offices with an ambiguous sense of duty. Provincial estates, therefore, did not so much leave privileged provinces open to exploitation as they created opportunities for the landed elite to advance their interests at the expense of both commercial groups and peasant tenants.[99] That Louis XIV was able to attract the reluctant cooperation of the Rouennais merchant community, on the other hand, is testimony to his success at dividing elite groups along lines of privilege and access to both power and resources in this *pays d'élection*.

---

suggests, towns in *pays d'élection* were also hit hard by extraordinary demands. See Table 4.6 and Bertucat, pp. 140-142.
[98] Temple, p. 80.
[99] This is the argument of James B. Collins (*Classes*, p. 10) in his study of the local rulers in Brittany.

PART III
CORPS AND CLIENTELES IN PUBLIC FINANCE

Chapter 5

Lenders and Money Handlers

To understand royal financial strategies and the responses of the elite to those strategies, historians need to account for the institutional specificities across the juridically unequal landscape that characterized early modern France. The previous chapters have shown how the corporate makeup and privileged contours of a province shaped elites' abilities to coalesce as they responded to royal financial demands. All this is not to suggest, however, that clienteles and personal relationships were not relevant. Indeed, personal relationships and clientele systems remained crucial both to the exercise of authority in general and to the administration of finances in particular throughout the history of old-regime France.[1] Corps and clienteles intersected to shape the process of state formation in the seventeenth and eighteenth centuries, and this is particularly true during the latter half of Louis XIV's reign, when a period of personal rule by the King met with a period of royal dependence on provincial institutions to provide financial intermediation.

Both individuals and corporations acted as financial intermediaries for the crown. Their relationships to one another, to the crown, to their clienteles of lenders and to the local ruling elite form the topics of the following two chapters. The present chapter focuses on the money handlers who provided valuable financial services to the crown but who often found themselves in precarious positions both with regard to the crown and to local populations. The following chapter examines the networks of lenders who supported the financial intermediation of privileged corps.

Introduction

Financiers, those who were charged with the responsibility of raising sums of money from the population and transferring them to the crown, long suffered an unfavorable reputation among the French. By providing liquid funds, they furnished essential services to a monarch who enjoyed only a rudimentary bureaucracy and whose financial options were further shackled by a poor credit

---

[1] See, for example, Julian Dent, 'The Role of Clientèles in the Financial Elite of France Under Cardinal Mazarin,' in J.F. Bosher, ed., *French Government and Society*, (London: Athlone Press, 1973), pp. 41-69.

reputation. Yet in doing so they often aroused the hostility of the populace. The arrival of tax farmers, for example, provided the spark for many of the uprisings of the 1630s and 1640s, and even being designated as collector of the *taille* within one's parish, a responsibility that most tried to avoid, typically brought the contempt of neighbors. The crown understood the poor reputation of financiers, and it used their poor image to justify pursuing them in Chambers of Justice and to seize what were deemed ill-gotten profits.[2]

For these reasons, it has become commonplace to view financiers as outsiders whose interests lay solely in their own enrichment and whose activities made possible the arbitrary strategies of an increasingly powerful monarch throughout the seventeenth century. This understanding is integral, for example, to the 'traditional' view that sees warfare as a catalyst for state development. Roland Mousnier argued, for example, that financiers stood in alliance with the crown and its commissioners, forming a governmental front able to mobilize resources and assert an autonomous will over and above the interests of local populations. At least for the period 1630-1660, William Beik sees the position of financiers in much the same terms. From the points of view of Languedocian taxpayers and office holders, financiers were outsiders who entered the province ready to exploit the local population by leasing indirect tax farms and by contracting to sell offices and privileges. Furthermore, as in the model put forth by Mousnier, these financiers enjoyed the political protection of intendants and military commanders who themselves often held a financial interest in their activities.[3]

Yet while Mousnier offers his model of a distinct and autonomous group of royal financiers allied with royal commissioners to explain how a succession of kings was able to construct a centralized monarchical state over the course of the seventeenth century, Beik sees an important change take place upon Louis XIV's assumption of personal rule. For Beik, the Mousnier model of financiers is specific to the troubled period spanning the ministries of Richelieu and Mazarin. After 1660, he argues, members of the local elite came to dominate the financial networks in Languedoc, and they ultimately integrated themselves into and even dominated the Kingdom-wide financial networks.[4] State finance was no longer perceived by the local elite as the exploitative domain of greedy outsiders, but rather as 'so many interlocking opportunities for investment, all controlled locally yet all tied to larger financial circuits.'[5] Granting local control over finances, Beik argues, was yet another means by which Louis XIV engineered a cooperative strategy of rule through the local elite, thereby linking the notables' prestige and authority to his own.

Was this transformation in financial systems from dominance by Parisian

---

[2] Mireille Touzery, *L'Invention de l'impôt sur le revenu* (Paris: C.H.E.F.F., 1994), pp. 15-20; Dessert, *Argent*, pp. 242-250.
[3] Mousnier, 'The Fronde,' p. 133; Beik, *Absolutism*, pp. 245-255.
[4] Beik, *Absolutism*, pp. 253-258.
[5] Ibid., p. 258.

financiers (the Mousnier model) to cooptation of local elites (the Beik model) evident everywhere in France upon Louis XIV's rise to personal power, or is the case of Languedoc somehow exceptional? Whereas several Languedocian families involved in local finance, such as the Sartre and the Bonnier, rose to Kingdom-wide prominence in the eighteenth century and came to dominate an integrated Paris-centered financial network, it is unlikely that such success would have been possible across the geographic board. There simply was not enough room at the top of eighteenth-century financial hierarchies for the local financiers of all other provinces to rise to the same heights as the Languedocians.[6]

Ultimate success on the level enjoyed by Languedocians, however, was not necessary for there to have been cooptation of local elites into royal finances under Louis XIV, and thus Beik's cooptation model may indeed apply to experiences outside Languedoc. Yet if changes like these did take place outside Languedoc, it remains to be seen how and why they came about and whether they were general or specific to certain provinces. The crown's financial conditions and its strategies to meet its changing needs may very well have determined any such shift from dominance to cooptation in state finances. The transformation that Beik describes in Languedoc came during a relatively flush period when Colbert was attempting to rein in privileges and debt and bring order to state finances, albeit with only limited success.[7] Yet, as detailed at a number of points throughout this work, the frontiers of royal finance lay with extraordinary affairs as Louis XIV's needs increased following 1688, and once more the crown came to depend heavily upon extraordinary *traités*, and thus on *traitants*. Was the change from the Mousnier model of dominance to the Beik model of cooptation able to withstand this renewed reliance on financiers, or were local elite groups once again displaced by outsiders in the raising and handling of money for the crown?

Local factors may also have determined the extent of any such shift toward local cooptation in financial activities. Distance from Paris might have made the Beik model of cooptation essential for raising funds in far away provinces. The

---

[6] Guy Chaussinand-Nogaret, *Les Financiers de Languedoc au XVIIIe siècle*, (Paris: S.E.V.P.E.N., 1970), pp. 29-81. Indeed, the main intent behind Chaussinand-Nogaret's book lies in explaining the exception of the Languedocian case.

[7] It has been commonplace to view Colbert as a reformer who tried to rationalize the King's finances. It is well known, for example, that Colbert strongly opposed the creation and sale of new offices and that he even attempted to buy back many of those already privately held. Such an austere program, though, began to fall apart for good with the outbreak of the Dutch War in 1672. Daniel Dessert points out, furthermore, that the crown never suspended the use of *traités* under Colbert, and that, in fact, the single largest extraordinary affair of the Old Regime was of his own creation: the *traité* to recover fines from the Chamber of Justice of 1661-1669 which the crown negotiated at 110,000,000 livres (*traité* Pierre de Champagne). Still, although figures are not available for the period under Colbert's ministry to accurately assess the crown's use of extraordinary *traités* during these years, it is likely that the period 1661-1689 saw a decrease in reliance on extraordinary *traités* relative to both the Fouquet years and the Pontchartrain years. See Dessert, *Argent*, pp. 158-167.

difficulties of governing in such distant provinces as Languedoc might have left the crown with no choice but to coopt locals in the interest of effective governance. On the other hand, institutions too might have shaped any such changes. Both Chaussinand-Nogaret and Beik suggest that the Estates of Languedoc were central to allowing the local elite to assume control over financial affairs in their province, but neither elaborates as to why estates might have mattered.[8] Would such a change as that described by Beik have been possible in provinces without estates, or was it a function of the specific institutional relationship between the crown and *pays d'États*? The present chapter addresses these questions by examining the ties that financiers in both Upper Normandy and Burgundy held with the crown, on the one hand, and with local populations, on the other, in the closing decades of Louis' reign.

Financiers as Intermediaries

Recent research suggests that financiers in the Old Regime functioned first and foremost as intermediaries for the crown. In return for the incomes they accrued collecting and handling public receipts, they were expected to advance the crown money. Thus, in whichever branch of royal finances they operated, be they venal office-holding direct tax collectors (*receveurs généraux* or *receveurs de la taille*), lease-holding indirect tax collectors (*fermiers*), or contractors investing in extraordinary affairs (*traitants*), they all had the same essential role – to advance sums to the crown, adhering to an agreed-upon timeline, and then to reimburse themselves, with interest, from the proceeds of their activities.[9]

Involvement in royal finances almost always required making substantial payments to the crown before gains were realized through tax collection or the sale of offices, *augmentations de gages*, privileges, or whatever may have been involved in an extraordinary *traité*. Financiers therefore had to have access to large sums of liquid funds, and this typically involved borrowing from their own clienteles of lenders.[10] *Traitants*, receivers, and tax farmers themselves did not always invest the greatest amount of personal wealth in royal finances. Rather, their financial backers provided much of the initial outlays of money required by the crown.

Indeed, there were several levels of involvement within each branch of royal finance that corresponded to different degrees of risk and anonymity. (See Figure 5.1). In extraordinary affairs, for example, the individuals under whose name contracts, or *traités*, were drawn were almost always mere straw men, or *hommes de paille*. These individuals, often designated as '*bourgeois de Paris*', lent their names to the companies of financiers who were the actual intermediaries. On paper,

---

[8] See Beik, *Absolutism*, p. 251; and Chaussinand-Nogaret, p. 19.
[9] Dessert, *Argent*, pp. 42-65.
[10] Ibid.

Legal designation	Capacity of involvement	Degree/type of risk	Degree of anonymity
Traitant	straw man	none	none
Caution	financial intermediary, *de facto traitant*	high financial and political risks	none
None: agreements drawn up by private contract	investors supporting *traitants*	medium financial risks, low political risks	high

Figure 5.1 Levels of involvement in extraordinary affairs

thus, Jean Jacques Clément, *bourgeois de Paris*, appears as the *traitant* who negotiated for the sale of the alternate offices of mayor and lieutenant mayor created by edict in December 1706 for the sum of 4,500,000 livres, but he likely had little if any financial interest in the affair, though he may have had a minor administrative role in the company.[11] Behind such straw men, then, were the actual intermediaries, or *defacto* financiers, designated legally as *cautions* or guarantors of the contracting *homme de paille*. They did not enjoy anonymity, since each agreement with the crown (*résultat*) had to be agreed to in writing by each *caution*. Their risks were the greatest of all involved, for not only was their financial solvency at stake, but in periods of crisis when the crown might use coercive means to add order to its financial situation, these intermediaries were often the first that the crown targeted.[12] The potential for gain, though, was also very high, as their return generally amounted to one-sixth of the total amount of the *traité* for which they contracted plus a ten per cent surtax levied on all purchasers of offices or *augmentations de gages*.[13] The clienteles of lenders who backed these *traitants*, on

---

[11] A.N., E 755^b, 21 December 1706, fol. 100.

[12] Dessert, *Argent*, pp. 238-257.

[13] The *cautions* of the above-mentioned Clément *traité* were some of the most prominent *traitants* of the period, including Claude Miotte, Jean Thévenin the elder, and Paul Poisson de Bourvallais. Fifteen *cautions* in all were listed for this *traité*; the share of each in the profits depended upon the stake they were able to bring into the association. *Traitants* formed ad hoc companies with one another to invest in specific extraordinary affairs. The acts of association, or the contracts establishing the companies, indicate the share of each member in the particular company, the amount each was to forward for initial costs, procedures for borrowing and accounting, and contingencies in case a member died before

the other hand, remained in most cases unknown to royal authorities, since their loan contracts were private and not notarized (*sous seing privé*). Their level of anonymity was thus the highest, and their risk was therefore almost entirely financial, although they were potentially subject to denunciations during proceedings of Chambers of Justice. Corresponding levels of involvement and risk characterized the collection of direct taxes and the farming of indirect taxes as well. Regardless in which branch of the system they were involved, financiers were alike in offering their services as financial intermediaries to the crown. Indeed, not only were their functions as intermediaries fundamentally the same, financiers from each branch of royal finance practiced cross-involvement, with especially receivers general investing in extraordinary *traités*.[14]

Daniel Dessert has uncovered the work and the world of these financier/intermediaries. He places little significance on the institutional relationships between provinces and the crown, since at the most basic level, all financiers operated in the same way. For Dessert, royal finances, directed from Paris, transcended provincial particularities.[15] Yet, as Dessert shows, while financiers acting in the mold of professional intermediaries formed a distinct Paris-centered professional group, they cannot be viewed as an autonomous corps allied with royal commissioners against the interests of locals as put forth by the Mousnier model. Locals may indeed have perceived them as outsiders, but at the same time they held strong financial ties with wide networks of individuals stretching across the Kingdom. Indeed, where the identities of their financial backers could be uncovered, Dessert found them to be almost exclusively of the nobility, both robe and sword, and of the clergy.[16] The profiteering of financiers may have undermined specific sets of elite interests, but other sets of interests overlapped rather neatly with their activities.

We are thus left with a very complicated initial understanding of the multi-tiered relationship between the crown, financiers and the provincial elite. Beyond the political questions focusing on interests, be they antagonistic or mutual between the parties (the questions addressed by Mousnier and Beik with differing results), lie the financial considerations (which Dessert studies) regarding who had moneyed

---

the dissolution of the company. For this particular company, see A.N., Min. Cent., XX, 441, 15 January 1713, *société*.

[14] Receivers general were well placed to invest as *traitants* in extraordinary finances. By delaying payment to the crown of direct tax revenues until the last possible moment, receivers had at their disposal liquid sums of money that they could place in short-term investments. In doing so, they were essentially lending the crown its own money. See Dessert, *Argent*, p. 203.

[15] 'Thus, whatever the juridical status of the tax district, the underlying contractual nature of the financier-crown relationship was the rule' (Dessert, *Argent*, p. 43). The translation is mine.

[16] Ibid., pp. 341-378.

ties with whom and who was financially dependent upon whom. Financial ties bound members of the local elite to financiers; political interests were not so unidirectional in either an antagonistic or mutual way, and it is in this realm where local institutions came to play a crucial role in influencing the relationships.

The Structures of Finance and the Position of Financiers

Burgundy—Pays d'États

As demonstrated in Chapter Three, the Estates of Burgundy prevented most of the extraordinary financial activity of professional *traitants* by repurchasing edicts in exchange for large sums of money paid to the King. Typically, whenever the estates repurchased edicts they did so before any *traité* was drawn up and before any company of financiers could contract to administer it. Yet the estates did not intervene in all cases to repurchase each royal edict that threatened to alter the privileges of the local elite, and there were thus cases in which *traitants* entered the province to sell offices, *augmentations de gages* or other privileges. In 1694, for example, a company of financiers contracting under the name of Dommartin obtained the rights to sell municipal offices throughout the Kingdom (colonels and officers of the bourgeoisie) for 2,000,000 livres, and there is evidence that an agent of this company sought buyers in Burgundy.[17] And in 1705, a company which formed around the straw man Claude Charpentier, *bourgeois de Paris*, agreed to an 80,000 livres *traité* for the sale of offices in the *maréchaussées* of Burgundy. This particular *traité* pooled the investments of four Parisians, corresponding thus to the Mousnier model of financiers as outsiders.[18]

On other occasions, the crown drew up *traités*, agreed to terms with companies of financiers, and *traitants* or their agents already began seeking purchasers within Burgundy when the estates stepped in to halt their activity. This was the situation when the estates repurchased and united the offices of mayor in 1696. By then, four years had passed since the King had created the offices for sale throughout the Kingdom, and a company of financiers doing business under the name of Antoine Gatte had already found some buyers when the crown agreed to the estates' offer to purchase and unite the Burgundian mayoralties.[19] At this point, the estates were

---

[17] A.N., G^7 1493. The municipality of Dijon paid the Dommartin company 26,400 livres to acquire these offices and unite them to the municipal corps. A.M.D., M 26, 20 July 1694.

[18] A.N., E 755^b, 21 April 1705, fol. 393. The four *cautions* comprising this company were Gabriel de Quenneville, Claude Joseph de la Chausse, Sr. Faurie, and Nicolas Genest de Launay *conseiller secrétaire du roi*. All lived in Paris at the time, and the first three were indicated as 'interressé dans les affaires de Sa Majesté', suggesting that they were involved in other financial activities.

[19] This was a Kingdom-wide *traité*, not specific to Burgundy, and the company consisted of some of the most important financiers of the period, including Paul Poisson de Bourvallais,

responsible on the one hand for paying Gatte the *finances* for those offices not yet sold and on the other for reimbursing the individuals who had already purchased offices.[20] In this particular affair, both the company of *traitants* and the estates acted as financial intermediaries for the crown: First a group of professional financiers forwarded the crown money to sell the offices, then the estates forwarded the financiers money to halt the sale. The crown received the proceeds for the sale of newly created offices, the financiers received the expected return on their investment, and the estates ended up as the single buyer in Burgundy, thereby preserving the province's privileged status.[21]

While it is thus true that in some cases companies of professional, Parisian-based, financiers profited from the sale of offices, *augmentations de gages* and privileges in Burgundy, most financial activity in the province centered on the office of Receiver General and Treasurer of the Estates (hereafter treasurer of the estates). The individual who filled this office was an agent of the estates. He was neither a royal officer, a contracting agent, nor a leaseholder of royal revenues. Rather, the estates granted a commission for this post to whomever they chose, and he remained in office as long as the estates wished.[22] More than the administrator of the province's finances, the treasurer of the estates was personally responsible for forwarding receipts to the Royal Treasury on behalf of the estates on a timely and regular basis, just as receivers general or *traitants* were responsible for making regular payments to the crown. This required that the treasurer have at his disposal his own clientele of lenders to whom he could turn when necessary. Essentially, the treasurer served as a financial intermediary for the estates who themselves intermediated finances for the crown.

During the final decades of Louis XIV's reign, the office of treasurer of the estates was filled by the Chartraire family, first by Antoine Chartraire to whom the estates conferred the office in 1685 after the previous treasurer Bazin died, then by his son François Chartraire de Bière who took over the responsibilities in 1709.[23] The Chartraire were a Burgundian family with strong ties to other members of the provincial elite, to Burgundian institutions and to the Condé clientele. Antoine married Elizabeth Marlaud in 1690 whose first husband held the office of counselor in the Parlement of Dijon. After the estates transferred the post of treasurer to François in 1709, Antoine purchased an office of counselor in the

---

Paulin Prondre, Pierre de la Croix and Jean Thévenin. For short biographies of these financiers, see Dessert, *Argent*, pp. 518-703.

[20] A.D.C.O., C 3503, *Registre des maires de la province de Bourgogne*.

[21] The estates were the single buyer of mayoralties in Burgundy with the exception of the municipality of Dijon which negotiated to repurchase and unite its own mayoralty and thus preserve its customary procedure for selecting its mayor.

[22] As governor, the Prince of Condé too played an important role in selecting the treasurer. See Pierre Lefebvre, 'Aspects de la "fidelité" en France au XVIIe siècle: le cas des agents des princes de Condé,' *Revue historique*, 507 (July-September 1973): 99-100.

[23] A.D.C.O., B 54, 22 June 1685, fol. 144; B 59, 12 July 1709, fol. 228.

Parlement of Metz which he held until he died in 1718.[24] François had been a counselor in the Parlement of Dijon and held the title of *conseiller honoraire* when he assumed the role of treasurer. That same year he married his second wife Benigne de la Michodière whose then deceased father had also been a counselor in the Parlement of Dijon and whose brother Claude was *chef du conseil* of the Prince of Condé. François himself was a *conseiller-agent* of Condé.[25] The Chartraire also had important Parisian connections which were crucial in piecing together a network of lenders to the estates. While Antoine was treasurer, François acted as his agent in Paris drawing up loan contracts with potential lenders to the estates. In 1701, for example, three of the *élus* of the estates gathered before a Parisian notary to ratify a loan contract by which François, acting as procurator of the estates, borrowed 100,000 livres in principal from Antoine Portail, *conseiller* and *avocat général* in the Parlement of Paris and Bertrand Tuffier, also *avocat* in the Parlement.[26] Thus the Chartraire family in Burgundy appears very much like the leading financial families of Languedoc in this same period. To the extent that financial matters devolved to the provincial level, the locally connected Chartraire profited from their handling of public receipts while developing financial ties on a Kingdom-wide, Paris-centered, scale.

As the Burgundian estates' treasurers, the Chartraire were involved in many different areas of money handling and intermediation. Whereas in provinces without estates the responsibilities of collecting taxes and raising extraordinary funds were usually divided between receivers (or farmers where indirect taxes were involved) and *traitants*, in Burgundy the treasurer of the estates was responsible for both ordinary and extraordinary financial activities by virtue of his one office. Thus, he received payment from receivers of the *taille* in each bailiwick and forwarded those sums to the crown as payment on behalf of the estates for such ordinary obligations as the *don gratuit*, the *subsistence* and the *exemption du logement*, and he was also involved on several different levels in extraordinary affairs. Whenever the estates negotiated a *rachat* with the crown, it became the treasurer's responsibility to pay the crown on a timely basis and to find lenders willing to invest in bonds on the estates (*rentes sur les États*). Then the treasurer was responsible for servicing and reimbursing those long-term loans with receipts from the specific indirect tax revenues controlled by the estates.

With such extensive involvement in the province's financial affairs, both ordinary and extraordinary, the treasurer of the estates enjoyed wide-ranging opportunities to profit. He pocketed a percentage of direct taxes paid to him by the receivers of the *taille*, and he retained a percentage of the money he handled both floating *rentes* for the estates and reimbursing *rentiers* on behalf of the estates.

---

[24] A.N., Min. Cent., XX, 377, 17 August 1690, *contrat de mariage*; XCII, 394, 1 February 1718, *extrait mortel*; XCII, 396, 16 May 1718, *notorieté*.
[25] A.D.C.O., 4E2/1633, 11 August 1709, *contrat de mariage*; Dessert, *Argent*, pp. 556-557.
[26] A.N., Min. Cent., XCII, 315, 26 May 1701, *ratification*. The Chartraire's position in the Condé clientele surely aided them in conducting affairs in Paris.

These portions represented rather small percentages of quite large sums, and they could thus potentially add up to significant amounts. In 1701, for example, the crown sent Antoine Chartraire an order (*mandement*) to pay the estates' ordinary obligations for the year which totaled 800,000 livres. Of this sum, the order specified that Chartraire's handling fees stood at the rate of 9 deniers/livre (3.75 per cent), totaling in this case 30,000 livres.[27] The treasurer also received fees from the estates. In the war-time year of 1705, for example, when the total expenses of the estates amounted to 3,457,945 livres, including 1,777,550 livres in payments made to the Royal Treasury for ordinary obligations along with 746,054 livres paid to the estates' creditors, Chartraire's fees paid to him by the estates amounted to 48,993 livres. In addition to this sum, he could count on his regular 9 deniers/livre handling fee from the crown, or 66,658 livres.[28] Furthermore, the estates paid their treasurer interest on any short-term loans that they asked of him. Thus, the treasurer of the estates profited by the same means as did receivers general and *traitants* – by retaining a percentage from the handling of funds and by lending short term. The treasurer of the estates, though, acting as the principal intermediary for the estates, had a hand in just about every transfer of funds that took place within Burgundy.

Though far from insignificant, the profits available to the estates' treasurers through their regular involvement in local financial activities actually paled in comparison to the profits accrued by many receivers-general or *traitants*.[29] At the same time, the estates' treasurers faced few risks, and their profits were practically assured since the fate of the office was closely tied to that of the estates. At no point, for example, did the crown demand payment from the treasurer for an *augmentation de gages* or use leverage against him in financial negotiations as it did to receivers general in *pays d'élection*. When François Chartraire saw his name included on a 1711 list of financiers from whom the crown was trying to force the purchase of *rentes*, he successfully argued that he should not be listed and that he in no way should be expected to pay 60,000 livres, since he had 'never entered into any *traité*, *soustraité*, farm, sub-farm, enterprise or troop provisioning, nor in any handling of His Majesty's money.'[30] As long as the estates remained vigorous, with

---

[27] A.N., E 698^c, 25 May 1700, fol. 445.

[28] A.D.C.O., C 3386. The remainder of the expenses included payments made to towns as reimbursement for their troop quartering (*étapes*), gifts to dignitaries, *gages*, public works within the province, fees paid to the chamber of accounts and the *élus* of the Estates, along with various miscellaneous expenses.

[29] In contrast, the *traitant* Paul Poisson de Bourvallais, to take as an extreme example, made such an enormous fortune through his involvement in extraordinary *traités* that he was taxed 4,400,000 livres by the 1716 Chamber of Justice, leaving almost none of his vast fortune for his widow. Dessert, *Argent*, p. 671

[30] A.N., E 836^b, January 1712, fol. 26. Beik (*Absolutism*, pp. 251-258) recounts that at one point, the crown abolished the office of treasurer of the Languedocian estates (*trésorier de la bourse*). That move, though, was part of a broader attack against the estates themselves, and once royal strategies began to change under Louis XIV, the office was reinstated, and the estates once again asserted control over provincial finances.

their financial autonomy supported by the coalition of local rulers, the office of treasurer remained sheltered behind the province's privileged status.[31] Furthermore, the more the estates responded to the political leverage wielded against them by the crown, and the more important an intermediary the estates became, the more the services of the treasurer were needed. As the estates borrowed ever larger sums under Louis XIV to pay for *rachats*, and as their importance for the crown and prominence as a major borrower increased therewith, so too did the importance of their treasurer along with his opportunities to profit personally.

The treasurer of the estates was not the only local financier to profit from the handling of public funds in Burgundy. There were, of course, the receivers of the *taille* underneath him involved in the collection of direct taxes on the bailiwick level. And beyond the collection and administration of direct taxes, the indirect taxes which the estates controlled, the *octrois de la Saône* and the *crues de sel*, offered opportunities for members of the local elite as well. The company chosen to lease the farm of the *octrois de la Saône* in 1689 when the estates first gained control over these revenues included four Burgundians and one Parisian.[32] In 1704, the estates leased the rights to collect the *octrois de la Saône* for an unprecedented twelve years to a company headed by Edmé Lamy, who was at the time receiver general of the *taillon* in Burgundy and Bresse.[33] His financial guarantors were Henry Quirot, auditor in the Dijon chamber of accounts, and Jean de la Coste d'Agey, *secrétaire du roi* in the chamber of accounts at Dole.

Lamy's professional prominence in Burgundy suggests that his role was more than that of a mere straw man within this company. In fact, following this twelve-year lease, he and his son Denis were the *cautions* for the successor lease held by the Chalonnais Nicolas Fabry.[34] Lamy began his career as a procurator in the Dijon chamber of accounts in 1678, then was receiver of fees for that court before finally becoming the receiver general of the *taillon* for Burgundy and Bresse in 1689.[35] Lamy was also prominent within the Condé clientele, and in 1711, upon the accession of Louis Henry de Bourbon as Prince de Condé, he was named the Prince's procurator and was given the responsibility of governing the revenues and

---

[31] The clergy, too, insisted that its treasurers remain independent and non-venal despite many royal attempts to change their status into crown-dependent intermediaries. See Michaud, pp. 51-64.

[32] The principal lease holder for this farm which was to last seven years was Philippe Pernin, bourgeois and counselor in the *grenier à sel* in Châlon sur Saône. The four *cautions* included another Châlonnais, Jean Baptiste Rioley, receiver of the King's farms, along with Claude Thierry, counselor and secretary in the Dijon chamber of accounts, Antoine Vauthier, bourgeois of Dijon and Pierre Mathurin de Belcourt, *avocat* in the Parlement of Paris. A.D.C.O., C 5366.

[33] As in Languedoc, the *taillon* was collected not by the treasurer of the estates, but by a separate individual holding a royal office of receiver. See Beik, *Absolutism*, p. 247.

[34] A.D.C.O., 4E2/1619, 7 October 1716, *acte passé entre Mrs. les élus et les Srs. Fabry et Lamy père et fils*.

[35] Arbaumont, *Armorial*, p. 263.

overseeing the farms of his Burgundian lands.[36] Farming the *octrois de la Saône* was thus one of the several affairs in which Lamy held an interest.

Clearly, the situation in Burgundy corresponds closely to the Beik model of financial activity centered on the local elite. Whether it was in handling direct taxes, indirect taxes or extraordinary finances, Burgundians performed the bulk of financial activities within Burgundy. To be sure, there was some involvement of outsiders; Parisians occasionally surfaced within the companies that farmed the *octrois de la Saône*,[37] and professional *traitants* at times entered the province armed with *traités* which the estates had not repurchased. Nonetheless, all the direct tax revenues (at least until the 1710 establishment of the *dixième*), a significant portion of extraordinary funds and the revenues from several indirect taxes were all controlled by members of the Burgundian elite who were able to position themselves to profit from royal exactions within their province.

Furthermore, this local elite that had a hand in the collection of revenues and the intermediation of finances overlapped closely with that same ruling coalition of privileged landholders that benefited from the estates' broader role of keeping land taxes to a minimum while preserving the privileged status quo. Edmé Lamy, for example, fits squarely within the ruling coalition, as I described it in Chapter Three. In 1714, he purchased the landed estate of La Perrière, which Louis XV elevated to the status of marquisate in 1725. He attained a noble title through his possession of an office of *secrétaire du roi*, for which he received letters of provision in 1709. And his close ties to the local robe elite were made stronger by his sons' careers: Antoine Benigne Lamy, seigneur de Samérey, became a counselor in the Parlement of Dijon in 1720, and Jean Denis, seigneur de Tillenet, who joined Edmé as *caution* for the Fabry lease of the *octrois de la Saône* in 1716, was a Dijonnais *maître des comptes*.[38]

This advantageous position of the Burgundian ruling coalition vis-à-vis local financial structures was largely a function of Burgundy's status as a *pays d'États*. The estates were able to fill their office of treasurer with whomever they chose, in conjunction with the wishes of the Condé princes, thus opening the way for a Burgundian to control the flow of direct tax revenues and to manage much of the extraordinary financial activity. Furthermore, the estates' willingness to repurchase edicts, beneficial to the ruling coalition by preserving the privileged status quo, directly affected financial structures in several ways: *Traitants* from outside Burgundy no longer had reason to enter the province, at least with regard to the specific *traités* repurchased; the treasurer of the estates assured the smooth transfer of funds from investors to the crown on behalf of the estates and then oversaw the

---

[36] A.D.C.O., 4E2/1635, 24 December 1704, *remise et subrogation des fermes*; A.N., Min. Cent., XCII, 357, 15 August 1711, *procuration*.

[37] One company, headed by Claude Mielle, was actually dominated by Parisians – it farmed the *octrois* between 1697 and 1700. A.D.C.O., C 5366. See Chapter Three for a brief discussion of this company.

[38] A.N. V¹ 183, 24 January 1709; Arbaumont, *Armorial*, p. 263.

eventual reimbursement of those debts; farmers, usually Burgundians and typically situated within the ruling coalition as Lamy was, collected the indirect revenues controlled by the estates which served to guarantee the loans; and investors in the estates' bonds received interest on their investments.[39] Without the estates, none of these financial ripples that effectively kept out Parisian-based financiers and instead benefited the Burgundian elite would have occurred.

The Généralité *of Rouen*—Pays d'Élection

Did the financial structures in Upper Normandy present similar opportunities for the local elite there to profit, or were the relationships between the crown, financiers and provincials more reminiscent of the Mousnier model of financial activity? Without provincial estates to intermediate finances and to shield local financiers, the crown certainly enjoyed more leverage in the selection and management of money-handlers, especially those at the top of the financial hierarchies. Venal office holders answerable to the crown, for example, were responsible for collecting direct taxes. Each of the *généralités* that comprised the Kingdom's *pays d'élection* had two receivers general who alternated years of exercise and who were responsible for collecting from receivers of the *taille* and passing the receipts to the Royal Treasury. Their functions were crucial for keeping funds flowing to the crown, and they were heavily involved in the transport of money and the circulation of bills of exchange. And within *généralités*, each *élection* had two receivers of the *taille*, again alternating years of exercise, responsible for collecting direct tax receipts from parish collectors and passing them to the receiver general. Although these offices of receiver were venal, their possession did not necessarily confer the right to handle direct tax revenues; that right came from the King and could be revoked and handed to another individual by commission at any time.[40]

Receivers were primarily employed for their services as intermediaries; as long as their accounts remained solvent and they could meet their financial obligations to the crown, they could expect to retain a hold over their post and continue handling direct tax receipts within their circumscriptions. In some cases, though, the crown did not hesitate to remove receivers from their exercise in any given year. From the fifteen *élections* that comprised the *généralité* of Rouen during the final decades of Louis' reign,[41] the crown took recourse to appointing its own handpicked collectors by granting year-long commissions thirteen times during the

---

[39] Chapter Six will focus on this last stage.
[40] Dessert, *Argent*, pp. 44-45.
[41] There were fourteen *élections* from 1691 to 1696, following the transfer of Pontoise to the *généralité* of Paris and before the creation of Eu which comprised parishes taken mostly from the *élection* of Arques. See Vannier, p. 13.

decade of the 1690s and eight times the following decade.[42] Fifteen of these commissions specified why the crown was designating its own handpicked agents. Of these, six reported cases where the crown actively intervened to strip the exercise of office away from receivers, either for reasons of insufficient *cautions*, for insolvency, or, in the case of Thomas Germain de Courcy whom Pierre Barbette replaced by commission in 1709, for 'irregular conduct in handling affairs.'[43] Other reasons for granting commissions to exercise the functions of receiver included vacancy due to death, incompatibility of the office holder, and civil disputes over the possession of the office.[44]

Receivers were therefore in a potentially vulnerable position in relation to the crown, and as intermediaries, they not only needed to fulfill their responsibilities to collect and transfer direct tax receipts, they also had to respond positively to any extraordinary requests for money. The crown often leaned upon receivers general to forward short-term loans, especially in order to fund the war effort. In June 1712, for example, François Guyot de Chenizot, receiver general of Rouen, obtained orders to advance 8829 livres per month for six months to support troop quartering in Rouen. He had already advanced 147,848 livres the previous four months and was still waiting to be reimbursed for that loan when he received these new demands.[45] Requests like these thus stretched the credit of receivers, and Chenizot gently reminded the *Contrôle Général* that he could not support such financial extensions indefinitely. Yet while receivers such as Chenizot bore the risk of lending on short term to the crown, unsure as they were of when they would be reimbursed, their returns could be quite rewarding. By August 2 of that same year, Chenizot was expecting an interest payment of 35,403 livres on his initial advance of 147,848 livres made some eight months earlier, amounting to a return of 24 per cent in less than a year.

In addition to these individual demands for short-term loans, which in fact were part of their responsibilities as intermediaries, receivers also faced extraordinary demands that targeted them as a corps. In 1688, the crown created a *traité* for the sale of vacant offices that had reverted back to the *parties casuelles*,

---

[42] A.D.S.M., 2B 142-150. It seems that some of the *élections* were more problematic for the crown than others; the 21 commissions granted to collect direct taxes during the twenty year period 1690-1710 were concentrated in five *élections*: Pontaudemer (7 different commissions), Andely (also 7 commissions), Chaumont et Magny (3), Gisors et Pontoise (2) and Rouen (2).

[43] A.D.S.M., 2B 150, fol. 95.

[44] The crown replaced M. le Grix, receiver in the *élection* of Pontaudemer, in 1690 and 1691 because he already held the office of lieutenant general in the *vicomté* of Pontaudemer and was thus considered incompatible; François Nicolle collected direct taxes in Andely by commission in 1694 while Jacques Chazot and his father's widow Anne du Val disputed ownership of the office. By 1696, Chazot was found to be the rightful owner, but he was insolvent, so direct taxes continued to be collected by commission in Andely. A.D.S.M., 2B 142, fols. 8 & 152; 2B 144, fol. 50; 2B 145, fol. 5.

[45] A.N., G^7 1112.

but rather than contracting with a company of *traitants* to sell those offices, it demanded loans from all of the receivers general against the proceeds of their sale, for which the receivers themselves then assumed the responsibility.[46] This was a relatively minor request that came just as the King's armies engaged themselves in the Nine Years' War; the close of war was when receivers, like all financiers, found themselves subjected to more serious pressures from a crown momentarily less dependent on their services and trying to put its financial house in order.

This was the case at the close of the Nine Years' War. The crown summoned all of the receivers general to Fontainebleau on October 5, 1699 where they were certain to face pressure to return part of their gains from the war years. Several excused themselves from attending but in their letters agreed to submit to whatever the 'company' of receivers agreed.[47] Meanwhile, the crown had drawn up a *traité* to recover the debts still owed to the Royal Treasury by financial officials from their exercise since 1690 (*traité des débets des comptables dans le royaume et des deniers revenants bons à Sa Majesté*) which, by the crown's calculations, totaled 1,600,000 livres. On October 4, the receivers general volunteered to take over the *traité des débets*, essentially agreeing to tax themselves up to five-sixths the value of the *traité*. Agreeing to this *traité* as they did the day before their reckoning in Fontainebleau, the receivers general surely were hoping to smooth over the King and his ministers; this arrangement also ensured that *traitants* from outside the group of receivers general would not be profiting at their expense.

The receivers general thus appear to have identified themselves and to have operated as a Kingdom-wide corps. The crown approached them as such in its negotiations, and they responded to the King's extraordinary demands as a unified company. These were not, as in the case of Burgundy, local financiers taking cover behind local institutions, and indeed their individual careers confirm this view of them as Paris-based outsiders engaged in provincial financial affairs.

The six individuals who held the post of receiver general of Rouen, either *ancien* or *alternatif*, between 1680 and 1715 had very few ties to Upper Normandy, and their financial careers, while centered in Paris, were rather Kingdom-wide in

---

[46] A.N., G^7 1492. The total value of the vacant offices was calculated at 5,002,981 livres, but the crown demanded much less from the company of receivers general, knowing that the offices would not sell anywhere near at par. The share of this total for which the receivers of Rouen were responsible, for example, was 389,170 livres, but the crown only demanded the sum of 58,000 livres from the two receivers general (*ancien* and *alternatif*) combined.

[47] A.N., G^7 1113. See, for example, the letter from Ferriol, receiver general of Grenoble: 'Uncertain as I am whether I could come tomorrow to Fontainebleau, I must answer your summons by saying that I will execute with submission the orders of M. the Controller General and that I accept in advance all that will be deliberated by my colleagues.' (Dans l'incertitude où je suis Monsieur, si je pourray me rendre demain à Fontainblaeu je réspons à la lettre que vous m'avez fait l'honneur de m'éscrire pour vous dire que j'executeray avec soumission les ordres de Mgr. le Contrôleur Général et que j'approuve par avance ce que sera déliberé par mes confrères).

scope.[48] These financiers built their careers in Paris, and their positions as receivers general of Rouen were just one of several areas of involvement in royal finances. Of the six receivers general, only Pierre Cousin was originally from Upper Normandy. Like the other five, though, Cousin established his career in Paris, in his particular case as a *créature* of Colbert. He served first as farmer general of the mint (*fermier général de la monnaie*) from 1672-74 then as farmer general of the King's domains from 1676-80. Thus he brought to his position of receiver general the perspective of a career financier, and it was by virtue of his experience in royal finances under the tutelage of Colbert, not of his Rouennais heritage, that Cousin held the post of *receveur général ancien* from 1677 to 1685.[49]

The careers of the other five receivers mirrored that of Cousin; they held posts in Paris that were not necessarily province-specific before becoming receivers general of Rouen. Pierre Alexandre was involved in troop provisioning, first as *trésorier payeur des troupes* in Italy and Ireland then as *commissaire ordinaire des guerres* during the 1680s and 1690s. He also held an interest in several sub-farms in Poitiers, Orléans and Tours before purchasing the office of *receveur général ancien* in 1704. Jacques Poulletier was also a *commissaire des guerres* before becoming receiver general of Rouen, and after he sold his post in 1704 he became first a *garde du Trésor Royal* and then intendant of finances in 1708.

It was typical of the receivers general to hold their primary residence in Paris even while exercising their offices and handling direct tax receipts from Upper Normandy. Pierre Cousin, the only Rouennais by origin, lived in Paris when he sold his office to Jacques Poulletier – Poulletier himself lived in Paris at the time of purchase and, twenty years later, still lived there when he sold the office to Pierre Alexandre, also a resident of Paris.[50] Their common residence in Paris and the financial contacts that developed there actually served receivers general well in their duties of transferring public funds through the use of bills of exchange. Also indicative of the Paris-centered professions of these receivers was their extensive involvement in extraordinary *traités* which allied them closely with other Parisian financiers.[51]

Less is known about the receivers particular of the *taille* who handled direct tax receipts within the *généralité* of Rouen at the level of *élections*. One could plausibly argue that the collectors further down the hierarchy and closer to the *taillables* in this multi-layered system where receipts passed through several hands

---

[48] Four individuals held the post of *receveur général ancien* of Rouen during these decades: Pierre Cousin, 1677-85; Jacques Poulletier, 1685-1704; Pierre Alexandre, 1704-1707; and François Guyot de Chenizot, 1707-1731. Two held the alternate office: René Aubry, 1669-1704 and Jean Marie de Vougny, 1704-1719.

[49] Unless otherwise noted, the career and family backgrounds of the receivers general come from the biographical notices in Dessert, *Argent*, pp. 518-703.

[50] A.N., Min. Cent., CXX, 156, 1 June 1685; CV, 998, 29 September 1704, *traités d'office*.

[51] Pierre Alexandre held interest in the fewest *traités*, three between 1696 and 1704; Jean Marie de Vougny was most heavily involved, investing in 39 different *traités* between 1693-1708.

from very small circumscriptions (the parish) to much larger ones (the *élection* or *généralité*) likely had closer ties to the tax-paying population. And just as geographic distance from Paris may have necessitated the cooptation of locals into financial networks, so too the need for information across what we might think of as cultural distances may have necessitated similar cooptation.

Unfortunately, the prosopographical studies of early modern financiers that have contributed to our understanding of the relations between finance and society have neglected this level of direct tax administration. Relevant source materials are scattered throughout notarial archives, so any comprehensive study of these 'smaller' financiers, even one centered on a specific *généralité*, would constitute a major undertaking. With a moderate amount of source material from the *généralité* of Rouen at hand, however, I can begin with some informed hypotheses.

By their nature these offices were more likely to attract members of the local elite as potential buyers. The sums handled by *receveurs particuliers*, the *cautions* required for their exercise, and the prices of the offices were all significantly less than the corresponding amounts for the *receveurs généraux*. Whereas Jacques Poulletier paid Pierre Cousin 300,000 livres in 1685 for the office of *receveur général ancien*, Anne Gaston de la Motte paid 8,500 livres in 1697 for each of the two offices of receiver of the *taille* in the newly created *élection* of Eu.[52] These offices were therefore considerably more accessible than those of receivers general which required both wealth and Parisian connections.

The letters of provision granted each time an office was acquired provide very scant information on the purchasers' origins and previous professions. Of the 39 letters from the period 1688-1717 representing 32 purchasers (seven purchased both the *anciens* and alternate offices of their *élection*), only two specify previous professions.[53] The above-mentioned de la Motte was a receiver in the *grenier à sel* of St. Valéry in the Caux region of Upper Normandy, and Claude Médard, who purchased both offices of *receveur de la taille* in the *élection* of Caudebec in 1703 and 1705, was formerly an *avocat* in the Parlement of Paris. The evidence is thus not only slim, but as yet inconclusive.

The different frequencies with which offices changed hands suggest that their holders had divergent career paths in mind. Within the thirty years spanning from 1688 to 1717, thirteen offices of receivers of the *taille* were bought and then sold again. The average tenure of the receivers who purchased these offices was 11 years. Only two of these thirteen receivers died while in possession of their office: Paul Charles Carpentier, *ancien* receiver of Eu, who died in 1716 after possessing his office for twelve years and Jean Boulanger, alternate receiver of Evreux for eight years until he died in 1704. Of the remaining eleven, all of whom purchased their offices after 1688 and sold them before 1717, some held their offices for a remarkably brief period of time and others for a much more significant period. The shortest tenure lasted two years; the longest spanned nineteen. Some, therefore,

---

[52] A.D.S.M., 2B 145, fol. 14.
[53] A.D.S.M., 2B 141-153.

appear to have used their offices as career stepping-stones perhaps on their way to a career in Paris, while others preserved their professional ties to Upper Normandy.

The handful of career profiles that we have at our disposal confirms this view. Jean Rolland Malet purchased his alternate office of receiver in Caudebec in 1703, and then less than two years later he sold it to Claude Médard who, as noted above, was an *avocat* in the Parlement of Paris.[54] Malet later made a name for himself as chief clerk of Controller General Desmaretz from 1708 to 1715, during which time he managed to gather a series of data on tax levels throughout the seventeenth century, data which today have become a valuable resource for historians.[55] Malet, therefore, acquired his office of receiver as a stepping stone to a more prominent and prestigious career in Paris, and his ties to Upper Normandy were probably not much stronger than those of the receivers general examined above who built their careers in Paris.

In contrast, Jean le Cordier held his office of *receveur ancien* in Pont de l'Arche for nineteen years. He had inherited it from his father Gilbert in 1697 and then resigned in favor of his son Jean Nicolas in 1715.[56] This office was therefore in the Cordier family for several generations, and it was not used expressly as a means for ascending to Parisian financial circles. Such stability in office holding suggests that a family like the Cordier had strong personal, professional and propertied ties to Upper Normandy and did not share the Parisian perspective of individuals like Malet and the receivers general. It seems likely, then that both Rouennais and Parisians were receivers of the *taille* in the *généralité* of Rouen during Louis XIV's final decades if we can understand these designations as indicative as much of outlook and perspective as of origin and birthplace.

As with the structures of direct tax collection, those of extraordinary affairs in *pays d'élection* were multi-layered, with professional Parisian financiers at the top of the hierarchy and below them their agents, or *sous-traitants*, with closer local ties and access to information about the provinces where the offices or privileges were sold. *Traitants*, like receivers general, were financiers who established their careers in Paris and who held interests in *traités* that spanned the Kingdom. To be sure, there were *traitants* of Norman origin. Jean Oursin, for example, had strong ties, both familial and financial, throughout Normandy and invested in *traités* that were both specific to Normandy and Kingdom-wide.[57] Yet Oursin lived in Paris,

---

[54] A.D.S.M., 2B 148, fols. 37 & 195.
[55] Collins, *Fiscal Limits*, pp. 108-109; Alain Guéry, 'Les Finances de la Monarchie Française sous l'Ancien Régime,' *Annales: E.S.C.*, 33 (1978): 216-239; Bonney and Bonney, *Malet*, pp. 9-47.
[56] A.D.S.M., 2B 145, fol. 46; 2B 152, fol. 17.
[57] Dessert, *Argent*, p. 661; A.N., Min. Cent., XX, 590, 27 June 1746, *inventaire après decés*. Oursin held a majority interest in the provisioning of *étapes* (troop movements) throughout the *généralité* of Rouen in 1707. He was also involved in 29 Kingdom-wide *traités* between 1701 and 1714, including the 1704 le Roux *traité* for the sale of offices of *échevins perpetuels* in all municipalities for 2.05 million livres and the Moreau *traité* of that same year for the sale of offices in chambers of account in Rouen, Dijon, Bretagne, Aix,

had many professional contacts in Paris and owed his extensive participation in royal finances to his Parisian ties.[58] This was the norm for *traitants*, just as it was for receivers general (themselves extensively involved in *traités*, as noted above). Even *traités* designed exclusively for the sale of offices or privileges specific to Upper Normandy had Parisian backers. The 1692 Godefroy *traité* for the sale of offices of police and inspectors of grain and cider in the town of Rouen had four financial backers (*cautions*) all living in Paris. These were Jean Blanchard, receiver general of the domains and woods of Caen; Jean Brunère seigneur de Montfort; Charles de Cheramboust; and Charles Boucher, *intéressé aux fermes de Sa Majesté*.[59] Four Parisians also backed the 1706 de Laulne *traité* for the sale of twenty offices of *maître voiturier par eau* in Rouen: Charles Savalette, *avocat* in the Parlement of Paris, Charles Bouchu, *secrétaire du roi*; and Louis Waubert and Jean du Mourier de St. Léon, both *intéressés dans les affaires du roi*.[60]

Below this level of Parisian-based *traitants*, their provincial agents, or *sous-traitants*, likely had closer ties to local populations. Yet as with the collection of direct tax revenues where little is known about the receivers at the lower levels, historians likewise know less about the *sous-traitants* active on the provincial level than they do about the Parisian-based *traitants*. The example of Robert Grisel of Rouen, though, offers some insight into who these provincial agents were.

As an agent in Rouen for several different companies of *traitants*, Grisel left many notarized traces of his professional activities. He was responsible for finding purchasers for various offices, and whenever he made a sale, a notary documented the transaction. Thus, on May 8, 1699, Grisel sold an office of *juré priseur vendeur de biens meubles* to Jacques Pierre Linot, royal sergeant in the viscounty of Rouen, for 250 livres. He acted here as the agent of François Godefroy, bourgeois de Paris, under whose name Parisian *traitants* had contracted to sell these offices of *priseurs vendeurs* throughout the three *généralités* of Normandy.[61]

Grisel, whose father was a procurator in the Parlement of Rouen, was a wealthy Rouennais bourgeois. At the time of his death, he owned at least two houses in Rouen along with land in the barony of Routot.[62] His participation in a number of *traités* as a sub-contractor suggests that it was possible for members of

---

Grenoble, Dole, Blois, Metz and Pau for 2 million livres. A.N., G^7 1494; BnF., Mss.Fr., 1103 & 11107.

[58] Parisians such as François Raffy, *receveur général des domaines en la généralité de Metz*, Mathieu Marchant, bourgeois, and Philippes de Lamet, *prestre docteur de la faculté de Paris*, testified before the corps of *secrétaires du roi* regarding the honesty and probity of Oursin's character at the time of his petition to join their corps. A.N., V^{2}38, 5 February 1705.

[59] A.N., E 611^a, 16 December 1692, fol. 433.

[60] A.N., E 767^a, 20 April 1706, fol. 272.

[61] A.D.S.M., 2E2/11, 8 May 1699, *vente d'office*. A second *traité* for which Grisel was a provincial agent was the 1694 *traité* of the *arrière ban* and the *traité des bourses communes* of the town and *généralité* of Rouen.

[62] A.D.S.M., 2E2/24, 1 July 1715, *inventaire après decés*.

the local elite to profit from royal financial activities, though finding buyers for such offices as *priseurs vendeurs de biens meubles* within a limited geographical area certainly did not enable Grisel to build the type of fortune erected by Parisian-based *traitants*.

As an agent of Parisian-based *traitants*, Grisel provided important services to his superiors. He likely presented himself as less of a threat to the local elite than did such outsiders as Claude Miotte or Paul Poisson de Bourvallais who profited immensely from their extensive involvement in extraordinary affairs.[63] Local agents also brought to the financial system intimate knowledge of the provinces in which they lived, and they filled a demand for simple manpower in the structures of extraordinary finance. *Sous-traitants* like Grisel embodied the ambiguous nature of extraordinary affairs in *pays d'élection*. Outsiders obviously profited to unparalleled extremes, but they were able to put on a somewhat friendlier face by coopting locals as *sous-traitants*.

Yet the system did not rest in a state of equilibrium where financiers and their agents freely and openly traded profits and services. Such a hierarchy as we find in the *généralité* of Rouen where Parisian-based financiers depended on local agents with stronger ties to the targeted communities gave rise at times to conflict not just pitting communities against outsiders but also dividing financiers from their agents. Thus, in 1706, the *cour des comptes aides et finances* in Rouen issued an order against local agents in Honfleur after Jean Dufaussey, farmer of the *aides* in the *généralité* of Rouen, complained that his agents, or sub-farmers, were opening the town gates 'at all hours of the night' to allow contraband to enter untaxed to the benefit, so the court speculated, of local cabaret operators (*cabaratiers*). By way of precedent, the court in its *arrêt* referred to a separate incident in 1691 in which sub-farmers in Falaise were found to be allowing smuggling, likewise at the expense of their patrons.[64] Where Paris-based financiers depended on locals for their access to information, and where the interests of their agents diverged to the point at which enforcement of contracts required the intervention of courts, simple domination of local interests by outsiders was not possible.

We therefore need a new model to understand the position of financiers in *pays d'élection* under Louis XIV as demonstrated by the Rouennais case. Outsiders, professional financiers from Paris, did not exclusively benefit from royal finances in Upper Normandy. There were opportunities for locals to benefit (at times at the cost of their patrons), albeit at the lower levels of the financial structures where the greatest fortunes were not to be made. Further, as Dessert argues, 'outsider' financiers held extensive financial links with local elites who provided them with credit. In Rouen, these local clienteles extended not just to the robe and sword nobilities and the clergy, but to the merchant elite as well. For this

---

[63] It remains to be seen, though, whether members of the local elite perceived *sous-traitants* as their peers taking advantage of local opportunities in royal finances (much like Beik's Languedocian elite) or as agents of exploitative professional financiers from Paris.

[64] A.N. AD XVI 9, *Arrêt de la Cour des Aydes de Rouen*, 16 November 1706.

reason, when the *receveur général des fermes* in the *généralité* of Rouen, La Houssaye, fled his creditors in 1713, the intendant Roujault feared that any impending bankruptcy proceedings against La Houssaye might also bring 'perhaps ten other merchants or bankers' to the point of bankruptcy.[65] Clearly, the Mousnier model of dominance exaggerates the autonomy and distinctiveness of the Parisian-based financiers.

Yet the Beik model does not hold for this *pays d'élection* either; the transformations in financial structures that he argues took place in Languedoc around 1660 simply did not occur in the *généralité* of Rouen. Parisians continued to dominate the upper levels of royal finances in Upper Normandy, and it was therefore they who profited disproportionately from handling Rouennais tax receipts and extraordinary funds. Where locals participated, they did so to fill a demand as agents of outside intermediaries. Local control over the flows of public money in this *généralité* remained minimal.

In Burgundy (and in Beik's Languedoc), on the other hand, while geography may have necessitated the cooptation of locals, the presence of estates was instrumental in creating the conditions for considerably greater local control over tax receipts and extraordinary affairs than otherwise would have been possible. Where Beik describes the increased involvement of the local elite in the handling of public money under Louis XIV, such a transformation is particularly important as an indicator of fundamental political shifts – shifts, though, specific to *pays d'États*, namely the strengthening of estates and the crown's increased reliance on their financial intermediation.

This hypothesis is consistent with the findings in previous chapters. As Louis XIV's needs multiplied beginning in 1689, he turned to the intermediation of provincial estates like those of Burgundy. Effective intermediation, though, required strengthened estates able to chart a course independent of the crown and to protect their positions as major borrowers. Thus, there were indeed some striking changes in financial structures under Louis XIV, but they were concentrated largely in *pays d'États*, and more than just opening up profitable opportunities in the handling of public receipts to the local elite, these transformations involved a fundamental shift of power from the King to estates.

If such changes were institution-specific, as I argue they were, they do not entirely explain Louis XIV's success in financing his major wars while effectively avoiding political instability. *Pays d'États* comprised less than one-third of French territory; the overwhelming majority of taxable wealth lay outside such provinces with estates. The crown still depended on the intermediation of Parisian financiers in *pays d'élection*, and outsiders still profited from the collection and handling of

---

[65] Roujault to Desmaretz, 14 May 1713, in Boislisle, *Correspondance*, 3: 490-491. La Houssaye's fraud against his creditors, among whom included the King, was sufficiently severe that even the protection of the Duke of Luxembourg, governor of Normandy, could not save him from imprisonment in the Bastille. Montmorency-Luxembourg to Desmaretz, 30 July 1714, A.N., G^7 543b.

funds in those provinces. Furthermore, there is no reason to think that the modifications to Mousnier's model detailed above that de-emphasize the distinctiveness and autonomy of Parisian financiers (i.e. their financial links with elite groups throughout the Kingdom and their use of provincial agents) represented innovations of Louis' personal rule. If, therefore, the financial structures did not change in *pays d'élection* between the ministries of Richelieu and Mazarin and the personal rule of Louis XIV, what did change?

The transformation must have come in the way Louis XIV responded to financial exigencies in light of the long history of contention over such matters. In particular, change occurred in the types of financial edicts the crown issued and in the types of *traités* created. Typical of the extraordinary *traités* by which Louis XIV tapped either the personal wealth or the credit of the privileged elite were those that targeted specific groups or corps for the sale of *augmentations de gages* or of new offices. (See Appendix 2). Louis' extraordinary affairs targeted privileged groups and pressured them through what essentially amounted to blackmail to provide financial support in order to preserve their privileged standings, much as described in the previous chapters. Louis took advantage of the tenuousness of privilege in conducting his extraordinary affairs. At no time, however, did he conduct a frontal assault on privilege or on privileged groups. He never sought to overturn privilege but rather to use it to his advantage.[66] In order to engage privileged elite groups as financial intermediaries, Louis for the most part respected the heritability of offices and the integrity of revenues by which corps guaranteed the loans they intermediated. Financial exigencies brought about a grudging respect for property and privilege.

By contrast, the crown's approach to extraordinary affairs during the ministries of Richelieu and Mazarin had produced at the very least the appearance of an assault on the privileged. The 1620s were marked by a sustained effort on the part of the crown to create *élections* in Guyenne, Languedoc, Burgundy, Dauphiné and Provence.[67] These steps amounted to much more than the creation and sale of new offices, since the successful establishment of *élections* in *pays d'États* necessarily undermined and ultimately rendered obsolete provincial estates. That was precisely the outcome in Dauphiné and Guyenne; in all five of these provinces the crown's attempts led to revolts.[68] Further, the crown's fateful decision to revoke the Paulette in 1648 targeted for attack the patrimonial interests of almost every royal venal office holder in the Kingdom and created much of the opposition behind the revolt of the judges in the first Fronde.[69]

Louis XIV avoided these types of frontal attacks on privilege and property

---

[66] This is the opinion also of Major (p. 337) and Beik (*Absolutism*, pp. 307-316). Compare Hurt, *Louis XIV*.
[67] Major, pp. 220-260; Collins, *Fiscal Limits*, p. 65.
[68] Collins, *Fiscal Limits*, pp. 65, 95.
[69] Ibid., p. 66; Moote, *Revolt*. Kettering (*Judicial Politics*, p. 247), however, downplays the significance of Mazarin's threats toward the Paulette in provoking judicial opposition at the outset of the Fronde in Provençe.

throughout his personal reign, even as war brought chaos to the state's finances. Indeed, such a change was necessary for there to have been any degree of cooperation between the crown and the provincial elite whose very status revolved around property and privilege. But privilege and the unequal access to privileged status also opened the door to a divide-and-rule strategy, one that Louis XIV perfected and employed particularly well toward the privileged elite of *pays d'élection*. In such provinces, *traitants* and *sous-traitants*, both Parisians and locals who enjoyed the financial backing of members of the elite from throughout the Kingdom, were ready to carry out and profit from Louis' strategies. Indeed, the privileged particularism of old-regime society proved for the most part a hostile context for group cohesion and coalition-building among the elite. *Pays d'États* presented the major exception. There, province-wide institutions allowed for broad coalitions of the elite to negotiate financial matters with the crown and to assert local control over both ordinary and extraordinary financial matters. As the following chapter demonstrates, these distinctions between broad privileged corps asserting local financial autonomy and many of the smaller, more particular corps extended as well to their ability to attract lenders as they intermediated finances for the crown.

Chapter 6

Intermediating Corps and Financial Clienteles*

Through his strategy of engaging privileged corps to act as financial intermediaries, Louis XIV tapped the financial support of a wide array of his subjects. The reach of extraordinary finances extended to not only short-term lenders and money handlers but also to venal office holders and, beyond them, the clienteles of lenders who supported the financial intermediation of privileged corps. Different scales of risk distinguished each area of involvement. As noted in the previous chapter, receivers, tax farmers, and *traitants* along with their financial backers faced steep risks, but their returns, at least, compensated for those risks. Venal office holders too faced risks, as creations of redundant offices could undermine the value of their investments. They depended on royal good will, therefore, and their desire to keep the King happy led them to borrow for the crown, thus exposing them to further risks as the guarantors of the King's debts. The lenders to privileged corps, on the other hand, faced the least risk, as their investments were guaranteed by either mortgaged offices or ear-marked revenues.

The 'traditional' model of state finances holds that lenders to the French crown were most often subjects of forced loans or of manipulations in privileges and property rights; that the crown frequently defaulted and that lenders thus parted with their money only for short terms and at high interest rates; and that the crown depended on tight-knit clienteles of lenders linked to ministers through close personal ties. The absolutist French state, the argument goes, was constitutionally incapable of ushering in a 'financial revolution' akin to those systems found in the Dutch Netherlands and in post-1688 England where governments funded long-term debt raised from anonymous and voluntary lenders.[1]

As this chapter demonstrates, French finances under Louis XIV were not in fact bound to stark choices between the tried and true absolutist policies and 'newer' constitutionally distinct arrangements. Through the intermediation of various privileged corps, certain features associated with the 'financial revolution' evolved: Voluntary, long-term, funded debt backed by privileged corps made

---

* A slightly different version of this chapter has appeared as Good Offices: Intermediation by Corporate Bodies in Early Modern French Public Finance, *Journal of Economic History*, 60 (2000): 599-626.
[1] North and Weingast, pp. 803-808; Tracy, *Financial Revolution*, pp. 1-3, 45, and 71-107; Brewer, *Sinews*, pp. 88-91.

possible reduced rates of borrowing. Yet there were no fundamental constitutional changes in old-regime France to accompany these developments in public finance. Indeed, privilege, so anathema to constitutional/parliamentary regimes, continued explicitly to underlie the whole system on which French finances rested.

As demonstrated throughout this work, few, if any, privileged corps were immune to the crown's financial pressure; if they hoped to keep newly created offices or privileges off the market they had no choice but to serve as financial intermediaries for the crown. The crown, for its part, realized important savings through such arrangements. The King posed a poor credit risk and could only attract voluntary lenders by paying a risk premium. As Figure 6.1 illustrates, the crown frequently paid more to borrow than the Estates of Burgundy paid. The uncertainties of wartime drove rates of royal bonds toward 7 or 8 per cent while the estates never had to pay more than 5.55 per cent to attract loans during war. Furthermore, lenders fully subscribed to the estates' bonds. The crown, on the other hand, was rarely able to sell its bonds at face value, except perhaps through recourse to forced loans, and so the yield on royal bonds (or the cost to the crown) was higher than the official rate. Thus, during the last years of the War of the Spanish Succession, the costs to the crown of raising voluntary loans continued to surpass the estates' costs, despite the lower official rates of royal loans that appear in Figure 6.1.[2]

Privileged corps, by contrast, could borrow at rates much lower than the crown, closer to the rates of between 4 and 5 per cent which private borrowers with good credit paid their lenders.[3] The crown therefore gave up much less in revenues granted to provincial estates or in *gages* paid to venal officer corps than what it paid to its own creditors leery of the risks of lending to the King. There were, however, important political ramifications to these arrangements of financial intermediation.[4]

The privileged corps that intermediated finances for the crown were not sovereign representative institutions. The very privileges by which they existed and which spelled out their prerogatives depended on continued royal recognition and good will. Provincial estates, where they existed, could claim certain rights based on custom, but the crown could, and in some cases did, circumvent them and raise taxes without their accord. Corps of venal office holders existed by virtue of the crown having initially created the property rights and privileges that constituted their positions, and while the crown was bound in theory to uphold property rights and contractual agreements, the history of royal defaults suggests that the practical reality was different. In short, the intermediation of finances by privileged corps

---

[2] François Velde and David Weir, 'The Financial Market and Government Debt Policy in France, 1746-1793,' *Journal of Economic History*, 52 (1992), pp. 19-22; Hoffman, Postel-Vinay and Rosenthal, 'Redistribution,' p. 261.
[3] Hoffman, Postel-Vinay, and Rosenthal, *Priceless Markets*, pp. 14-25.
[4] The attention of historians has focused mostly on the political impact of these financial arrangements in the pre-Revolutionary era at the end of the 18th century. See Bien, 'Offices'; and Bossenga, *Politics*.

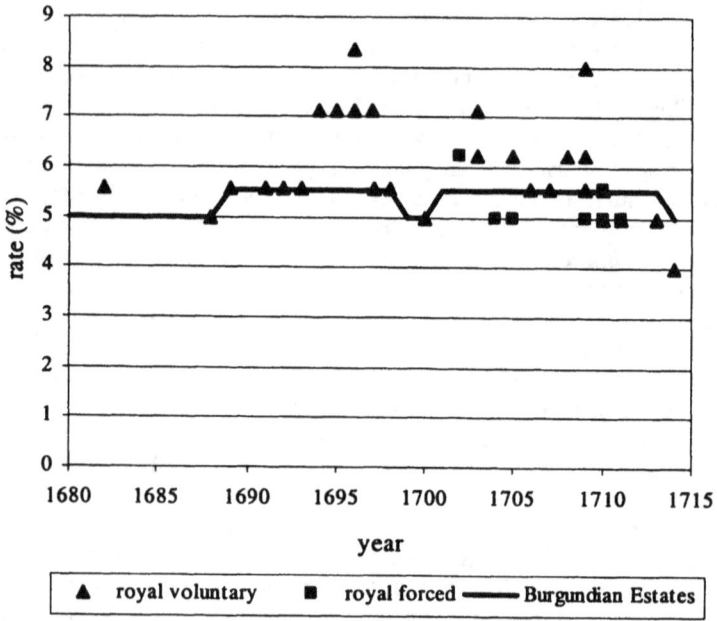

Source: François Forbonnais, *Recherches et considérations sur les finances de France depuis l'année 1595 jusqu'à l'année 1721, (Liège: Cramer, 1758)*; A.D.C.O., C 4577-4584.

Figure 6.1 Comparative interest rates of rentes

was distinctly different from the sovereign parliamentary control over taxing and borrowing seen in the both the sixteenth-century Dutch case and the post-1688 English case. Indeed, it was largely their dependence on the crown for the continued recognition of their status that drove privileged corps to accept their positions as financial intermediaries; failure to do so might have led to their circumvention and undermining by the crown. On the other hand, if the crown expected to reap any financial gains from borrowing through intermediaries, some level of political power needed to devolve to the intermediating corps so that they could assure their lenders that their investments were reasonably safe.

In this corporate society of old-regime France, not all privileged corps were created equally in terms of their political impact. Some were stronger and more independent than others, able to offer guarantees and assurances to a wide array of lenders, as evidenced through their borrowing records. Different types of corps attracted networks of creditors that varied in scope and make-up. Indeed, identifying the lenders to privileged corps offers keen insight into the corporate intermediaries themselves. The greater the ability to turn to lenders with no apparent personal or political ties to the corps to whom they lent, the more those corps must have required some form of political strength in order to guarantee that debt. The data on lenders, presented here, suggest that provincial estates in particular were on the forefront of intermediation for the crown. While the innumerable venal officer corps altogether raised significantly more than estates, individual provincial estates nonetheless raised very important amounts, and they did so with stronger guarantees offered to wider clienteles of lenders. To show how and why these divergent experiences in intermediation developed, I will first examine the private credit market in France under Louis XIV and the roles of brokers and intermediaries within that market. I will then turn to the methods by which different corps guaranteed their debts and the resulting risks for lenders. Identifying the lenders, then, will not only indicate which corps were most successful in attracting a wide array of investors, but why some might have been more successful than others.

Private Markets and Public Intermediaries

Recent research has shed considerable light on private credit markets in old-regime France. Despite a lack of lending or deposit institutions within the early modern French economy, private capital markets were quite dynamic both in rural and urban settings. Notaries played an important role in matching borrowers with lenders and providing information to the lenders about borrowers. During Louis XIV's reign, the most common long-term instrument for borrowing was the perpetual *rente* which entitled the lender to receive annual interest payments on his or her principal at or below the legally designated maximum rate (usually 5 per cent). In accordance with usury laws, while the lender received interest payments on the capital, he or she could not demand repayment of the principal, and *rentes* were amortized only when borrowers chose to repay the principal. Not even the death of either the borrower or the lender terminated a perpetual *rente*.[5]

Information was thus crucial, since lenders needed strong assurances that the collateral pledged by borrowers would be preserved in its value and integrity over potentially indefinite time periods. There was no national registry of mortgages, and thus there was no sure way for lenders to know whether a borrower's property served as collateral several times over to different lenders or whether mortgaged property even remained in the borrower's possession. Notaries were well placed to provide this type of information in matching borrowers and lenders and were therefore crucial to the functioning of the private credit market.

Still, notaries could not completely resolve the problem of asymmetric

---

[5] Jean Laurent Rosenthal, 'Credit Markets and Economic Change in Southeastern France, 1630-1788,' *Explorations in Economic History*, 30 (1993): 129-157; Philip T. Hoffman, Gilles Postel-Vinay, and Jean Laurent Rosenthal, 'Private Credit Markets in Paris, 1690-1840,' *Journal of Economic History*, 52 (1992): 293-306.

information. Parisian notaries, for example, did not fully develop their potential as brokers until some time after the settlement of the Law Affair.[6] A borrower's reputation thus remained crucial for instilling confidence in potential lenders, and for that reason members of the elite, those whose status tended to signify wealth and the secure possession of property, found willing lenders much easier than did the non-elite. Much of the private credit activity thus represented a transfer of funds among the elite, between those with capital to lend and those with both property to mortgage and the reputation to back up this *crédit*.[7]

The crown was long aware of the shackles placed on the credit market by the lack of any public information on mortgages, and there were several attempts to create a central registry in which all creditors would have to declare their liens on mortgaged property. Most notably, Louis XIV tried to create a central registry of mortgages by his edict of April 1673, and then Louis XV tried again by another edict in June 1771. The motivation behind these reform attempts was clear. A commission studying the edict of 1771 referred to the secrecy of mortgaged property (*'la clandestinité de l'hypothèque'*) and the risk for lenders of not knowing whether borrowers had already mortgaged their property as the primary reasons why a central registry was needed.[8]

Opposition from the parlements, though, forced the crown to withdraw these reform measures each time before they went into effect. In response, the crown set up a commission in 1775 to study the reasons for this resistance, and it found that most opposition sprang from a concern for privacy. Perhaps more relevant to the final decades of the eighteenth century, a period when political thinkers became increasingly concerned about royal despotism, than to the period of Louis XIV's reign was the fear that public information on mortgages could aid the crown in its search for taxable wealth.[9] What remained constant throughout the early modern period, though, was the importance of dignity and the feeling that such a universal requirement to declare publicly private patrimonial matters would violate the status and dignity of certain individuals. Members of the elite who enjoyed a high level of status and dignity, the very same individuals who were politically well placed to oppose these royal edicts, also benefited from the common use of reputation as a

---

[6] Hoffman, Postel-Vinay, and Rosenthal, *Priceless Markets*, pp. 96-113.

[7] The very word *crédit*, signifying the ability to borrow, was very much bound up with the concept of reputation. See Jay M. Smith, 'No More Language Games: Words, Beliefs, and the Political Culture of Early Modern France,' *American Historical Review*, 102 (1997): 1413-1440. Hoffman et al. found that of their sample, 64 per cent of Parisian borrowers from 1730 to 1788 were nobles and venal officers; among lenders, 39 per cent were nobles and officers and 33 per cent were merchants, bourgeois, notaries and financiers. See Hoffman, Postel-Vinal, and Rosenthal, 'Private Credit Markets,' pp. 294-99.

[8] A.N., E 3707¹, *Résumé du projet de la loi sur les hypothèques*.

[9] A.N., K 871, *Réflexions générales et particuliers sur le projet d'Édit portant établissement des offices de conservateurs des hypothèques*, 1770.

gauge of credit worthiness, and mortgage information made public might have seriously undermined their ability to borrow based upon their *crédit*.[10]

While these attempts ended in failure and the crown was never able to overcome opposition to the creation of central mortgage registries, Louis XIV did establish strong incentives to declare mortgages held on privately possessed government offices. According to the edict of February 1683, creditors who registered their liens on offices held priority claims over them in the event of default.[11] Thus only nine years after revoking his attempt at overall mortgage reform, Louis XIV succeeded in establishing a source of public information regarding the credit activity surrounding offices.

Why were offices an exception to the crown's otherwise bleak record of establishing public mortgage information? One answer surely lies in the semi-public nature of offices as property and the greater degree of royal prerogative in fixing the property rights of office holding. As well, the edict of February 1683 also suggests that Louis recognized the importance of offices as a source of royal credit and the need for office holders to be able to borrow against those offices in order to intermediate royal finances.[12] With mortgage information made public, Louis could count on office holders to tap up to the full market value of their offices or the capital value of any anticipated increases in *gages*. Office holders across the board would be able to offer transparent assurances to their lenders that reliance solely upon personal reputation might not have allowed. Indeed, it was likely a combination of their reputations as members of the elite and the public disclosures regarding their mortgageable property that enabled office holders to make up a disproportionate share of the borrowers on the Parisian private credit market.[13]

If we turn away from individual borrowers and focus instead on privileged corps, we see that they and their lenders confronted the same sets of issues in terms of information and security. What follows focuses specifically on borrowing by venal officer corps on the one hand and by provincial estates on the other. Both types of corps agreed to act as financial intermediaries for the crown in order to prevent changes in their privileged status. Both borrowed important sums of money for the crown, acting as guarantors of those debts and servicing their subsequent obligations with either *gages* paid or revenues granted by the crown. Yet important differences separated the two as well.

The assurances that each of these types of corps offered their lenders differed in form and, as we will see, in effectiveness. When venal officer corps borrowed

---

[10] A.N., K 871, *Réflexions générales*. See also Hoffman, Postel-Vinay, and Rosenthal, 'Redistribution,' p. 265, and Smith, 'No More Language Games,' pp. 1413-1440.
[11] Louis-Lucas, 2: 398.
[12] See Chapter Two.
[13] Hoffman, Postel-Vinay and Rosenthal group nobles and officers into a single category in their study of Parisian borrowers and lenders. Comprising only 9 per cent of the Parisian population, these groups made up 64 per cent of the private borrowers from 1730 to 1788 and borrowed 85 per cent of the money on the market in these years. See 'Private Credit Markets,' p. 299.

for the crown, they mortgaged the offices and the incomes accruing to them (the *gages*) that were the personal property of their members. For example, when the office-holding members of the *bureau des finances* in Rouen sought a loan from the dean of the Rouennais parlement, M. Duplessis Puchot, they agreed to pledge as collateral not only the office of treasurer of France which they were repurchasing and uniting to their corps but also the offices individually possessed by the members of the corps.[14] It was common practice for venal officer corps to stipulate that all members remained equally responsible for the timely payment of interest on *rentes* taken out in the name of the corps, and this obligation extended as well to members who joined after the loans were taken.[15]

Such mortgages, though, were only as secure as the private property rights over the mortgaged items, and as property with a semi-public quality, offices conferred a shaky guarantee. Succession rights, for example, could be altered or undermined by the crown. The ministries of Richelieu and Mazarin had used that legal leverage to gain political concessions from office holders earlier in the century, a strategy that ultimately backfired and resulted in conflict. After assuming personal rule, Louis XIV showed greater respect for the patrimonial possession of offices than did his predecessors. As I argued in Chapter Two, the negotiations over renewing the heritability of offices had by his reign become transparent and predictable, with few important offices ever reverting back to the crown for resale. As the succession rights of offices strengthened, so too did their use as mortgageable instruments. Indeed, with the incentive established to declare liens and the strengthened succession rights, Louis XIV showed himself to be interested in facilitating the mortgaging of offices in more ways than one.

In theory, therefore, loans to venal officer corps during Louis XIV's reign were safe investments for which lenders had legal recourse in the event of default. Indeed, the high credit risk for which the crown was at this point well known was, in these cases, transferred from the lenders to the office holders. Their own privately possessed offices, legally considered real property, as well as the incomes accruing to those offices guaranteed the loans, leaving the officers in the position of having to service their debts with their own savings whenever the crown was late in paying their *gages*. Office holders found themselves in just such a bind in 1709, when, in the midst of the War of the Spanish Succession and a severe harvest shortfall, the crown fell into arrears in its *gages* payments for the first time since the 1640s. Unlike the King, venal officer corps were legally bound to uphold their own contractual commitments, and they thus had to search for alternative revenue sources to service their debts. Reception fees levied against new office holders were an alternate revenue source at this point, but they raised the costs to new-

---

[14] A.D.S.M., C 2297.
[15] See, for example, the deliberations of the *parlementaires* of Rouen that mention loans taken out 'in collective name and in solidarity' among all the members. A.D.S.M., 1 B 226.

comers of entering into the venal office system and made offices a less attractive investment.[16]

While lending to venal office holders entailed less risk than lending to the crown, there remained, to be sure, definite uncertainty and risk for lenders. In cases of default, foreclosure was a lengthy and costly process, where claims were prioritized in ways that at times left some creditors with only a pittance of their original principal, and where debtors who enjoyed political connections had numerous possibilities to appeal and delay final decisions.[17] Even creditors who enjoyed political connections and influence had difficulty at times foreclosing on mortgaged offices. A retired counselor in the Parlement of Dijon, Richard Vallon de Mimeure, tried for three years to prevent his debtor Étienne Millière, likewise a counselor in the Parlement of Dijon, from exercising his office which he had pledged as collateral for a loan now in default. Millière, Mimeure argued, had gone to great lengths to 'vex and exhaust' his creditors through a series of appeals until an *arrêt* from the King's council finally blocked him from taking his seat on the Dijon bench, clearing the way for the office to be seized and auctioned.[18]

At times, the crown added to the uncertainties by changing the rules in cases of foreclosure or by encouraging 'redundant' mortgages on offices. In 1698, at the close of the Nine Years' War, the crown reimbursed a series of *augmentations de gages* that had been acquired at the beginning of the war and that their holders, in many cases, had pledged as collateral in order to acquire. Creditors, seeing the revenues upon which they held claims dry up, took measures to secure repayment of their principal. The crown, however, wished to free office holders as quickly as possible from any encumbrances that their creditors might place on their offices, so it issued an *arrêt* stipulating that creditors' claims would be judged 'summarily' in each province or *généralité* by the intendant. Creditors, in this case, could not take their claims to courts for adjudication.

More threatening to creditors than 'evoking' foreclosure cases into the jurisdiction of intendants were the occasional decisions on the part of the crown, in order to facilitate future lending by office holders, to change the order in which claimants held priority on *gages*, thereby making it possible for office holders to pledge their offices and their *gages* twice over. An *arrêt* in 1692 aided office holders in paying their *prêts*, and thus in gaining admission to the *droit annuel*, by stipulating that any lenders who provided loans for those *prêts* would be reimbursed from the *gages* paid to those office holders in 1692 and 1693 'with preference over all other creditors, even over those whose money had been used for the purchase of the offices.' A similar *arrêt* in 1702 offered 'special privilege' to individuals willing to lend to holders of hereditary offices for their payment of taxes meant to confirm that heredity. The *arrêt* ranked the 'special privilege' of the

---

[16] Doyle, *Venality*, pp. 52-53, and 71. Bien reports that in 1711, the *secrétaires du roi* of the Grande Chancellerie in Paris were owed 1.8 million livres in unpaid *gages*. See '*Secrétaires*,' p. 163.
[17] Hoffman, Postel-Vinay, and Rosenthal, *Priceless Markets*, pp. 63-64.
[18] A.N., AD IX 448, *Arrêt du conseil*, 28 January 1688.

new lenders 'concurrently with those who will have sold the said offices or lent their money for their acquisition, and with preference over all other creditors.'[19] The risks of lending to office holders thus extended beyond the typical delays and costs of foreclosure to the uncertainty that the crown might weaken some creditors' claims in order to strengthen others'.

Contradictions were thus becoming apparent within the policy of engaging corps of venal office holders as financial intermediaries. Office holders sought lenders in order to preserve their succession rights – the rights necessary in order to borrow against those very offices – yet the string of debts in many cases taken to preserve that heritability required a reshuffling of creditors' claims on those offices, which in turn weakened their potential as mortgageable property. The limits of this system of financial intermediation through venal officer corps were clearly being reached as the crown scrambled for extraordinary financial support during these war years.

No such reshuffling of claims, on the other hand, arose from the intermediation provided by provincial estates. In the period under study here, estates typically mortgaged crown-granted revenues whenever they borrowed from the public. The Estates of Burgundy, as demonstrated in Chapter Three, secured their loans with revenues from the *octrois de la Saône* and the *crues de sel*, indirect revenues that the crown granted to the estates over definite time periods. Like mortgages on venal offices, these loans were only as secure as the estates' hold over the revenues. Since the crown was the original grantor of the earmarked revenues, it could, and in fact did, try on several occasions to redirect them for its own benefit. Each time, though, the estates appealed for the preservation of their credit reputation, and in fact they almost always succeeded in protecting the integrity of the revenues under their control. The estates also vigorously supervised the accounts of tax farmers who leased the rights to collect these taxes and pursued delinquent financiers to the point of condemning some to debtors' jail.[20] Occasionally, commercial slumps caused the earmarked revenues to diminish. This was the case in 1691 when the returns from the *crues de sel* fell short of the obligations assigned to them. Concerned about their credit and 'not wanting their lenders to suffer any harm', the estates opted not to reschedule their debt and instead ordered their administrators to set aside the necessary amounts from other funds. The estates thus understood the importance of the guarantee they offered their creditors, and they appear to have had the discretionary authority to make up at least slight and occasional shortfalls.[21]

Another important difference separated estates from venal officer corps as intermediaries. The Estates of Burgundy used their crown-granted revenues both to pay the interest and to reimburse the principal owed their lenders in accordance with an informal schedule. Venal officer corps, on the other hand, used their *gages*

---

[19] A.N., AD IX 448, *Arrêt du conseil*, 2 September 1692; AD IX 449, *Arrêt du conseil*, 11 April 1702.
[20] See Chapter Three.
[21] A.D.C.O., C 3018, *Décrets des États*, 1691.

to pay only the interest on their debts. Because they borrowed with perpetual *rentes*, neither provincial estates nor venal officer corps were legally required to repay the principal borrowed. The Estates of Burgundy, however, chose to adhere to a repayment schedule. This practice likely reassured lenders since the estates offered no tangible assets on which lenders could foreclose. Creditors were entirely dependent on the estates' ability as an intermediary to preserve their hold over mortgaged revenues, and failing that, no property served as collateral. Does this suggest that loans to venal officer corps were safer investments than loans to provincial estates since tangible assets (i.e., offices) backed them up, or did the Burgundian estates' adherence to their repayment schedule instill greater confidence in their lenders than venal officer corps were able to? The available evidence on who lent to these different corps will speak to these questions.

The Data

Two primary data series that I have gathered offer comparative insight into how privileged corps pieced together their lending clienteles. The first of these series brings together the individuals and organizations who lent to the Estates of Burgundy. The second consists of lenders to various venal officer corps in both Upper Normandy (the *généralité* of Rouen) and the province of Burgundy along with the lenders to the municipality of Dijon.[22] The sources of these data series are detailed in Appendix 3. The first series is complete. It contains evidence of all *rente* contracts undertaken by the Estates of Burgundy between 1681and 1715. It contains 5,756 contracts totaling 34,308,852 livres in principal. The second series, on the other hand, comprised of 647 contracts totaling 2,671,877 livres in principal, captures a sample of borrowing by a selection of officer corps within the two regions during this same period. Both data series contain information on certain social indicators of lenders, including their titles, professions, residences, and gender, and comparisons can be made across series and over time about the make-up of the lending clienteles. Using these series to compare total borrowing, though, would be misleading since only the first is all-inclusive.

Finally, I have compiled a third data series that groups together lenders to individual office holders in Upper Normandy who borrowed to purchase increases

---

[22] The municipality of Dijon is a territorial corps like the Estates of Burgundy. I have grouped its borrowing records with those of venal officer corps, though, because it borrowed much of its funds in the same manner as officer corps, offering newly united offices as collateral and paying the interest on its loans with *gages* from those offices. When the town borrowed 26,400 livres to repurchase and unite the offices of colonel, major, captains and lieutenants of the bourgeois guard in 1694, for example, those offices were offered as the primary collateral, and in addition lenders were given rights to claim the 'funds and revenues, both patrimonial and crown granted of the said town' in case of default. This is very similar to the practice by venal officer corps of offering their newly united offices as collateral in addition to pledging shared responsibility and to offering up their individual offices as further collateral. A.M.D., M 26.

Table 6.1 Borrowing by Estates of Burgundy

5 year period	Number of contracts	Amount, livres Nominal	Amount, livres Real*	Average contract size, nominal livres
1681-1685	251	1546964	1546964	6163.2
1686-1690	232	1929300	1867562	8315.9
1691-1695	587	2961221	2555534	5044.7
1696-1700	684	4121260	3367069	6025.2
1701-1705	1068	5345142	4302839	5004.8
1706-1710	1663	7814693	6103275	4699.2
1711-1715	1271	10590272	7667358	8332.2
Total	5756	34308852	27410601	5960.5

*Adjusted to 1679 livre.

Source: See Appendix Three.

in their *gages*.[23] The debtors here are office holders who borrowed as individuals rather than as corps to meet the crown's demands. I will use this third series to study borrowing over time by individual office holders, but it is less useful in providing social information on lenders. This already small data set is handicapped by incomplete information regarding the occupations, titles and residences of lenders, and the work by Hoffman et al. based on notarial sources can likely better address this sector of the private credit market.

Borrowing Over Time

Examining the changing levels of borrowing over the period 1681-1715 by the Estates of Burgundy, by venal officer corps of both Upper Normandy and Burgundy, and by individual office holders in Upper Normandy presents some surprises. Borrowing by the Estates of Burgundy grew steadily over the last decades of Louis XIV's reign, as Table 6.1 presents, increasing from about 1.5 million livres borrowed during the five years from 1681 to 1685 to over 10.5 million livres during the last five years of the reign. This seven-fold nominal increase, or five-fold real increase when adjusted to the changing silver content of the livre, over this period corresponds to the growing role of the Burgundian

---

[23] This data series includes 148 contracts totaling 473,292 livres from the same time period as the others. The sources for this series are the same as for the second. See Appendix 3.

Table 6.2 Sample of officer corps borrowing in Burgundy and Rouen

5 year period	Number of contracts	Amount, livres Nominal	Real*	Average contract size, nominal livres
1681-1685	16	117889	117889	7368.1
1686-1690	28	113350	109723	4048.2
1691-1695	84	377250	325567	4491.1
1696-1700	24	64370	52590	2682.1
1701-1705	134	597128	480688	4456.2
1706-1710	190	581459	454119	3060.3
1711-1715	171	820431	593992	4797.8
total	647	2671877	2134568	4129.6

*Adjusted to 1679 livre.

Source: See Appendix Three.

estates as a financial intermediary for the crown. Their importance as a provider of extraordinary funds increased significantly during the War of the Spanish Succession, reaching new heights in 1710 when the estates agreed to a 1 million livre repurchase of edicts in addition to the 2.4 million livre repurchase of the capitation tax.[24]

Borrowing by both venal officer corps and individual office holders also increased over this same period. (See Tables 6.2 and 6.3). Both data samples present significant increases in the final fifteen to twenty years of Louis' reign, roughly during the War of the Spanish Succession, and both indicate that this increase continued and reached its peak right into the last five years of the reign.

This expansion in borrowing came just as constraints against such growth were hardening. Louis XIV's personal reign coincided with a long period of stagnation punctuated by occasional crises in the private credit market. In particular, frequent monetary and interest rate manipulations hampered the growth of credit. In Paris, the nominal levels of indebtedness on the private capital market showed little movement between the years 1662 and 1715, increasing only slightly in the last ten years of this period from roughly 170 million to 200 million livres.

---

[24] Not all of the 34.3 million livres that the estates borrowed between 1681 and 1715 was for payment of ordinary and extraordinary obligations. Some of the loans, especially during the last years of Louis' reign, were raised to reimburse old bonds or to refinance outstanding debt at lower rates. These figures thus do not correlate precisely to changing debt levels, but represent instead the sum of all credit contracts undertaken by the estates.

Table 6.3 Sample of individual office-holder borrowing in Rouen

5 year period	Number of contracts	Amount, livres		Average contract size, nominal livres
		Nominal	Real*	
1681-1685	8	17400	17400	2175.0
1686-1690	14	22170	21460	1583.6
1691-1695	16	29600	25545	1850.0
1696-1700	27	78283	63957	2899.4
1701-1705	22	99549	80137	4525.0
1706-1710	43	104495	81611	2430.1
1711-1715	18	121795	88180	6766.4
total	148	473292	378290	3197.9

*Adjusted to 1679 livre.

Source: See Appendix Three.

The doubling of borrowing by venal officer corps within the same time frame and the even greater increase in borrowing by individual office holders appears to have diverged significantly from the overall stagnant direction of the private credit market.[25] These were also the years when the payment of *gages* fell into arrears and could thus not be offered as firm collateral. Indeed, venal officer corps such as the *bureau des finances* in Rouen and the parlements of both Rouen and Dijon, still under pressure to meet their obligations to the crown, advertised quite forcefully their difficulties finding lenders.[26]

Thus, contrary to assertions that the crown's 1709 default in *gages* payments signaled the end of venality as a major source of financing for the War of the Spanish Succession, royal pressure on office holders to intermediate extraordinary finances drove a steady expansion of their borrowing.[27] Furthermore, only a small portion of the borrowing by venal officer corps and individuals detailed in these data represents refinancing. The Chamber of Accounts of Dijon borrowed 149,081

---

[25] True, the Parisian private capital market in this period might not be an entirely neutral basis for gauging the activity of venal officer corps – the two trends were likely inversely correlated as the massive build-up of government debt between roughly 1702 and 1714 drew capital away from private borrowers.
[26] Hoffman, Postel-Vinay, and Rosenthal, 'Redistribution,' p. 260; Idem., *Priceless Markets*, pp. 50-68; Bien, 'Secrétaires,' p. 163; Doyle, *Venality*, pp. 37-38.
[27] Compare Doyle, *Venality*, p. 52.

livres in 1714 at 4.16 per cent to reimburse loans which had been floated earlier at 5.55 per cent, and the municipality of Dijon refinanced some of its debt contracts on only an irregular and infrequent basis to satisfy creditors' requests for reimbursement, even though it was under no legal obligation to do so.[28] The remainder of the sources that provide the data for these samples (series 2 and 3) contain only evidence of new borrowing to satisfy new royal demands. Any precise quantification of the total debt held by venal officers would constitute a significant undertaking involving widely dispersed notarial documents. Still, we can infer from these data that the nominal debt level of venal office holders, both as individuals and as corps, increased in the final decades of Louis XIV's reign while it stagnated among private borrowers in general.

Corps/Lender Contacts

Who were the lenders who fueled this expansion in borrowing by both the Estates of Burgundy and venal officer corps? To compare how these different types of privileged corps pieced together their clienteles of lenders, I have categorized the lenders in both data series into three categories: lenders with direct personal or professional contacts with the corps to which they lent, those with indirect personal or professional contacts, and those with no apparent contacts at all. The first group in both series consists of individuals from the intermediating corps themselves and their family members. The second group represents members of the elite who likely had some professional or personal contacts with members of the intermediating corps or who at the very least shared common interests as local rulers, and the final group brings together all those with no obvious contacts or connections, either professional or personal, with the corps to which they lent. Grouping lenders into these categories serves to measure the role of personal relations in piecing together lender clienteles and the ability of corps to reach beyond their immediate contacts in attracting investors.

Among those lending to the Estates of Burgundy, the first category of lenders, those with direct personal or professional contacts, includes individuals who were among the *élus* or who attended the estates as deputies for either of the three orders, along with their family members and/or widows; agents of the estates, including the treasurers Chartraire and their family members, along with the receivers of the *taille* who collected revenues for the estates under the treasurer; and the Condé princes and their domestics or clients who, as members of the most prominent clientele group of Burgundy, had close ties to the most prominent

---

[28] A.D.C.O, B 6 bis. The total borrowing activity of the Chamber of Accounts between 1682 and 1714 amounted to 1,287,479 livres. In 1695, the municipality of Dijon borrowed 12,570 livres from Jean Gault, treasurer of France in Burgundy, to reimburse the procurator Joseph Fallavier. A.M.D., M 24.

Table 6.4 Lenders' contacts with borrowing corps

Borrowing corps	Contact type	Number of contracts	Value, livres	Percentage	Average value of contracts
Estates of Burgundy	direct	899	7696818	22.43	8561.53
	indirect	2714	13368102	38.96	4925.61
	none	2143	13243932	38.6	6180.09
	total	5756	34308852	100	5960.54
venal officer corps	direct	187	767649	30.97	4105.10
	indirect	225	1013122	40.87	4502.76
	none	183	697882	28.16	3813.56
	total	595	2478653	100	4157.49

institution of the province.[29] Lenders who held indirect professional or personal contacts correspond to our understanding of the local coalition of rulers and include members of the local (Burgundian) nobility and clergy along with town officials who themselves were not deputies but who by virtue of their titles or positions were represented, albeit indirectly, in the estates. Also included are Burgundian judicial and financial officers who as members of the local ruling coalition benefited from the position of the estates in protecting provincial privileges. Finally, by process of elimination, lenders with no apparent contacts to the estates include, in the most general terms, the Burgundian non-elite as well as non-Burgundians.

Identifying individuals who held direct personal or professional contacts with venal officer corps was a simpler task. They include officers of the corps themselves along with their family members and/or widows.[30] For each venal officer corps, this circle of lenders with direct contacts was much more limited in scope than was the corresponding group of lenders to the Burgundian estates, since there was no rotation of membership within venal officer corps. The category of lenders who held indirect ties to officer corps includes other office holders who were from the same province but who were lending to corps other than their own,

---

[29] Several sources served to identify the deputies to the estates. From archival records, I gathered lists of all deputies who attended the meetings of 1694, 1697, 1700, 1703, and 1712. I also gathered the complete lists of *élus* for each triennality from 1679-1718. A.D.C.O., C 3018-3019, *Registres des transcriptions des décrets des États*. Finally, there is the published list of deputies who attended each of the meetings in the chamber of the second estate in Beaune and Arbaumont, *La Noblesse*, pp. 36-60.

[30] The sources usually indicated whenever lenders were office holders of the corps themselves. I also used Arbaumont, *Armorial*, to help identify family members of officers in the Chamber of Accounts of Dijon.

Table 6.5 Lenders' contacts with officer corps, Burgundian versus Norman

Province	Contact type	Number of contracts	Value, livres	Percentage	Average value of contracts
Burgundy	direct	184	738449	38.69	4013.3
	indirect	204	716922	37.56	3514.3
	none	147	453436	23.75	3084.6
	total	535	1908807	100	3567.9
Normandy	direct	4	29200	5.12	7300.0
	indirect	21	296200	51.98	14104.8
	none	36	244446	42.9	6790.2
	total	61	569846	100	9341.7

along with members of the local nobility or clergy. Again, the lenders with no apparent contacts include mostly non-locals and the non-elite.

Using these categories of lenders as a basis of inquiry, some important distinctions can be drawn between the lenders to whom the Estates of Burgundy turned and those to whom venal officer corps turned as they sought funds to support royal extraordinary demands. The Estates of Burgundy borrowed from 1680 to 1715 between one-fifth and one-fourth of their funds from individuals with direct contacts to that institution, slightly less than 40 per cent from individuals with indirect contacts, and about the same amount from those with no apparent links, either personal or professional. (See Table 6.4). Of the 34.3 million livres that the estates borrowed between 1681 and 1715, they were able to attract 13.2 million from individuals outside the local network of notables with personal or professional ties to the estates.

Venal officer corps, on the other hand, depended more on their professional and personal contacts to raise extraordinary funds. Almost one-third, or 30.97 per cent, of the principal borrowed by officer corps came from individuals with direct personal contacts to those corps – a group much more circumscribed than the corresponding group for the Burgundian estates.[31] Individuals with indirect contacts lent slightly more than 40 per cent of the total principal to the venal officer corps, and those with no obvious ties at all lent only 28 per cent. Officer

---

[31] The social identity of the lenders for 52 of the 647 contracts in this data series could not be found, and thus I could not determine with confidence whether they had personal or professional contacts with the corps to whom they lent. The following calculations are based upon the remaining 595 contracts that total 2,478,653 livres in principal. See the comments in Appendix 3.

corps, then, appear to have depended more on the personal and professional contacts of their members to attract lenders than the Estates of Burgundy.

The data suggest that geography played a role in piecing together lending clienteles, and this is most notable in comparing the creditors of Burgundian officer corps with those of Norman corps. Here, the second data series presents some shortcomings: Lenders to Norman officer corps are not nearly as well represented in this sample as lenders to Burgundian corps. Nonetheless, the figures in Table 6.5 suggest at least tentatively that there were differences in the borrowing patterns of the two groups of venal officer corps, with Burgundian corps depending to a much greater degree than their Norman counterparts on personal and professional contacts to attract lenders. Rouen is relatively close to Paris, and members of the office holding elite from that city likely had professional contacts with Parisian notables. My system of classification, however, would not capture such links within the credit networks. Also, because of the prominent commercial sector there, local merchants were more likely to have lent to officer corps in Normandy than in Burgundy. Again, merchants would not show up in my classification scheme as having informal ties to venal officer corps, though in the Rouennais case they shared space at the top of the local hierarchy, and they were surely well placed to make informed investments in venality.[32] Both of these factors suggest why the Rouennais were able to reach a wider clientele of lenders with no apparent personal or professional contacts.

Non-institutional distinctions, therefore, mattered. The Rouennais case suggests that geography and socio-economic structures affected the make-up of lending clienteles to intermediating corps. Still, institutions mattered as well, and if we keep geographical distinctions aside by considering borrowing by just Burgundian corps, my argument that the estates depended less on personal ties than did venal officer corps is actually strengthened. Whereas the Estates of Burgundy borrowed almost forty per cent of their funds from individuals and institutions with no clear personal or professional contacts, Burgundian officer corps could only fund about twenty-four per cent of their borrowing from individuals across such barriers, and a full 38.7 per cent came from individuals with direct ties to the corps.

Considering once more the two data sets in their entirety, if we examine the borrowing patterns over time, there appear again important differences separating the estates from venal officer corps. I have divided both data series into two periods, 1680-1700 (period 1) and 1701-1715 (period 2). The first period includes about nine years of relative peace until 1689, then the Nine Years' War, and about two or three years of peace following that war. Period 2 encompasses roughly the duration of the War of the Spanish Succession followed by the last two years of Louis' reign. The second period also coincides with the fast-paced expansion of borrowing by both the Burgundian estates and venal officer corps.

The Estates of Burgundy show slight change in their borrowing patterns between periods 1 and 2. There was a minor increase in the proportion of lenders with direct contacts and a larger increase in that of lenders with no clear contacts at

---

[32] Bardet, *Rouen*, p. 192.

Table 6.6 Lenders' contacts with borrowing corps, two periods

Borrowing corps	Contact type	Period 1			Period 2		
		Number of contracts	Value, livres	Percentage	Number of contracts	Value, livres	Percentage
Estates of Burgundy	direct	281	1968867	18.7	618	5727951	24.1
	indirect	1003	5513183	52.2	1711	7854919	33.1
	none	470	3076695	29.1	1673	10167237	42.8
	total	1754	10558745	100	4002	23750107	100
Venal officer corps	direct	86	398972	60.3	101	368677	20.3
	indirect	38	137777	20.8	187	875345	48.2
	none	24	125143	18.9	159	572739	31.5
	total	148	661892	100	447	1816761	100

all at the expense of those with indirect contacts. The overall dependence on the local elite to furnish capital diminished as the estates found that they could turn elsewhere to satisfy their growing demand for investors. (See Table 6.6). Venal officer corps, on the other hand, saw greater change over these two periods in their contacts with lenders. In period 1, less than one-fifth of the money lent to officer corps came from individuals with no contacts at all, and individuals with direct personal and professional contacts provided a full 60 per cent of their funds. Then, as demand for money increased, the greatest expansion occurred in the proportion of funds provided by lenders with indirect links to the corps.

The large proportion of funds provided to officer corps by lenders with direct contacts, by members of the corps themselves or by their family members, in period 1 is striking. Essentially, officers were borrowing from themselves, or perhaps across generations within the same families, in order to finance, as corps, the extraordinary transfers of funds expected by the crown. This peculiarity suggests much about venal officer corps as financial intermediaries. To begin with, they seemingly did not enjoy the prestige and prominence needed to attract lenders in large numbers and instill confidence as guarantors of public debt during the final decades of the seventeenth century. Yet at the same time, since the members of these corps were more or less borrowing from themselves (or from family members), there is no reason why they could not instead have lent directly to the King as individuals by purchasing *augmentations de gages* and paying the principal out of their own pockets into the King's coffers. That they chose not to do so and to negotiate instead as corps suggests that organizing themselves and dealing with the King as such provided assurances in their negotiations that they would not otherwise have had as individuals. Strength, therefore, appears to have come from numbers, size and prominence, and groups of notables sharing a set of functions and privileges held stronger bargaining positions with the crown than individual notables on their own. The threat of an uncooperative parlement or chamber of accounts surely instilled greater responsibility in the crown in meeting *gages* obligations than the lesser threat of disgruntled individual magistrates here and there. The changes that we see in period 2, then, came as the crown called upon officer corps to borrow greater amounts of money to help meet the costs of the War of the Spanish Succession. Members of officer corps apparently did not enjoy the financial flexibility to provide as great a portion of the funds themselves, but most of the financing still had to come from fellow members of the local elite.

Overall, thus, the Estates of Burgundy were more capable of reaching outside the immediate circle of local elite groups in attracting lenders. As Hoffman et al. have argued, the problem of asymmetric information, or the inability of lenders to know for certain the status of debtors' collateral, led lenders in France to restrict their loans largely to borrowers with whom they had close contacts. Data from the Parisian credit market toward the end of the seventeenth century, where roughly 40 per cent of all loans in the form of *rentes* were made to individuals of the same family, profession or neighborhood, bear out these constraints.[33] The Estates of Burgundy, however, were succeeding in overcoming the barriers caused by asymmetric information, as they managed to attract greater proportions of 'anonymous' lenders. What accounts for this success in piecing together a wider clientele of lenders? One possible explanation might lie with the interest rates that the different types of corps paid their lenders. If the estates paid higher rates than venal officer corps, then the significance of their wider lending clientele would be diminished. We could simply argue that the estates attracted investors from afar (both socially and geographically speaking) by virtue of the greater returns on their bonds. The data, though, do not support such an argument.

Figure 6.1 shows that the estates paid 5.55 per cent on their bonds during wartime, and then as peace came, they typically reduced their rates to 5 per cent, as they did in 1698 and again in 1714. Venal officer corps did not leave such thorough records of their debt management as the Burgundian estates did, so it is more difficult to reconstruct the rates they paid. Some indications exist, though, for both the chamber of accounts and the municipality of Dijon. Records from the chamber of accounts mention paying a rate of 5.55 per cent for loans floated in 1702 and 1705, and the municipality paid likewise for loans floated in 1694 and 1704. Then, following the crown's lead, the chamber of accounts reduced the rates on almost all its *rentes* to between 4.166 per cent and 4.55 per cent in 1713 and 1714. Only during these final few years was there any divergence between the rates paid by the estates and those paid by other Burgundian corps, and this divergence was temporary. By 1717 virtually all corporate intermediaries were following the trends of the private credit market and reducing rates in the midst of

---

[33] Hoffman, Postel-Vinay, and Rosenthal, *Priceless Markets*, pp. 62-68.

the Law Affair.[34] Furthermore, the divergent patterns of borrowing by these two types of intermediaries easily predated these last few years of the reign when they were paying slightly different rates.

If interest-rate differentials do not explain the estates' relative success in reaching beyond local notables to borrow funds, the answer must therefore lie in the ability of the estates to assure potential lenders of the safety of their investments. But the question remains how they were able to offer such assurances. We can begin by eliminating some explanations that the evidence does not support.

Mortgage laws designed to extend legal recourse to lenders in case of default fail to explain why lenders were attracted to investing in the estates. While it is true that the crown managed to weaken mortgages on offices at the margin, nonetheless mortgage laws fell short of providing any concrete assurances to the estates' creditors that lenders to officer corps lacked. If anything, the reverse is true, since lenders to officer corps retained legal recourse to tangible assets for the life of their perpetual *rentes*, while the estates offered no such tangible assets as collateral.

Nor can we argue, as Daniel Dessert does in the case of individual financiers and money handlers, that a more politically influential clientele of lenders made the bonds of the Burgundian estates less likely targets of forced default by the crown.[35] The financiers studied by Dessert were part of a highly personalized financial system wherein their loans from the politically connected made them less likely targets of selective default. Colbert himself had observed that Fouquet had borrowed from '*presidents à mortiers*, [and from] other presidents and counselors of all the sovereign courts... not only to improve that merchandise (i.e. to ensure financial liquidity at the best possible terms) but also to shield the gifts that he made to many of his friends.'[36] Fouquet's clientele of lenders consisted largely of his political clients; forty years later the Estates of Burgundy were able to borrow for the crown without such heavy reliance on personal ties to the politically connected. Only about 26 per cent of funds from outside the Burgundian elite came from judicial or financial officers, 14 per cent came from the sword nobility and 6 per cent came from clergymen. Less than half of the funds that the estates raised from outside their professional and personal contacts, then, came from elite groups that might have assured the relative safety of their bonds. Meanwhile, women, both widowed and unmarried, provided almost one-fourth of these funds, and bourgeois, merchants and professionals provided about one-fifth.[37] Any political clout provided by creditors must have come from those elite individuals with personal or professional ties, either direct or indirect. But here, too, any such explanation falls short.

---

[34] Hoffman, Posel-Vinay, and Rosenthal, 'Redistribution,' p. 261.
[35] Dessert, *Argent*, p. 366.
[36] Colbert, 'Mémoires sur les affaires de finances pour servir à l'histoire,' in Clément, ed., v. 2, p. 42
[37] Tables 6.7 and 6.8 offer a social and professional breakdown of the lenders who had no clear contacts with the intermediating corps.

Indeed, the *élus* expressed a preference for local Burgundians over non-Burgundians as lenders, but this was not part of any strategy to assure the relative good standing of their *rentes*. Rather, they were interested in assuring that locals, regardless of their status or political position, benefited from the relatively secure investment opportunities already made available by the estates. While the *élus* actively sought certain types of lenders, it was not with the express purpose of recruiting politically prominent investors.[38]

Further, the close-knit nature of the privileged elite, especially in a provincial capital like Dijon which was known more as an administrative than a commercial center, undermines any 'prominent clientele' argument. Members of the elite with direct or indirect ties to the Estates of Burgundy also held direct or indirect ties with many of the venal officer corps of that province, and many prominent Burgundians lent to both the estates and to the local officer corps.[39] The local elite groups lending to the estates were not distinct from the elite groups lending to officer corps, and it is unlikely that they assured the safety of the estates' debts while not also assuring the safety of officer corps' debts. There is no evidence that the estates sought a heavy presence of the elite among their bondholders; nor is there any indication that the estates' bonds were made any safer by such presence.

A related argument might point to the Condé princes as responsible for assuring the safety of the Burgundian estates' debt, not by virtue of holding the debt themselves (Louis III de Bourbon, prince de Condé purchased only two *rentes* during this period, both in 1696 for a total of 40,000 livres in principal) but by virtue of their role as provincial patrons. This argument has two problems. First, the Condé princes were also the political patrons of such key Burgundian corporations as the parlement and the chamber of accounts. Had they enhanced the financial independence of the estates, we would also expect them to have enhanced the financial independence of the officer corps as well, thereby strengthening their ability to attract lenders. This was clearly not the case. Secondly, the political prominence of the Condé princes within Burgundy declined after 1740, yet the estates still attracted a wide network of lenders, indeed even wider than under Louis XIV.[40] The estates were thus succeeding in piecing together an increasingly anonymous clientele of lenders, and they did so without relying on the support of any particular patrons either inside or outside their clientele of lenders.

Reputation, therefore, must have played an important role in attracting a wide

---

[38] In 1713 the *élus* reimbursed 422,257 livres to Lyonnais creditors with principal borrowed from Burgundians. In their deliberations, they recognized '...that it is to the advantage of individuals from this province to be able to invest their money in *rentes* on the estates in the place of those who are not natives of the province.' A.D.C.O., C 4562.

[39] Jean Baptiste Canabelin and André Bernard Bernardon, both *maîtres des comptes* in the chamber of accounts, lent extensively to both their own corps and to the estates. And François Chartraire de Bière, treasurer of the estates, held a number of the estates' *rentes*, and he lent 6,300 livres to the municipality of Dijon in 1706.

[40] Kettering, *Patrons*, pp. 91-94; Mark Potter and Jean Laurent Rosenthal, 'Politics and Public Finance in France: The Estates of Burgundy, 1660-1790,' *Journal of Interdisciplinary History*, 27 (1997), pp. 594-611.

clientele of lenders to the estates. As already suggested, reputation, or *crédit*, was particularly important for individuals borrowing on the private credit market given the lack of public information on mortgaged holdings. Because of their semi-public nature and their relative prominence, privileged corps could likely count on their reputations surpassing in prominence and visibility those of 'average' private borrowers on the market. If interest rates were no more attractive than those paid by venal officer corps, if mortgage laws did not make the estates' bonds safer, and if the political prominence of lenders or patrons did not serve to provide explicit assurances, a well advertised reputation as a responsible borrower must have been key to the estates in attracting a large network of lenders. It remains to understand how a particularly favorable reputation evolved.

The estates approached their role as financial intermediary with much vigor and insisted on preserving an independent hold over the revenues by which they serviced their debt. Their ability to protect the integrity of mortgaged revenues, even when confronted by a crown ready to redirect them, and their resulting ability to adhere to their schedule of reimbursements surely attracted creditors leery of lending capital in an era marked by frequent interest rate changes and monetary manipulation. In such an environment, creditors to the estates held a distinct advantage since they could at any point count on having their principal reimbursed to them in the near future. The average duration of the estates' loans was about five years through the 1680s and 1690s, increasing to about eight years the following decade and to ten years in the 1710s. The estates' policy of regular reimbursement enhanced liquidity and offered a greater range of options to investors holding the estates' bonds. Lenders could take their capital, once reimbursed to them, and invest elsewhere should they find superior assets on the market; likewise they could more easily protect their investments from anticipated devaluations by keeping their reimbursed principal in specie.[41] More often, though, lenders chose to keep their money invested in the estates' bonds by turning around and purchasing newly issued *rentes*.[42]

By contrast, the *gages* paid to venal officers only allowed for payment of interest to their lenders. There was no systematic attempt by venal officer corps to reimburse regularly their creditors. Indeed, they did not have the financial wherewithal to do so other than by seeking funds from members' own savings or personal credit networks, and so lenders to venal officer corps found themselves typically locked into their investments with no reimbursement in sight.

There were thus real benefits in terms of liquidity to lending money to the estates over lending money on the private market or to other royal financial intermediaries who did not regularly reimburse their debts. Indeed, the mere adherence to their reimbursement schedule surely enhanced the estates' reputation as a credible borrower. While the estates never offered their creditors a written

---

[41] Hoffman, Postel-Vinay, and Rosenthal (*Priceless Markets*, pp. 69-95) make a convincing case that both lenders and borrowers anticipated monetary manipulations into the future, though not always accurately.
[42] Potter and Rosenthal, 'Politics,' pp. 592-594.

commitment to keep to a fixed schedule of debt management, lenders knew which future revenues were earmarked for their reimbursement. Information largely determined the allocation of capital in old-regime credit markets, and the estates, for their part, understood the importance of publicizing their intent and sticking to their promises in order to enhance their reputation among potential lenders.[43] We have already seen the estates' concern in 1691 when a commercial slump threatened their reimbursement schedule. In extraordinary circumstances, furthermore, the estates enhanced the liquidity of their bonds even beyond what their reimbursement schedule allowed: Planning to cut interest rates from 5.55 to 5 per cent, the estates in 1713 offered to reimburse any creditors their principal if they were unwilling to accept that decline in payments.[44] And this concern for liquidity along with this vigilant attitude in defense of their bondholders lasted as long as the estates were in the business of guaranteeing public debt. In deliberations toward the end of the eighteenth century, administrators of the estates admitted that it was of 'wise administration' to reimburse their debts on a timely and anticipated basis and that the practice would prove 'useful when [they] borrow again.' Only a strong hold over their mortgaged revenues made such a strategy possible for the estates.[45]

Political distinctions, then, namely their ability to manage their debt independently with revenues controlled locally, explain the Burgundian estates' success in assuring investors and in piecing together a wide clientele of lenders. Venal officer corps, meanwhile, depended on the crown's timely payment of *gages* merely to pay the interest on their debts, and failing that, only by virtue of the officers' personal solvency were interest payments made on time to the lenders. Furthermore, the crown could, and did on occasion, alter the claims of creditors on mortgaged offices. No such intervention occurred in the estates' management of their debt. Venal officer corps were not as well positioned to intermediate finances for the crown with the same degree of independence as the Estates of Burgundy.

It would be mistaken, however, to dismiss venal officer corps as politically irrelevant during this period. My findings suggest that as *individual* corps they did not enjoy the financial autonomy and the political strength that characterized provincial estates. The Estates of Burgundy were larger and more prominent than most venal officer corps in terms of the size of their deputation, their jurisdictional reach and the funds under their control. Size surely aided the estates in promoting their reputation. They also had the experience of handling royal funds, and they were therefore well placed to assert control over mortgaged revenues and manage

---

[43] On the importance of information in allocating capital, see Hoffman, Postel-Vinay, and Rosenthal, *Priceless Markets*, passim.

[44] A.D.C.O., C 4562, *Extrait des registres des deliberations des élus*, 10 November 1713.

[45] A.D.C.O. , C 4569, 18 February 1773. The full statement from the estates' deliberations is quoted in Potter and Rosenthal, 'Politics,' p. 589. On the estates' eighteenth-century measures to enhance the liquidity of their bonds, see Mark Potter and Jean Laurent Rosenthal, 'The Development of Intermediation in French Credit Markets: Evidence from the Estates of Burgundy,' *Journal of Economic History*, 62 (2002): 1024-1049.

their debt without interference from the crown.[46]

Yet taken together, the countless number of venal officer corps across the kingdom intermediated considerably more debt for the crown than the handful of provincial estates. No single venal officer corps rivaled the Burgundian estates in terms of financial autonomy and effective intermediation, but venality as a whole proved a crucial source of extraordinary funds for Louis XIV, and the extent of its spread during these decades carried with it long-term political costs just as great for the crown as the relative intensification of autonomy and power in the provincial estates. These political costs, the legacy left by the financial drain of Louis XIV's wars, will be considered by way of conclusion to this work.

---

[46] If indeed size mattered in effectively intermediating finances for the crown, then the kingdom-wide corps of *secrétaires du roi* about which Bien writes and bases many of his conclusions may not be entirely representative of venal officer corps in general. See 'Secrétaires,' and 'Manufacturing Nobles: The Chancelleries in France to 1789,' *Journal of Modern History*, 61 (1989): 445-486.

Chapter 7

Conclusion

Louis XIV's wars and financial strategies imposed upon the French crown a complex set of short and long-term costs, both financial and political in nature. To close this study, I first focus on the short-term impact of extended warfare by examining how the Regency government of Louis XV confronted the liquidation of the practically unmanageable debt left by its predecessor. I then place Louis XIV's financial strategies in a broader historical perspective. Such a view allows for both a theoretical assessment of French absolutism and an understanding of the forces that drove long-term political change within the early modern French state.

Financial Default and Reform under the Regency

Louis XIV died on September 1, 1715, bringing to close the longest reign of old-regime France. The impact of his reign, though, extended well into the eighteenth century. Above all, the financial and political consequences of his final war-torn decades as King weighed upon his successors.

The financial costs of Louis' last two wars were tremendous. The crown's total outstanding debt grew by a real factor of about seven between Colbert's death in 1683 and 1715.[1] Whereas the debt at the close of the reign totaled about two billion livres, ordinary revenues only amounted to between 100 and 150 million livres per year during the last five years of the reign.[2] This roughly two billion livre-debt included mostly long term loans floated through direct solicitation, such as *rentes sur l'hôtel de ville de Paris* or *rentes sur la gabelle*, and short-term loans in the form of paper money. Added to this figure should be the capital value of offices, said to have increased by somewhere between 542 million and 639 million livres, roughly doubling the nominal value of outstanding offices.[3] And in addition to these were the debts that Louis created through the intermediation of provincial estates, municipalities and the Assembly of the Clergy. As a result of Louis XIV's wars and his strategies to finance them, his successors found throughout the

---

[1] See Chapter One

[2] Briggs, *Early Modern France*, p. 218; Guéry, 'Les Finances,' p. 225.

[3] The estimates are from Marion, *Histoire*, 1:64; and Doyle, *Venality*, p. 51. *Augmentations de gages* alone amounted to 205 million livres in added capitalization of offices between 1683 and 1714. A.N., K 886, *État des augmentations de gages aliénées par le roy depuis l'année 1683 jusques et compris l'année 1714*.

eighteenth century that any attempt to reform venality or abolish corporate privileges forced them immediately to confront the issue of the large levels of public debt held and guaranteed by privileged corps.[4]

The financial condition of the French crown was thus disastrous upon Louis XIV's death, and it remained for the Regency of Louis XV to steer the government back to a financially sound footing through a combination of default, coercion and reform. Financial default typically followed some of the more costly wars of old-regime France, and in the aftermath of the War of the Spanish Succession, the monarchy began to go down this path in the final two years of Louis XIV's reign. After having paid its creditors interest rates of 5.56 to 6.25 per cent on their *rentes* throughout the war, the crown reduced the rate first to 5 per cent in 1713 and then to 4 per cent the following year.[5] Default through interest rate reductions and monetary manipulation became especially severe by 1720. In the interim, the duc de Noailles, president of the *Conseil des Finances*, was charged with the responsibility of charting a course for financial reform.

Noailles replaced Desmaretz as the crown's chief financial official under the Regency, and it was thus he who assumed management of the debt left by Louis XIV. In an attempt to balance expenses with receipts, Noailles directed the crown's finances along a rather well-tried course of both default and reform. Continuing the measures first taken in 1713, Noailles intended to convert as much of the short term debt as possible into long term perpetual *rentes* and then to reduce to 4 per cent the interest paid on any long term debts which were not already reduced.[6] Then, to further decrease expenses, Noailles targeted the venal office system for reform. Edicts suppressing offices, *augmentations de gages*, and privileges had already grown in frequency, from a trickle to a 'flood' at the time of Louis' death, and Noailles added to the deluge with his first edict of suppression in October 1715 that targeted seven intendants of finance and six intendants of commerce. An edict in December of that same year reduced the number of offices in Chancelleries throughout the Kingdom. These were followed by forty-four edicts in 1716 and seventeen in 1717, all targeting specific offices, privileges, or surtaxes for suppression.[7]

A few of these edicts suppressed only individual offices, such as the February 1716 edict that called for the suppression of the office of president in the bailiwick of Mâcon. Most, however, targeted sets of offices for suppression, and these typically included the types of offices that Louis XIV had favored in his creations,

---

[4] Bien, '*Secrétaires*,' pp. 153-168; Bossenga, *Politics of Privilege*.
[5] Hoffman, Postel-Vinay, and Rosenthal, 'Redistribution,' pp. 270-272.
[6] I am focusing here on attempts by Noailles and the Regency to reduce expenses, including the debt burden, through default or reform. For a discussion of reform attempts on the revenue side of the equation, see Touzery, pp. 1-54.
[7] Doyle, *Venality*, p. 44; A.N., G^7 1567/1568, *Table des édits et déclarations portant supression d'offices et de droits rendus depuis et compris le mois d'octobre 1715*.

namely administrative offices and those related to troop provisioning.[8] In fact, most edicts targeted those offices that had been created after 1688 as little more than instruments of war finance.

The breadth of offices covered in these edicts suggests ambitious intentions on the part of the Regency, yet the results fell far short of such intentions. To begin with, not all of the offices created by Louis XIV had found purchasers. Those offices that existed only on paper were likely the first that the Regency targeted for suppression. Their abolition changed little and cost the crown nothing. For those offices that had found buyers, the crown faced the obvious hurdle of reimbursing their *finances* before they could be liquidated, and given its financial condition the crown was in no position to afford such costly reimbursements on the scale necessary to bring significant contraction to venality.

Some offices were included within the crown's debt consolidation, their capital value converted into *rentes* paying 4 per cent.[9] Yet the monarchy was seeking ways to wipe out debt altogether, not merely to convert one form to another. Lacking a fund to finance the reimbursement of offices akin to a *caisse d'ammortissement*, Noailles was left having to find creative means of financing the liquidation of offices, and the methods decided upon were often either ineffective or counterproductive. While the crown suppressed the venality of municipal offices by an edict of September 1714, for example, municipalities were left with the burden of financing the necessary reimbursements.[10] Those that could not afford to do so with the revenues from either their patrimonies or their *octrois* retained the burdensome structures of venality within their municipal governments.

In some cases, the crown had to create offices in order to finance the liquidation of others. In an edict amending the June 1715 decision to suppress a number of offices in the Chancelleries, the crown first specified that those offices created 150 or 200 years prior would be reimbursed based on the *finances* originally paid rather than their present market values. As for those offices of more recent creation and those with *augmentations de gages* attached that proved more costly to liquidate, the edict stated that their reimbursement would be financed by 'proceeds from the creation of other new offices.'[11] On other occasions, the crown suppressed public charges only to transfer their functions to existing offices. In these instances, the crown would demand payment from the office holders whose

---

[8] Some examples include the July 1716 edict for the suppression of offices of pig inspectors; the August 1716 edict suppressing all offices of masters of bridges (*maîtres des ponts*); and the November 1716 edict for the suppression of offices of treasurers, general payers of pensions and gratifications of military officers.
[9] Doyle, *Venality*, p. 48.
[10] A.N., G[7] 1553.
[11] '...le fonds même qui proviendra de la création des nouveaux offices.' A.N., E 3644, 14 December 1715, fol. 34.

functions and jurisdictions expanded in order to reimburse holders of the suppressed offices.[12]

Unable to fund on its own the reimbursement of offices, the Regency could not match its ambitions with results. One recourse remained – the Chamber of Justice which opened in March 1716 and closed in March 1717. These judicial proceedings that carried with them a historically notorious reputation were used not only to retire debts through default but to gain back through coercion the profits obtained by financiers from their handling of public funds.[13] Chambers of Justice had the authority to jail financiers and even to hand down the death penalty, but they typically culminated with orders for financiers to pay fines and taxes. They thus represented rather blunt political tools by which the crown could rein in its overall debt. In drawing up its tax roll, the Chamber in 1717 specified how payment was to be made, and in this way, the crown retired not only specific debt issues but offices as well.[14] The final tax roll of the proceedings included 15.7 million livres in fines to be paid with surrendered offices and 2.8 million in *augmentations de gages*.[15]

Overall, the effectiveness of the Chamber of Justice in lessening the crown's debt burden was quite moderate. The total taxes levied against financiers as part of the final accommodation that put an end to the proceedings amounted to about 219.5 million livres, a figure eclipsed by the approximately 2 billion livres (plus the capital value of offices) in outstanding debt that the crown had faced in 1715. As it had done with previous Chambers of Justice, the crown intervened toward the end of this one in 1717 to draw up the moderated tax roll, fearing that extreme judgments against financiers would have compromised the financial standing of not only the financiers themselves but of their politically prominent backers.[16]

The Regency government thus came out of the Chamber of Justice in 1717 still facing debts that placed any fundamental reform of venality and any permanent reduction of expenses beyond its reach. The only remaining path for the Regency to arrive at a sound financial footing was to extend the default even further.

A massive default came indeed in 1720 with the collapse of the Law scheme. John Law had devised a complicated system joining together a Royal Bank, a

---

[12] The February 1716 edict that suppressed the office of president in the bailiwick of Mâcon transferred the functions and *gages* of that office to the lieutenant general of the same bailiwick.

[13] An eighteenth century legal encyclopedia defined the chamber of justice as 'a sovereign tribunal or commission of the royal council temporarily established to search out those who have embezzled royal funds.' J.F. Bosher, '"Chambres de Justice" in the French Monarchy,' in *French Government and Society 1500-1850*, ed. J.F. Bosher (London: Athlone Press, 1973), p. 20.

[14] While the Regency was unsure how it was going to finance the liquidation of several offices of payers and controllers of *gages*, at least one of those offices was to be surrendered as payment for a fine levied by the Chamber. A.N., E 3651, 20 February 1717, fol. 81.

[15] Dessert, *Argent*, p. 275.

[16] Ibid., p. 271.

trading company and indirect tax farms as a means of servicing the crown's debt, invigorating commerce and enriching both the King and his subjects.[17] He received royal letters patent to found a general bank in May 1716, and he raised the initial capital by exchanging bank shares for both coin and government paper.[18] Law was initially successful in creating public confidence in bank issues, and in December 1718 his general bank was converted into the Royal Bank by declaration of the King.

Meanwhile, Law's trading company, the Company of the West, was established in August 1717. Law intended the trading company and the bank to complement each other. The bank would provide credit, and the trading company would put that credit to profitable use. The crown continued to benefit from the swap of royal debt for shares in this expanding operation. The shares paid a return of two per cent, half of what holders of the crown's *rentes* were receiving prior to this arrangement, and the King paid the bank three per cent on the swapped debt it held.[19] In September 1718, the company was granted the royal tobacco farm, and by 1719 all was in place as Law had originally envisioned. The company collected taxes, printed money and held a monopoly over large areas of overseas trade. Adding to the semblance of success, a speculative frenzy began to drive up the price of shares toward the end of 1719.

The bubble quickly burst the following year, however. A series of royal moves failed to prop up the troubled currency, and indeed some of the crown's actions actually harmed public confidence in what had by then become the only legal tender.[20] The final blow to the paper currency came on August 29 when an edict announced that bills of 1,000 livres and 10,000 livres would be stripped of all value as legal tender on October 1 and that those of 100 livres and 10 livres would face the same fate on May 1 of the following year. This was the final signal for those who had not already done so to rid themselves of these soon to be worthless bank notes. Debtors took advantage of the situation to repay their debts with the collapsed paper currency, and because the notes were still the only legal tender, creditors had to accept them at face value as reimbursement. Debtors did not even

---

[17] A recent assessment of the life and works of John Law can be found in Antoin E. Murphy, *John Law: Economic Theorist and Policy-Maker*, (Oxford: Clarendon Press, 1997).

[18] Law initially offered 1,200 shares at 5,000 livres each, payable one-fourth in coin and three-fourths in government paper, or *billets d'État*. Marion, *Histoire*, 1:93.

[19] Hoffman, Postel-Vinay, and Rosenthal, 'Redistribution,' p. 277.

[20] Letters patent in January 1720 stipulated that bank notes would thereafter be the only legal currency for all transactions. An *arrêt du Conseil* of 27 February prohibited anyone from holding more than 500 livres worth of coin. A declaration of March 11 prohibited the use of gold or silver coins, and an *arrêt du Conseil* of April 6 stipulated that all payments thereafter be made with bank notes even if contracts had called for payment specifically in coin. In addition to these measures, Law embarked on a program to manipulate the value of specie so as to drive people to exchange their coins for bank notes. See Thomas Kaiser, 'Money, Despotism, and Public Opinion in Early Eighteenth-Century France: John Law and the Debate on Royal Credit,' *Journal of Modern History* 63 (March 1991): 16.

need to have their own savings in paper to benefit. Throughout the Kingdom, individuals renegotiated their debts by borrowing paper currency at 2 per cent to reimburse their original creditors whom they were likely paying 4 or 5 per cent. There was thus a massive shift of wealth as a result of the collapsed Law scheme that favored debtors over creditors. Not only did interest rates fall to 2 per cent, many creditors were left holding nearly worthless paper in the end.[21]

The lenders to privileged corps were not immune to these monetary shocks. The Estates of Burgundy, for example, renegotiated their loans down to 2 per cent, and as with all private transactions after January 1720, they had no choice but to service their debts with the soon to be worthless paper money. The estates' participation in this default drew some opposition from creditors who refused to accept reimbursement in paper money. The most widely publicized case was that of Elizabeth Rouillé. Her late husband, Sr. Bouchu, marquis de Saneergarre and counselor of state, had lent 11,000 livres to the estates in 1711 at 5.56 per cent, a rate that was later reduced to 3 per cent in 1719.[22] The loan was originally backed by revenues from the *octrois de la Saône* anticipated to accrue beginning in 1737. Rouillé was thus not expecting to be reimbursed her principal until at the earliest 1737. When the estates tried to reimburse her loan in 1720 with paper money, the only legal tender at the time, she refused to accept the payment and sued the estates.

The estates had the support of the crown in this matter, for it was in accordance with the various *arrêts* and edicts announced in the first months of 1720 that they acted to reimburse their creditors with paper money. The estates also asserted that they could reimburse their loans whenever they chose and that they were under no obligation to wait until the mortgaged revenues came due. Their response to Rouillé's complaint stated: 'Nowhere in the *rente* contract is there stipulation that reimbursement cannot come before 1737; ...furthermore *rentes* are by their general nature amortized at the pleasure of the debtor.'[23] In the end, Elisabeth Rouillé and the few other holdouts who had joined her in opposition had to accept reimbursement in paper. Judging by this case, the Estates of Burgundy

---

[21] Hoffman, Postel-Vinay, and Rosenthal, *Priceless Markets*, pp. 78-85; Pierre Dardel, 'Influence du Système de Law sur la situation économique de la Haute Normandie,' *Actes du 81e Congrès National des Sociétés Savantes, Section d'Histoire Moderne et Contemporaine*, (Rouen-Caen, 1956): 121-140. Some individuals were well placed to broker paper currency. The Norman *traitant* Jean Oursin, for example, entered into several hundred contractual arrangements as a lender throughout the years 1719 and 1720, providing paper currency, in most cases at interest rates of 2 or 2.5 per cent, to those seeking to renegotiate their debts. A.N., Min. Cent., XX, 590, 27 June 1746, *inventaire après decés*.
[22] Documents which contain testimonies and decisions in this case are found in A.N., H¹ 104, 1er Dossier; and A.D.C.O., C 4563.
[23] A.N., H¹ 104, 1er Dossier, *Mémoire pour les élus généraux des États de Bourgogne, défendeurs et demandeurs contre dame Elisabeth Rouillé*.

profited from the Law affair to redistribute as much of their debt as possible with the cheaper paper money coursing through the economy.[24]

As the largest single debtor, the crown naturally came out of the Law affair with a much reduced debt load.[25] As part of the Law scheme liquidation, the crown in early 1721 converted all of the paper money brought forth, whose face value totaled almost 2.5 billion livres, into perpetual *rentes* totaling 1.5 billion livres in principal and paying interest of 2 to 2.5 per cent. Individuals from all corners of the Kingdom presented their currency for conversion. Indeed, it is easy to understand how the paper could have spread so far given the wave of renegotiations that swept across the Kingdom in 1720.[26] Creditors like Elisabeth Rouillé, who as a *rentier* of the Burgundian estates once held one of the safest investments in the Kingdom, found themselves presenting otherwise worthless paper currency for conversion at a discount into royal *rentes* now paying less than half the interest paid before the initial rate reductions in 1713 and 1714.

The financial relief that the crown experienced after 1720 came at some cost to both the credit market as a whole and to the crown in particular. The financial system took years to recover, given the universal, across-the-board, losses experienced by creditors.[27] Confidence in monetary stability returned only slowly and hesitantly, hindering the recovery of the credit market.[28] Political confidence in the crown suffered as well. Doubts lingered throughout the eighteenth century whether the absolute monarch could well be trusted ever again to establish a centralized institution of public credit. Monetary manipulation thereafter came to be associated with despotism.[29]

Such was the legacy of Louis XIV's wars and his strategies for financing those wars. Reform of such costly structures as venality, which had actually been strengthened as part of Louis' financial strategies, was beyond the reach of his cash-strapped successor. It thus took a massive default that involved indiscriminate redistribution in the private market as well as among royal creditors to lighten the crown's debt load.

---

[24] Hoffman, Postel-Vinay, and Rosenthal, (*Priceless Markets*, pp. 69-95) argue that both debtors and creditors tried to anticipate royal monetary moves and negotiate or terminate their loan contracts accordingly.

[25] Hoffman, Postel-Vinay, and Rosenthal (Ibid., p. 87) estimate the monarchy's default in real terms as it stood in 1721 at 1.5 billion livres.

[26] 511,009 individuals presented paper currency for conversion, of whom 107,936 were Parisian and the remainder were provincials. See Marion, *Histoire*, 1:109; Dardel, 'Influence du Système,' pp. 121-140.

[27] Personal links between borrowers and lenders did not provide any significant guarantees against renegotiation or repayment during those crucial months of 1720. Widows in particular came out of the collapsed affair quite poorly since as a group they were heavy net lenders. Hoffman, Postel-Vinay, and Rosenthal, 'Redistribution,' p. 278.

[28] 'Confidence had so totally fallen following these events that neither the King nor individuals had any creditworthiness (*crédit*) left' (Marion, *Histoire*, 1:102).

[29] Kaiser, p. 26; Hoffman, Postel-Vinay, and Rosenthal, 'Redistribution,' p. 279.

Warfare and Absolutism

In many ways, Louis XIV's personal reign ended in 1715 much as it had begun in 1661. Both his decision to govern personally and his death fifty-five years later followed upon the heels of long periods of warfare during which the crown relied heavily on extraordinary financial measures that targeted especially members of the elite. Both episodes then opened the door to financial defaults and Chambers of Justice. Attempts at financial reform also followed in each case. Both Colbert in the 1660s and the duc de Noailles in the years following 1715 enjoyed only limited success at reform; neither was able to change any fundamental structures. One might reasonably ask if any lasting political changes occurred during Louis XIV's reign, or if, on the other hand, political developments merely followed a war-driven cycle in which periods of relative financial ease along with reform and accommodation alternated with periods of war, increased financial demands and political division.

Important changes did indeed take place under Louis XIV, changes which affected in meaningful ways the relationship between the crown and the Kingdom's elite and which lasted well beyond his reign. The model of political change that has informed this study places the monarchy on a 'learning curve' in which kings and their ministers acted to avoid the political costs that their predecessors faced as they attempted to finance war. In other words, historical constraints acted along with structural constraints to shape the monarch's options for financing war. Louis XIV's strategy, by which he averted the widespread political conflict of the first half of the century, consisted of securing the individual and corporative hold over privilege and then using the element of privilege as leverage in negotiations. The patrimonial possession of offices, for instance, strengthened during Louis' personal reign as the negotiations over renewal of the *droit annuel*, necessary for extending the heritability of offices, became transparent and predictable, easing the uncertainty that had plagued these negotiations earlier. In contrast, during the ministries of Richelieu and Mazarin, the crown had threatened to revoke the heritability of offices in an attempt to gain political and financial concessions from venal office holders, while during Colbert's ministry, uncertainty abounded regarding the property rights of office holding. Likewise, Louis abandoned any serious attempt to undermine estates. Provincial privileges, namely the prerogative to assert local financial autonomy through estates, were strengthened, at least in those provinces where estates existed upon Louis' assumption of personal rule. As long as they remained obedient, privileged corps could be useful to the crown, as Louis found, and he thus secured their underlying privileges and property rights and compelled them into intermediating finances for his war effort.

Louis targeted privileged corps by creating or threatening to create redundant offices or privileges. To preserve and protect their privileged positions, and in the case of venal officer corps to protect the investments of their members, corps paid the crown to keep such new creations off the market. With the heritability of offices firmly established, venal officer corps could mortgage their members' offices and incomes (*gages*) to finance those extraordinary payments. The crown then increased their *gages* which they used to pay interest on their debts. Likewise, provincial estates were able to assert a strengthened hold over crown-granted revenues in order to provide the crown with extraordinary funds. A fundamental change thus took place in how the crown targeted the elite for financial support. Whereas Richelieu and Mazarin took negotiating stances that threatened to undermine universally the very claims to privileged status enjoyed by members of the elite, Louis XIV shored up the private hold over both offices and privileges and then targeted specific groups to intermediate finances.

Louis' strategies, however, were not without consequence. As our model of political change suggests, his approach to war finance, while successfully avoiding the costs borne by the crown in the 1630s and 1640s, created new sets of costs that the monarchy would have to confront in the eighteenth century.

Indeed, those costs extended beyond the *financially* enumerable costs which I have detailed above. *Political* costs, too, were borne, namely in the form of the relative shift in political power toward corps that was necessary in order to create out of them effective intermediaries. Because of these political costs, this approach to funding war remained limited in both scope and time. Existing provincial estates, especially those in larger provinces such as Languedoc and Brittany, not to mention Burgundy, proved indispensable for their ability to borrow large sums for the crown. Yet despite their effectiveness in providing financial support, the crown limited the revenues alienated to a few in each province, and it made no moves to create other similar bodies capable of intermediating finances to such an extent.[30]

Louis XIV did, on the other hand, create waves of new offices, tapping the personal wealth of elites and aspiring elites and engaging venal officer corps to borrow for his war effort. Yet even this expansion was largely limited to Louis' personal reign, slowing to a halt after 1715 and reversing itself under the Regency.[31] Never again would venality provide such important levels of war finance. Meanwhile, it is true that existing provincial estates continued to provide extraordinary payments to the crown throughout the remainder of the Old Regime, but any growth in their borrowing to fund such payments was outweighed in relative terms by the crown's turn to the direct solicitation of loans as its primary means of raising extraordinary finances. Louis XIV's successors turned their backs in large part on financial intermediation by privileged corps, unwilling to accept the political costs of devolved authority.

The unwillingness of Louis XIV's successors to embrace his financial strategy along with its political implications highlights what is probably the most fundamental difference distinguishing French finances from those of her maritime rivals that successfully ushered in financial revolutions. Aside from this brief and

---

[30] Beik, *Absolutism*, pp. 245-78; Collins, *Classes*, pp. 218-26.

[31] The capital value of all venal offices was not significantly greater in 1789 than it was in 1722 following a significant rollback. Nominal values were approximately 750 billion *livres* in 1722 and 850 billion in 1789. Doyle, *Venality*, pp. 55-60.

exceptional period during the latter half of Louis XIV's reign, the French crown from the seventeenth century through the end of the Old Regime demonstrated a virtually unyielding refusal either to share financial authority with or to disclose financial matters to elites and aristocrats clamoring for power and influence.[32] The financial intermediation undertaken for the French crown by privileged corps thus never amounted to the sovereign command over revenues and debt management enjoyed by the Dutch States as early as the sixteenth century and by the post-1688 English Parliament. Whereas the authority of those political bodies developed largely without reference to royal authority, in France the prerogatives of provincial estates and venal officer corps alike derived from the crown.[33] Indeed, the very privileges by which these French corps existed and which made possible their financial intermediation were conferred by and thus dependent upon the crown. Louis XIV did not merely choose a financial strategy that made use of existing arrangements. As King, he was the source of much of the power and authority that he ceded to privileged corps in return for their financial intermediation.

As we have seen, however, corps were not malleable institutions that could be made to respond with equal effectiveness to the crown's demands. Much more than conduits for patron-client ties or channels for the crown to extend its authority during this period of highly personalized rule, corps also shaped and channeled local expressions of political and financial interest. The shift in power toward privileged corps gravitated especially toward provincial estates because, as we saw with the Estates of Burgundy, such a shift resonated with a coalition of elites whose interests were well served by the estates' strengthening. No other institution, whether in *pays d'États* or *pays d'élection*, provided an arena for such extensive coalition building, and estates were thus in the best position to assert the political will necessary for effective financial intermediation. Yes, the crown itself provided much of the impetus for the shift in power that made possible effective financial intermediation, but local powers, arrayed in and around corps, negotiated their

---

[32] Louis XVI rejected all attempts by the Assembly of Notables in 1787 to establish a financial oversight committee. Proposals put forth that same year for the creation of provincial assemblies met with less intransigence on the King's behalf. These assemblies, though, were envisioned as having very limited powers restricted to the administrative realms of tax partitioning and collecting. See Jean Egret, *The French Pre-Revolution, 1787-1788*, Wesley D. Camp, tr., (Chicago: University of Chicago Press, 1977), pp. 31-35 and 64-71.

[33] While the Spanish crown was initially instrumental in creating a funded debt under the States of Holland, the long history of political decentralization in the Low Countries enhanced the degree of local financial autonomy early on. Once the 'novel expedients' of 1542 created a funded debt for the first time, the royal government thereafter played a diminishing role in managing that debt and in authorizing future loans. Thus, Charles V inadvertently helped create the conditions for permanently placing the provinces of the Low Countries in a financially advantageous position vis-à-vis the Spanish crown. See Tracy, *Financial Revolution*, pp. 34-35 and p. 97.

responses and shaped outcomes along lines largely determined by the given institutional parameters at the foundation of this corporate society.

Warfare, thus, did not produce political change reminiscent of 'modern' state building. Modern appearances, such as representative bodies assuming responsibility for debt management and borrowing from anonymous voluntary markets, rested upon a foundation of privilege that was only strengthened by the turn to intermediation by privileged corps. And contrary to the models of political change put forth by Weberian historical sociologists, the costs of warfare, which reached particular heights during this latter half of Louis XIV's reign, did not drive a wedge between the crown and the Kingdom's elite. Indeed, Louis XIV's strategies to meet the financial costs of warfare in many ways brought the two camps closer together within their underlying interdependent political and economic relationships. Louis' approach to funding his wars entrenched privilege and local particularism and in some cases enhanced the power and prestige of elite groups. To be sure, the privileged elite throughout the Kingdom bore many of the costs of warfare; the crown's extraordinary measures imposed upon notables both material taxes and enhanced financial risks. Overall, the costs of extended warfare in all likelihood weighed more heavily upon the Kingdom's elite than any benefits, be they political or financial, and elite support in many cases was compelled by an astute crown capable of using privilege as an effective bargaining chip. Nonetheless, royal ideology and a sense of mutual interest drove much of the elite support for the crown's war effort, and the crown notably resisted any systematic long-term undermining of elite property or privilege. All indications from the latter half of Louis XIV's reign suggest that royal power and elite power were interdependent and that state power was necessarily based on that interdependence.

France on the European Stage

The French monarchy was both unwilling and unable to usher in a full-fledged financial revolution. Yet such was not the only option to a sovereign engaged in war in the seventeenth century. Too often, historians measure the success or the propriety of (backward) French finances against the Whiggish yardstick of the forward looking English system.[34] Yet a broader look at Europe in this period of warfare uncovers other sets of options available to rulers seeking the financial means to take to the battlefield.

In Brandenburg-Prussia, political compromises in the latter half of the seventeenth century established a fiscally effective balance of power, where authority to tax evolved to the central government while nobles received in turn enhanced authority over their landed estates.[35] Alternately, the Duchy of Savoy under the leadership of the reformist Duke Victor Amadeus II (1675-1730)

---

[34] See, for example, North and Weingast.
[35] See Chapter One.

presented a model of efficient administration. A land survey, begun in April 1697 accompanied attempts to equalize the burden of direct taxation from community to community and to enhance revenues overall, and intendants on the French model were sent throughout the provinces between 1696 and 1701 to bring the more marginal under central control. These reforms did not fully come to fruition until later in the eighteenth century, and we also must not underestimate the importance of foreign subsidies in supporting the Savoyard war effort. Still, sound management paid off for the Dukes. Despite temporary loss of territories to French invasions – Savoy, Nice, and portions of Piedmont were all occupied by French troops during both conflicts, the Savoyard state came out of the War of the Spanish Succession with a total debt load measuring less than three times annual ordinary revenue, and through careful management, interest on the consolidated debt dropped to between 4 and 5 per cent by 1713.[36]

We are left, therefore, with three sets of responses, which we could term the English 'financial-revolution' model, the Prussian 'compromise model', and the Savoyard 'administrative model', though to be sure, there are elements within these models that overlap. Still, they are sufficiently distinct so that each in their own way proved not only instrumental in helping to meet the costs of war, but also pivotal in setting the political courses for these states in the eighteenth century.

Louis' strategy relied on a watered-down combination of administrative effectiveness and political compromise that ended with elements of the financial revolution emerging. Land surveys on a Kingdom-wide level were out of the reach of the crown, and the newly created *dixième* tax on income, intended to lessen the relative direct-tax burden on the peasantry, depended on declarations of wealth from the taxed subjects themselves. Still, the newly created capitation and *dixième* taxes together altered the fundamental relationship between King and subjects, bringing taxpayers under the more direct authority of royal administration.[37] Intendants saw their authority expand on a number of fronts, managing the fiscal system and conveying information to the office of the Controller General, though they certainly fell short of displacing local interests from involvement in the handling of revenues. With the distances involved and the strength of provincial particularism, Louis XIV's administration nonetheless achieved some remarkable successes in charting and then enforcing a financial course.

Compromise, though, was necessary. Without ushering in the explicit tradeoffs that Prussian electors/kings did, and without demarcating such sharp distinctions between noble spheres of authority and royal prerogative, Louis oversaw an informal compromise that secured elites' underlying property and privileges and that expected in turn their obedience and their involvement, albeit at some sacrifice to them, in financial matters. The shape of this compromise, informal as it was,

---

[36] Geoffrey Symcox, *Victor Amadeus II*, (London: Thames and Hudson, 1983), p. 201; Carlo Capra, 'The Italian States in the Early Modern Period,' in Bonney, ed., *Rise*, pp. 428-434; Storrs, pp. 74-121.

[37] Kwass, *Privilege*.

differed from province to province depending upon a region's social structures and privileged status; it was, nonetheless, an integral feature of wartime rule with which Louis simply could not have dispensed.

Across Europe, in polities as distinct in their governing institutions and social structures as England, Prussia and the Duchy of Savoy, 'states' faced wartime financial challenges of unprecedented degree in this period from 1688 to 1715, and the models of war finance that developed in response were pivotal in setting the political courses for the eighteenth century. In each case, political change ensued from a confluence of underlying social structures, historically conditioned crown/elite relationships, and the short-term necessity common to all to meet the growing costs of war.

As France embarked upon her period of war in 1688, Louis XIV had the advantage of hindsight and avoided the costly politics of conflict that sowed division between the ruling elite and the crown. As a result, he succeeded in meeting international challenges without descending down the path toward political chaos and institutional collapse. His successors, on the other hand, were left facing the financial and political burdens of his strategies. They thus held a different perspective, and they reversed the political course charted by the Sun King. Intent on financing the wars of the eighteenth century without expanding on Louis XIV's political balance, his successors in the end paid the ultimate political price with the demise of the absolutist state.

Appendix 1

Merchants and the Rouennais Town Council

Though we know their identities from the records of municipal deliberations, there is little direct information about individual *échevins* from notarial documents or family papers that would allow a detailed analysis of their fortunes and business interests.[1] Any conclusions are therefore of a provisional nature. The records of the municipal deliberations offer professional background information on a few of the *échevins*, such as Baudouin de Talvenne, elected *échevin* in 1695 as a former *trésorier de France* in the *bureau des finances* in Rouen. A few *échevins* were designated as seigneurs, such as Pierre Hébert, seigneur de la Plenière, elected to serve in 1710. Commercial interests, though, were the most common among the elected municipal officers.[2] In his very brief report *'pour l'instruction du duc de Bourgogne'* in 1698, the intendant of Rouen, Yves-Marie de la Bourdonnaye, mentioned the Asselin family, dominant on the town council throughout the seventeenth century, as one of the region's most notable families of *'négociants'* worth a fortune of 700,000 to 800,000 livres.[3] He also makes indirect reference to Jean Etienne le Couteulx, *échevin* in 1683, 1689 and 1701, who was one of the region's major bankers and whose family rose to kingdom-wide prominence within eighteenth century banking circles.

In what stands as a veritable 'who's who' in Rouennais society, Claude Pellot, First President of the Parlement of Rouen, offers a useful description of the town council and its members from 1670 to 1683. Though his observations were limited to the decade prior to the period under study here, a few of the individuals mentioned as *échevins* by Pellot were still active on the town council during the following decades, such as le Couteulx, Nicolas Turgis and Nicolas Marye. Of the five *échevins* whose professional life Pellot described, three were indicated as being involved in commerce: the above mentioned le Couteulx along with the *'négociant'* Lemarchand and the merchant Fermanel d'Espiney. One *échevin*, de Mézenguemare-Brice, held the judicial office of *conseiller* in the Parlement of

---

[1] A.M.R., A28-30.
[2] Bardet, *Rouen*, p. 100.
[3] Hurpin, p. 111.

Rouen, and one, a certain de Gauville, was listed as living from his investments (*'vit de ses rentes'*).[4]

In this guide to Rouennais society, Pellot also lists those who, in his opinion, were the 'principal bourgeois and merchants.' Several of those listed served as *échevins* during the following decades, such as M. Tabouret, elected *échevin* in 1686 and described by Pellot as 'bourgeois ... no longer involved in commerce.' Two merchants who conducted commerce with Spain were involved in municipal governance, Louis Gueroult and le Tellier. Pellot also listed here the above-mentioned le Couteulx, Nicolas Turgis and Nicolas Marye, and finally Le Boullenger, cloth merchant, elected *échevin* in 1707.[5]

The town council consisted of six *échevins* chosen every three years by an electoral council of forty notables. A list of the triennial town councils from 1680 through the triennality beginning in 1716 follows. I have added codes for the occupations of the *échevins*. Occupation codes 1, 2, and 3 indicate involvement in commerce at some point in their careers. A full explanation of the codes follows the list.

---

[4] Claude Pellot, *Notes du Premier Président Pellot sur la Normandie, 1670-1683*, ed. G.A. Prevost (Paris: Auguste Picard, 1915), pp. 124-128.

[5] Ibid., pp. 128-132. Besides listing his banking activities, Pellot also notes that le Couteulx was a cloth merchant.

Appendix 1

	Family name	First name(s)	Occupation code
1680	Du Four		1,4
	Le Tellier		1
	Crevel		0
	Turgis		1
	Asselin	Jacques	1,3
	De La Motte		0
1683	Bultran		0
	Boutren de Corneville		0
	Euon		1
	Godefroy	Pierre	1
	Le Couteulx	Jean Etienne	1
	Desdames		0
1686	Asselin	Jacques	1,3
	Tabouret		1
	Turgis	Jean	1
	Bouthan		0
	Baudoin de Tallevanne		5
	Benet		0
1689	Le Couteulx	Jean Etienne	1
	Le Bac de Trouville		0
	Baudoin de Tallevanne		5
	Godefroy		0
	Dehors		0
	Locquet		0
1692	Boutren de Corneville	Claude	0
	Marie	Nicolas	1,2,3
	Bigot de Heaume	Jacques	0
	Gueroult	Andre	1
	Le Canu	Eustache	0
	Le Carpentier	Louis	0
1695	Baudouin de Talvenne		5
	Godefroy	Pierre	0
	du Resnel du Belley		0
	Marie	Nicolas	1,2,3
	Asselin	Nicolas	1
	Le Planquois	Guillaume	0
1698	de Trouville le Ber		0
	Dehors		0
	de La Motte Bomichel		0
	Le Planquoy		0

	Family name	First name(s)	Occupation code
1698	Le Baillif	Philipes	1,2
	Marlot	Nicolas	0
1701	Le Couteulx	Etienne	1
	Le Carpentier	Louis	0
	Bigot	Jean	0
	Roland	Jacques	0
	Planterose	Pierre	1,2,3
	de Rouves	Denis	0
1704	Godefroy	Pierre	0
	Marye	Nicolas	1,2,3
	de Moy de Verger	Michel	0
	Hellot	Pierre	0
	Judde	Nicolas	1,3
	de Vaudichon	Louis	0
1707	Bigot de Heaume		0
	Le Bailiff	Philippes	1,2
	Le Boullanger	Robert	1,2,3
	Bocquet	Robert	0
	Cecile	Francois	1,2
	Le Bailiff	David	1,2,3
1710	Marye	Nicolas Etienne	1,2,3
	de Moy du Verger		0
	Hebert de la Pleiniere	Pierre	6
	Cabeuil	Nicolas	1,2
	Deschamps	Charles	0
	Judde	Louis	1,2
1713	Le Baillif	Philippes	1,2
	Bocquet	Robert	0
	Le Couteulx	Jean Etienne	1
	Denis	Gilles	7
	Planterose	Francois	1,2
	Taillet	Pierre	0
1716	Rolland		0
	de Verger		0
	Planterose	Thomas	1
	Le Marquis	Pierre	0
	Cecile	Meslon	1,2
	Pommeraye	Nicolas	0

Occupation codes:
0 = unknown
1 = merchant; involved in commerce
2 = member of post-1710 municipal financial company
3 = served at least once as *prieur des consuls* (presiding officer of Chamber of Commerce or the *juridiction consulaire*)
4 = *secrétaire du roi*
5 = former *trésorier de France*
6 = seigneur
7 = lawyer (*avocat*)

Appendix 2

Privilege and Louis XIV's 'Divide-and-Rule' Strategies

The growth in the number and value of extraordinary financial treaties (*traités extraordinaires*) in the decades after 1689 presented expanding opportunities for individuals to enter into financial activities with the expectation of making significant returns. In this favorable context for get-rich-quick schemes, the office of the Controller General received hundreds, and in peak years thousands, of proposals from *traitants* or aspiring *traitants* (technically *'donneurs d'avis'*, or givers of advice) hoping to involve themselves in extraordinary affairs.[1]

Individuals from practically all social stations communicated their ideas to the *Contrôle Général*. Some examples include the 1691 proposal by the Dijonnais writer de Launay to tax the income of local tax farm agents who, in his opinion, took their employ simply to benefit from tax and troop lodging exemptions,[2] or the 1692 letter from the comte de St. Maiole offering to share his idea for the creation of a number of offices deemed absolutely necessary and not the least bit harmful to the interests of anyone.[3] Women, too, offered their ideas.[4] Madame de Beuvron of Rouen sent a proposal in 1703 to erect into venal offices the positions of guild masters.[5]

The motivations driving the authors of these schemes varied somewhat, but the dominant impulse was clearly financial gain. Most hoped that if the King accepted their idea they would be chosen to invest in and profit from the affairs. The unnamed author of a proposal to sell licenses to cabaret owners and inn keepers in Burgundy closed his letter by stating 'If the proposal is agreeable to Monseigneur (the *Contrôleur Général*), there are financially solvent individuals who will offer a

---

[1] A.N., G^7 694 - G^7 726. Proposals from this period fill 33 boxes in the *Archives Nationales* and number in the thousands, making any quantitative study of them a major undertaking. Françoise Bayard (*Monde*, pp. 80-83), however, has done just that for the slightly more manageable period 1599-1653 from which she gathered 526 proposals that laid out explicit programs for raising money.
[2] A.N., G^7 694.
[3] A.N., G^7 695.
[4] Bayard, *Monde*, p. 93.
[5] A.N., G^7 698.

considerable sum for the king's profit.'[6] Others were looking more for social advancement than investment opportunities. In a relatively modest proposal, a certain Le Breton suggested the creation of one single office of president in the *présidial* of Auxerre which he himself offered to buy for 9,000 livres, and in an appeal to the sympathy of the Controller General, M. Vernon, curé of Notre Dame de Grâce près la Seine, did not request any financial remuneration for his proposal to create offices but merely asked to be granted a benefice in a town, for he was 'dying in the country.'[7]

While profit and social advancement were clearly the primary motivations, one also gets a sense from reading these proposals that envy or resentment toward specific groups or corps played a part as well. This is particularly true in the schemes that begin with denunciations and then end with proposals to tax the offending groups or to create new offices. The above mentioned de Launay of Dijon proposed his levy on the agents of tax farms to correct the 'fraud committed by several individuals who are practically alone in enjoying all sorts of exemptions and privileges.' And Morin, a Rouennais writer, proposed in 1693 to create a new chamber of appeals in the Parlement of Rouen for those who lost their cases in other chambers. Morin did not think too highly of the existing *parlementaires* whom he deemed incapable of rendering justice in all its integrity and who, despite requirements of nobility, were all 'sons of merchants.' The First President of the parlement, whose opinion he apparently respected, was right in his assessment of the court as a parlement of cousins, Morin exclaimed.[8]

Whatever the motivation, whether it be profit seeking, social advancement, resentment or a combination of all three, this flood of proposals for extraordinary affairs signifies a conjuncture between Louis' increased demand for money, especially after 1689, and his increased willingness to use privilege as a financial tool. Privilege and the unequal access to privileges enjoyed by different groups in old-regime France made possible this proliferation of proposals and, more fundamentally, the crown's reliance upon extraordinary affairs during these decades. The authors of these proposals understood the possibilities presented by the crown's financial needs, and they targeted privileges deemed undeserved, privileges considered undervalued from which the crown could reap more money, or privileges which would be useful and for which there would be a demand. By pointing out such areas where change in the privileged status quo could be profitable, the individual authors of these proposals were only all too happy to volunteer their neighbors, their townsmen, or anyone other than themselves as

---

[6] A.N., G^7 694. Bayard (*Monde*, pp. 89-93) points out that as a general rule, the authors of proposals accepted by the crown received only a small portion of what they had expected, whether they were hoping for a one-time payment or a percentage of the returns. It is possible that her conclusions may not hold as well for the period 1689-1715, however, when the returns for *traitants* were fairly well fixed at 1/6 plus ten per cent of the total value.
[7] A.N., G^7 694.
[8] A.N., G^7 695.

objects of potential *traités*. In a society that valued the status quo and shunned 'nouveautés', the crown could forge ample alliances with people willing to alter the status quo of others. Juridical inequality and the presence of privileged corps throughout society opened the door for Louis XIV to a strategy that included a strong dose of 'divide-and-rule' during his time of financial need.

Appendix 3

Data Sources for Lending Clienteles

Data in the first series in Chapter Six come from records compiled by the Estates of Burgundy. The estates kept very detailed records of their loans in registers drawn up to track each *rente* issued.[1] Scribes listed in these registers the names of lenders along with, in most cases, their occupations, residences and titles. They also listed the amounts borrowed and the interest payments due annually. If holders of these *rentes* sold them on the secondary market before the estates reimbursed their principal, the new purchasers were indicated. And for most contracts, the date of reimbursement was later marked in the margin beside the original information.

Several sources provided data for the second series. The *bureau des finances* in Rouen gathered copies of *quittances des finances* for all offices in the *généralité* of Rouen and compiled them in registers.[2] These were the receipts drawn up each time either an individual office holder or an officer corps purchased a new office or acquired an *augmentation de gages*. If the purchaser borrowed any or all of the capital, the treasurers writing the *quittances* listed from whom the funds were borrowed. From these four registers, I have extracted evidence of borrowing by numerous officer corps, including the *bureau des finances* itself, various *élections* and bailiwicks of the *généralité*, the *cour des comptes aides et finances*, along with various corps of administrative officers such as the community of 48 salt porters of Rouen or the wood millers of the same town.[3]

In Burgundy, members of the chamber of accounts drew up a list in 1713 of all its creditors from whom the corps had borrowed collectively, indicating the original dates of the loans. The municipality of Dijon retained copies of the notarial acts by which it borrowed funds for the repurchase of offices and for other extraordinary purposes.[4] Also, registers compiled by the chamber of accounts which contain letters of provision and some *quittances des finances* for Burgundian

---

[1] A.D.C.O., C 4577-4584.
[2] A.D.S.M., C 1370-1373.
[3] Series P in the *Archives Nationales* contains scores of registers of *quittances des finances* for offices throughout the kingdom and would therefore provide much the same information on a wider scale. Indeed, a comprehensive history of the financial aspect of venal offices under Louis XIV could be written largely from this series. The registers of the *bureau des finances* in Rouen, however, offer the advantage of focus, since they detail the transactions of one specific *généralité*.
[4] A.D.C.O., B 6 bis; A.M.D., M 24 & 26-27.

offices include *quittances* that indicate the lenders to various bailiwicks of the province.[5]

Finally, for the third data series, information on lenders to individual office holders in Upper Normandy came from the same registers of *quittances* compiled by the *bureau des finances* in Rouen that provided data on lenders to venal officer corps.

There are two potential weaknesses in the second data series, on which much of my argument depends: the limited number of contracts on which it is based relative to the first data set and the greater proportion of contracts for which social indicators remain unknown. Most of these shortcomings stem from the Rouennais sources; data from Burgundy on the borrowing activity of the chamber of accounts and the municipality of Dijon are complete for the periods indicated, and they are much more inclusive of information on social indicators. Of the 52 contracts in this second series that I have tagged as problematic, only 14 come from Burgundian sources (comprising less than 1% of the Burgundian contracts in this series). Clearly, the Rouennais data is the most incomplete and poses the greatest potential difficulties. These shortcomings in my data are by no means fatal to my conclusions, however. Indeed, in the Corps/Lender Contacts section of Chapter Six where I separate the Rouennais from the Burgundian data in this series, my argument regarding institutional differences in borrowing practices holds up to scrutiny.

---

[5] A.D.C.O., B 53-61, *Enregistrements de la Chambre des Comptes*.

Bibliography

Archival Sources

Archives Nationales

AD IX 448-449, *Archives Imprimées*, financial matters.
AD XVI 9, *Archives Imprimées*, towns and provinces.
E 611^a, E 698^c, E 755^b, E 767^a, E 818^b, E 824^b-825^a, E 836^b, King's council, *arrêts*.
E 1810, 1819-1821, 1823, 1830, 1838, 1845, 1853, 1872, 1874, 1889, 1919, 1924, 1932, 1957, King's council, *arrêts*.
E 3644, Edicts and declarations, financial matters, 1715-1718.
E 3651, Council of the Regency, financial affairs, 1715-1718.
E 3707^1, King's council, edicts and debates concerning mortgage regulations.
G^7 543b, Correspondence of Secretaries of State.
G^7 694-726, Proposed traités.
G^7 1112-1113, Correspondence between *receveurs généraux* and *contrôleurs généraux*.
G^7 1138-1139, Correspondence and memoirs related to the *dixième*.
G^7 1323-1325, *Revenus casuels*; Correspondence and notes on the *rachat de l'annuel*.
G^7 1492-1494, *Traités*, correspondences, notes, tables.
G^7 1543, *Traités, trésoriers de l'extraordinaire de guerre, lettres de bourgeoisie*, etc.
G^7 1553, *Traités, subdélegués de M.M. les intendants*, mayors, lieutenant mayors.
G^7 1567/68, Regency – suppression of various offices.
G^7 1763, Chambers of Accounts of Aix, Blois, Dijon and Dole.
H^1 99, Estates of Burgundy.
H^1 104, Burgundy, divers affairs, 1723-1728.
H^1 105, Burgundy, intendancies.
H^{1*} 140^b, Burgundy, municipal *octrois*, 1696-1697.
H^1 1588/44, Documents on the *généralité* of Rouen, 1700-1712.
K 871, Legislation on regulation of mortgages.
K 886, Memoir by Mgr. le Duc de Noailles on the administration of finances.
V^1 183, Offices, letters of provision.
V^2 38, *Secrétaires du roi*, testimonies by peers on public morals.
Minutier Central, études XX, XCII, CV, and CXX

Bibliothèque Nationale de France

fond français:
Mss. Fr. 7012, 'Venalité des Charges,' anonymous memoir.
Mss. Fr. 11103, 11107, Tables of *traités*.
Mss. Fr. 18230-31, Offices.

Archives Départementales de la Côte d'Or

B 6, B 6bis, Chamber of Accounts, financial affairs.
B 53-61, Registers of the Chamber of Accounts.
C 327, Offices.
C 361 ter., *Dixième*.
C 2982-2983, Estates, Registers of privileges.
C 2998-3002, Registers of original decrees of the Estates.
C 3018-3019, Transcriptions of decrees of the Estates.
C 3330, Estates, *Cahiers de remonstraces*.
C 3353, Correspondence of the Estates.
C 3375-3391, Reports on administration by the corps of the élus.
C 3498-3499, Accounts of the Estates.
C 3503, Mayors of Burgundy.
C 3505, Municipal offices.
C 3524, Municipal *octrois*.
C 4562-4563, 4569, 4577-4584, Estates, *rentes*.
C 5366-5367, *Octrois*.
C 5808, *Dixième*.
4E2/1619, 4E2/1633, 4E2/1635, Notarial records.

Archives Municipales de Dijon

M 24, 26-27, Municipal loans.

Archives Départementales de la Seine Maritime

1B 212, 217, 222, 226-227, Secret registers of the parlement.
2B 139-153, Registers of the Chamber of Accounts.
C 222, Municipal *octrois*.
C 1071, Offices.
C 1370-1373, *Bureau des finances, quittances des finances*.
C 2297, Secret register of the *bureau des finances*.
C 2346, *Bureau des finances*, correspondences.
2E2/11, 2E2/24, Notarial records.

Archives Municipales de Rouen

A 28-30, Municipal deliberations.

Published Sources

Basnage, Henri. 'Traité des Hipotèques.' In *Les Oeuvres de Maitre H. Basnage*. 3rd edn. Rouen, 1709.
Boislisle, A.M. de, ed. *Correspondance des contrôleurs généraux des finances avec les intendants des provinces*, 3 vols. Paris: Imprimerie Nationale, 1874-97.
Clément, Pierre, ed. *Lettres, instructions, et mémoires de Colbert*, 7 vols. Paris: Imprimerie Impériale, 1861-1873.

Colbert, Jean Baptiste. 'Mémoires sur les finances de France pour server à l'histoire.' In *Lettres, instructions, et mémoires de Colbert*. Edited by Pierre Clément. Paris: Imprimerie Impériale, 1861-1873, 2: 17-68.
Davot, Gabriel. *Traité sur diverses matières en droit français*, 8 vols. Dijon, 1751-1765.
Depping, Georges Bernard, ed. *Correspondance administrative sous le règne de Louis XIV*, 4 vols. Paris: Imprimerie Nationale, 1850-1855.
Guyot, Pierre Jean Jacques Guillaume, ed. *Traité des droits, fonctions, franchises, exemptions, prérogatives et privilèges annexés en France à chaque état, soit civil, soit militaire, soit ecclésiastique*, 4 vols. Paris, 1786-87.
Hurpin, Gérard. *L'Intendance de Rouen en 1698*. Édition Critique du Mémoire 'Pour l'Instruction du Duc de Bourgogne.' Paris: Comité des Travaux Historiques et Scientifiques, 1984.
Isambert, François André. *Recueil général des anciennes lois françaises, depuis l'an 420 jusqu'à la Révolution de 1789*, 29 vols. Paris: Belin-Le-Prieur, 1821-1833.
Ligou, Daniel. *L'Intendance de Bourgogne à la fin du XVIIe siècle*. Édition Critique du Mémoire 'Pour l'Instruction du Duc de Bourgogne.' Paris: Comité des Travaux Historiques et Scientifiques, 1988.
Louis XIV. *Mémoires for the Instruction of the Dauphin*. Translated by Paul Sonnino. New York: The Free Press, 1970.
Pellot, Claude. *Notes du Premier Président Pellot sur la Normandie, 1670-1683*. Edited by G.A. Prevost. Paris: Auguste Picard, 1915.
Smedley-Weill, Anette, *Correspondance des intendants avec le contrôleur général des finances, 1677-1689*, 3 vols. Paris: Archives Nationales, 1991.

Secondary Works

d'Arbaumont, Jules. *Armorial de la Chambre des Comptes*. Dijon, 1881.
Anderson, Perry. *Lineages of the Absolutist State*. New York: Verso, 1974.
Arandel de Condé, Gérard d'. *Les Bourgeois de statut à Rouen, 1664-1790*. Rouen, 1971.
Arbassier, Charles. *L'Absolutisme en Bourgogne: L'Intendant Bouchu et son action financière*. Dijon: Thorey, 1919.
Aston, Trevor, ed. *Crisis in Europe, 1560-1660*. London: Routledge, 1965.
Bardet, Jean-Pierre. *Rouen aux XVIIe et XVIIIe siècles: les mutations d'un espace social*. Paris: S.E.D.E.S., 1983.
Bayard, Françoise. *Le Monde des financiers au XVIIe siècle*. Paris: Flammarion, 1988.
Beaune, Henri, and Arbaumont, Jules d'. *La Noblesse aux États de Bourgogne de 1350 à 1789*. 1864. Reprint. Geneva: Mégariotis Reprints, 1977.
Behrens, C.B.A. *Society, Government, and the Enlightenment*. London: Thames and Hudson, 1985.
Beik, William. *Absolutism and Society in Seventeenth-Century France: State Power and Provincial Aristocracy in Languedoc*. Cambridge: Cambridge University Press, 1985.
——, 'État et société en France au XVIIe siècle: la taille en Languedoc et la question de la redistribution sociale.' *Annales: E.S.C.* 39 (1984): 1270-1298.
——, 'A Social Interpretation of the Reign of Louis XIV.' In *L'État ou le Roi*. Edited by Neithard Bulst, Robert Descimon, and Alain Guerreau. Paris: Éditions de la Maison des sciences de l'homme, 1966, pp. 145-160.
——, *Urban Protest in Seventeenth-century France*. New York: Cambridge University Press, 1997.

Benedict, Philip. *Rouen During the Wars of Religion.* Cambridge: Cambridge University Press, 1981.
Bercé, Yves-Marie. *Croquants et nu-pieds: les soulèvements paysans en France du XVIe au XIXe siècle.* Paris: Gallimard, 1974.
Bernstein, Hilary J. 'The Benefit of the Ballot? Elections and Influence in Sixteenth-century Poitiers.' *French Historical Studies* 24 (2001): 621-652.
Bertucat, Charles. *Les Finances municipales de Dijon depuis la liquidation des dettes (1662) jusqu'en 1789.* Dijon: Nourry, 1910.
Bien, David. 'Manufacturing Nobles: The Chancelleries in France to 1789.' *Journal of Modern History* 61 (1989): 445-486.
——, 'Offices, Corps and a System of State Credit: The Uses of Privilege Under the Ancien Regime.' In *The French Revolution and the Creation of Modern Political Culture.* Edited by Keith M. Baker, 4 vols. Oxford: Pergamon Press, 1987, 1: 89-114.
——, 'Property in Office under the Ancien Régime: The Case of the stockbrokers.' In *Early Modern Conceptions of Property.* Edited by John Brewer and Susan Staves. New York: Routledge, 1996, pp. 481-494.
——, 'The *Secrétaires du Roi*: Absolutism, Corps and Privilege Under the Ancien Regime.' In *De l'Ancien Régime à la Révolution Française.* Edited by Albert Cremer. Göttingen: Vandenhoeck & Ruprecht, 1978, pp. 153-168.
Bonney, Margaret and Bonney, Richard. *Jean Roland Malet: premier historien des finances de la Monarchie Française.* Paris: Comité pour l'Histoire Économique et Financière de la France, 1993.
Bonney, Richard, ed. *Economic Systems and State Finance.* Oxford: Clarendon Press, 1995.
——, *The King's Debts: Finance and Politics in France, 1589-1661.* Oxford: Clarendon Press, 1981.
——, *Political Change in France Under Richelieu and Mazarin, 1624-1661.* Oxford: Oxford University Press, 1978.
——ed. *The Rise of the Fiscal State in Europe, c. 1200-1815.* Oxford: Oxford University Press, 1999.
——, '*Le Secret de leurs familles*: The Fiscal and Social Limits of Louis XIV's *Dixème*.' *French History* 7 (1993): 383-416.
——, 'The Struggle for Great Power Status and the End of the Old Fiscal Regime.' In *Economic Systems and State Finance.* Edited by Richard Bonney. Oxford: Clarendon Press, 1995, pp. 315-390.
Bosher, J.F. '"Chambres de Justice" in the French Monarchy.' In *French Government and Society, 1500-1850.* Edited by J.F. Bosher. London: Athlone Press, 1973, pp. 19-40.
Bossenga, Gail. 'City and State: An Urban Perspective on the Origins of the French Revolution.' In *The French Revolution and the Creation of Modern Political Culture.* Edited by Keith M. Baker, 4 vols. Oxford: Pergamon Press, 1987, 1: 115-140.
——, *The Politics of Privilege: Old Regime and Revolution in Lille.* Cambridge: Cambridge University Press, 1991.
Breen, Michael P. 'Legal Culture, Municipal Politics and Royal Absolutism in Seventeenth-century France: The *Avocats* of Dijon, 1595-1715.' Ph.D. diss., Brown University, 2000.
Brenner, Robert. 'The Agrarian Roots of European Capitalism.' In *The Brenner Debate.* Edited by T.H. Aston and C.H.E. Philpin. Cambridge: Cambridge University Press, 1985, pp. 213-327.
——, *Merchants and Revolution: Commercial Change, Political Conflict, and London's Overseas Traders, 1550-1653.* Princeton: Princeton University Press, 1993.

Brewer, John. *The Sinews of Power: War, Money and the English State, 1688-1783.* New York: Knopf, 1989.
Brewer, John and Staves, Susan, eds. *Early Modern Conceptions of Property.* New York: Routledge, 1996.
Briggs, Robin. *Early Modern France, 1560-1715.* Oxford: Oxford University Press, 1977.
Capra, Carlo. 'The Italian States in the Early Modern Period.' In *The Rise of the Fiscal State in Europe, c. 1200-1815.* Edited by Richard Bonney. Oxford: Oxford University Press, 1999, pp. 417-442.
Chaussinand-Nogaret, Guy. *Les Financiers de Languedoc au XVIIIe siècle.* Paris: S.E.V.P.E.N., 1970.
Collins, James B. *Classes, Estates and Order in Early Modern Brittany.* New York: Cambridge University Press, 1994.
———, 'Les Conflits des élites locales dans la France moderne: le cas Breton.' *Cahiers d'histoire* 45 (2000): 645-674.
———, *Fiscal Limits of Absolutism: Direct Taxation in Early Seventeenth-Century France.* Berkeley and Los Angeles: University of California Press, 1988.
———, *The State in Early Modern France.* New York: Cambridge University Press, 1995.
Dardel, Pierre. 'Influence du système de Law sur la situation économique de la Haute Normandie.' *Actes du 81e congrés national des sociétés savantes: Rouen-Caen, 1956, Section d'histoire moderne et contemporaine.* Paris: Bibliothèque National, 1957, pp. 121-140.
De Vries, Jan. *The Economy of Europe in an Age of Crisis, 1600-1750.* Cambridge: Cambridge University Press, 1976.
Dent, Julian. 'An Aspect of the Crisis of the Seventeenth-century: The Collapse of the Financial Administration of the French Monarchy (1653-61).' *The Economic History Review,* 2nd Series, 20 (1967): 241-256.
———, 'The Role of Clientèles in the Financial Elite of France Under Cardinal Mazarin.' In *French Government and Society, 1500-1850.* Edited by J.F. Bosher. London: Athlone Press, 1973, pp. 41-69.
Descimon, Robert. 'The Birth of the Nobility of the Robe: Dignity versus Privilege in the Parlement of Paris, 1500-1700.' In *Changing Identities in Early Modern France.* Edited by Michael Wolfe. Durham: Duke University Press, 1997, pp. 95-123.
Dessert, Daniel. *Argent, pouvoir et société au Grand Siècle.* Paris: Fayard, 1984.
Dewald, Jonathan. *The European Nobility, 1400-1800.* Cambridge: Cambridge University Press, 1996.
———, *The Formation of a Provincial Nobility: The Magistrates of the Parlement of Rouen, 1499-1610.* Princeton: Princeton University Press, 1980.
Dickson, P.G.M. *The Early Modern Financial Revolution in England: A Study in the Development of Public Credit, 1688-1756.* New York: Macmillan, 1967.
Downing, Brian. *The Military Revolution and Political Change.* Princeton: Princeton University Press, 1992.
Doyle, William. 'The Price of Offices in Pre-Revolutionary France.' *The Historical Journal* 27 (1984): 831-860.
———, *Venality: The Sale of Offices in Eighteenth-century France.* Oxford: Clarendon Press, 1996.
Dubost, François. 'Absolutisme et centralisation en Languedoc au XVIIe siècle, 1620-1690.' *Revue d'histoire moderne et contemporaine* 37 (1990): 369-397.
Duby, Georges, ed. *Histoire de la France rurale,* 4 vols. Paris: Seuil, 1975-1977.

Dumont, François. *Une Session des États de Bourgogne, la tenue de 1718.* Dijon: Imprimerie Bernigaud et Privat, 1935.
Dupâquier, Jacques, ed. *Histoire de la population Française,* 4 vols. Paris: Presses Universitaires de France, 1988.
Durand, René. 'Le Commerce en Bourgogne à la veille de la Révolution Française.' *Annales de Bourgogne* 2 (1930): 224-233.
Durand, Yves. *Les Fermiers Généraux au XVIIIe siècle.* Paris: Presses Universitaires de France, 1971.
Esmonin, Edmond. *La Taille en Normandie au temps de Colbert, 1661-1683.* Paris: Hachette, 1913.
Farr, James R. 'Consumers, Commerce and the Craftsmen of Dijon.' In *Cities and Social Change in Early Modern France.* Edited by Philip Benedict. London: Unwin Hyman, 1989, pp. 134-173.
——, *Hands of Honor: Artisans and Their World in Dijon, 1550-1650.* Ithaca: Cornell University Press, 1988.
Félix, Joel. 'Les Dettes de l'État à la mort de Louis XIV.' *Comité pour l'histoire économique et financière de la France: Études et Documents* 6 (1994): 606-08.
Foisil, Madeleine. *La Révolte des Nu-Pieds et les révoltes normandes de 1639.* Paris: Presses Universitaires de France, 1970.
Forbonnais, François. *Recherches et considérations sur les finances de France depuis l'année 1595 jusqu'à l'année 1721.* Liège: Cramer, 1758.
Ford, Franklin L. *Robe and Sword: The Regrouping of the French Aristocracy After Louis XIV.* Cambridge: Harvard University Press, 1953.
Giesey, Ralph. 'Rules of Inheritance and Strategies of Mobility in Pre-Revolutionary France.' *American Historical Review* 82 (1977): 271-289.
Gordon, Robert W. 'Paradoxical Property.' In *Early Modern Conceptions of Property.* Edited by John Brewer and Susan Staves. New York: Routledge, 1996, pp. 95-110.
Goubert, Pierre. *Beauvais et le Beauvaisis de 1600 à 1700,* 2 vols. Paris: E.H.E.S.S., 1960.
Guéry, Alain. 'Les Finances de la Monarchie Française sous l'Ancien Régime.' *Annales: E.S.C.* 33 (1978): 216-239.
——, 'Le roi dépenser: le don, la contrainte, et l'origine du système financier de la monarchie française d'Ancien Régime. *Annales: E.S.C.* 38 (1984): 1241-1269.
Hamon, Philippe. *'Messieurs des finances': Les grands officiers de finances dans la France de la Renaissance.* Paris: C.H.E.F.F., 1999.
Hamscher, Albert N. *The Conseil Privé and the Parlements in the Age of Louis XIV: A Study in French Absolutism.* Philadelphia: The American Philosophical Society, 1987.
——, *The Parlement of Paris after the Fronde, 1653-1673.* Pittsburgh: University of Pittsburgh Press, 1976.
t'Hart, Marjolein. 'Cities and Statemaking in the Dutch Republic, 1580-1680.' *Theory and Society* 18 (1989): 663-687.
——, 'The Emergence and Consolidation of the "Tax State": The Seventeenth Century.' In *Economic Systems and State Finance.* Edited by Richard Bonney. Oxford: Clarendon Press, 1995, pp. 281-293.
Hoffman, Philip T. and Norberg Kathryn, eds. *Fiscal Crises, Liberty and Representative Government, 1450-1789.* Stanford: Stanford University Press, 1994.
Hoffman, Philip T.; Postel-Vinay, Gilles; and Rosenthal, Jean-Laurent. *Priceless Markets: The Political Economy of Credit in Paris, 1660-1870.* Chicago: University of Chicago Press, 2000.

———, 'Private Credit Markets in Paris, 1690-1840.' *Journal of Economic History* 52 (1992): 293-306.
———, 'Redistribution and Long-Term Private Debt in Paris, 1660-1726.' *Journal of Economic History* 55 (1995): 256-284.
Holt, Mack. 'Culture populaire et culture politique au XVIIe siècle: l'émeute de Lanturelu à Dijon en février 1630.' *Histoire, Économie et Société* 16 (1997): 597-615.
Hurt, John J. *Louis XIV and the Parlements: The Assertion of Royal Authority.* Manchester: Manchester University Press, 2002.
———, 'Les Offices au Parlement de Bretagne sous le règne de Louis XIV: Aspect financiers.' *Revue d'histoire moderne et contemporaine* 23 (1976): 3-31.
———, 'The Parlement of Brittany and the Crown: 1665-1675.' *French Historical Studies* 4 (1966): 411-433.
Jouanna, Arlette. *Le Devoir de révolte.* Paris: Fayard, 1989.
Kaiser, Thomas. 'Money, Despotism, and Public Opinion in Early Eighteenth-Century France: John Law and the Debate on Royal Credit.' *Journal of Modern History.* 63 (1991):
Kettering, Sharon. 'Brokerage at the Court of Louis XIV.' *Historical Journal* 36 (1993): 69-87.
———, *Judicial Politics and Urban Revolt in Seventeenth-century France.* Princeton: Princeton University Press, 1978.
———, *Patrons, Brokers, and Clients in Seventeenth-Century France.* Oxford: Oxford University Press, 1986.
Kruger, Kersten. 'Public Finance and Modernisation: The Change from Domain State to Tax State in Hesse in the Sixteenth and Seventeenth Centuries, A Case Study.' In *Wealth and Taxation in Central Europe: The History and Sociology of Public Finance.* Edited by Peter-Christian Witt. New York: Berg, 1987, pp. 49-62.
Kwass, Michael. *Privilege and the Politics of Taxation in Eighteenth-century France: Liberté, Égalité, Fiscalité.* New York: Cambridge University Press, 2000.
Labrousse, C.-E. *Esquisse du mouvement des prix et des revenus en France au XVIIIe siècle,* 2 vols. Paris, 1933.
Lachiver, Marcel. *Les Années de misère: la famine au temps du Grand Roi.* Paris: Fayard, 1991.
Lachmann, Richard. *Capitalists in Spite of Themselves.* New York: Oxford University Press, 2000.
Laurent, Robert. *L'Octroi de Dijon au XIXe siècle.* Paris: S.E.V.P.E.N., 1960.
Lavisse, Ernest. *Histoire de France depuis les origines jusqu'à la Révolution,* 9 vols. Paris: Hachette, 1900-1911.
Le Roy Ladurie, Emmanuel. *The Peasants of Languedoc.* Translated by John Day. Chicago: University of Illinois Press, 1976.
Lefebvre, Pierre. 'Aspects de la "fidelité" en France au XVIIe siècle: le cas des agents des princes de Condé.' *Revue historique* 507 (1973): 59-106.
Ligou, Daniel. 'Les Élus Généraux de Bourgogne et les charges municipal de 1692 à 1789.' *Actes du 90e congrés national des sociétés savantes: Nice, 1965, Section d'histoire moderne et contemporaine.* Paris: Bibliothèque National, 1966, pp. 95-119.
Louis-Lucas, Paul. *Étude sur la vénalité des charges et fonctions publiques,* 2 vols. Paris: 1882.
Lüthy, Herbert. *La Banque Protestante en France de la Révocation de l'Édit de Nantes à la Révolution,* 2 vols. Paris: S.E.V.P.E.N., 1959.
Lynn, John A. *The Wars of Louis XIV, 1667-1714,* New York: Longman, 1999.

Major, J. Russell. *From Renaissance Monarchy to Absolute Monarchy: French Kings, Nobles, and Estates.* Baltimore: The Johns Hopkins University Press, 1994.

Marion, Marcel. *Histoire financière de la France depuis 1715,* 6 vols. Paris: Rousseau, 1927-1931.

Mathias, Peter, and O'Brien, Patrick. 'Taxation in England and France, 1715-1810: A Comparison of the Social and Economic Incidence of Taxes Collected for the Central Governments.' *Journal of European Economic History* 5 (1976): 601-650.

Michaud, Claude. *L'Église et l'argent sous l'Ancien Régime: les receveurs généraux du clergé de France aux XVIe-XVIIe siècles.* Paris: Fayard, 1991.

Moote, A. Lloyd. *The Revolt of the Judges: The Parlement of Paris and the Fronde, 1643-1652.* Princeton: Princeton University Press, 1971.

Mousnier, Roland. 'The Fronde.' In *Preconditions of Revolution in Early Modern Europe.* Edited by Robert Forster. Baltimore: The Johns Hopkins University Press, 1970, pp. 131-159.

———, *Fureurs paysannes: les paysans dans les révoltes du XVIIe siècle.* Paris: Clamann-Levy, 1967.

———, *La Monarchie absolue en Europe du Ve siècle à nos jours.* Paris: Presses Universitaires de France, 1982.

———, *La Plume, la faucille et le marteau.* Paris: Presses Universitaires de France, 1970.

———, 'Recherches sur les soulèvements populaires en France avant la Fronde.' *Revue d'histoire moderne et contemporaine* 5 (1958): 81-113.

———, *La Vénalité des offices sous Henry IV et Louis XIII.* Paris: Presses Universitaires de France, 1971.

Murphy, Antoin E. *John Law: Economic Theorist and Policy-Maker.* Oxford: Clarendon Press, 1997.

Nachison, Beth. 'Absentee Government and Provincial Governors in Early Modern France: The Princes of Condé and Burgundy, 1660-1720.' *French Historical Studies* 21 (1998): 265-297.

Nagle, Jean. *Le Droit de marc d'or des offices.* Geneva: Droz, 1992.

North, Douglass and Weingast, Barry. 'Constitutions and Commitment: The Evolution of Institutions Governing Public Choice in Seventeenth-century England.' *Journal of Economic History* 49 (1989): 792-821.

Oliver-Martin, François. *Organisation corporative de la France d'Ancien Régime.* Paris: Receuil Siry, 1938.

Ormrod, W.M.; Bonney, Margaret; and Bonney, Richard, eds. *Crises, Revolutions and Self-Sustained Growth.* Stamford, UK: Shaun Tyas, 1999.

Pagès, Georges. *La monarchie d'Ancien Régime en France (de Henri IV à Louis XIV).* Paris: Armand Colin, 1928.

Picard, Charles le. *Catalogue des maires et échevins de la ville de Rouen et des prieurs des consuls depuis leur institution jusqu'en 1790.* Louviers, 1895.

Porchnev, Boris. *Les soulèvements populaires en France de 1623 à 1648.* Paris: S.E.V.P.E.N., 1963.

Potter, Mark and Rosenthal, Jean-Laurent. 'The Burgundian Estates' Bond Market: Clienteles and Intermediaries, 1660-1790.' In *Des personnes aux institutions: réseaux et culture du crédit du XVIe siècle au XXe siècle en Europe.* Edited by Paul Servais. Louvain, Belgium: Bruylant-Academia, 1997, pp. 173-195.

———, 'The Development of Intermediation in the French Credit Markets: Evidence from the Estates of Burgundy.' *Journal of Economic History* 62 (2002): 1024-1049.

———, 'Politics and Public Finance in France: The Estates of Burgundy, 1660-1790.' *Journal of Interdisciplinary History* 27 (1997): 577-612.
Rabb, Theodore K. *The Struggle for Stability in Early Modern Europe*. New York: Oxford University Press, 1975.
Richard, Jean, ed. *Histoire de Bourgogne*. Toulouse: Privat, 1978.
Richet, Denis. *La France moderne: l'Esprit des institutions*. Paris: Flammarion, 1973.
Ricommard, Julien. 'L'Édit d'avril 1704 et l'éréction en titre d'office des subdélégués des intendants.' *Revue historique* 195 (1945): 24-35.
Robin, Pierre. *La Compagnie des secrétaires du roi*. Paris: Receuil Siry, 1933.
Root, Hilton. *The Fountain of Privilege: Political Foundations of Markets in Old Regime France and England*. Berkeley and Los Angeles: University of California Press, 1994.
———, *Peasants and Kings in Burgundy: Agrarian Foundations of French Absolutism*. Berkeley and Los Angeles: University of California Press, 1987.
Rosenthal, Jean-Laurent. 'Credit Markets and Economic Change in Southeastern France, 1630-1788.' *Explorations in Economic History* 30 (1993): 129-157.
Rothkrug, Lionel. *Opposition to Louis XIV: The Political and Social Origins of the French Enlightenment*. Princeton: Princeton University Press, 1965.
Roupnel, Gaston. *La Ville et la campagne au XVIIe siècle*. Paris: Armand Colin, 1955.
Saint-Germain, Jacqus. *Samuel Bernard, le banquier des rois*. Paris: Hachette, 1960.
Saint-Jacob, Pierre de. *Les Paysans de la Bourgogne du Nord au dernier siècle de l'Ancien Régime*. Paris: Société des Belles Lettres, 1960.
Salmon, J.H.M. 'Venality of Office and Popular Sedition in Seventeenth-Century France: A Review of a Controversy.' *Past and Present* 37 (1967): 21-43.
Schaeper, Thomas J. 'The Creation of the French Council of Commerce in 1700.' *European Studies Review* 9 (1979): 313-329.
Schnapper, Bernard, *Les Rentes au XVIe siècle: Histoire d'un instrument de crédit*. Paris: S.E.V.P.E.N., 1957.
Skocpol, Theda. *States and Revolutions*. Cambridge: Cambridge University Press, 1979.
Smedley-Weill, Anette. *Les Intendants de Louis XIV*. Paris: Fayard, 1995.
Smith, Jay M. *The Culture of Merit: Nobility, Royal Service, and the Making of Absolute Monarchy in France, 1600-1789*. Ann Arbor: The University of Michigan Press, 1996.
———, 'No More Language Games: Words, Beliefs, and the Political Culture of Early Modern France.' *American Historical Review* 102 (1997): 1413-1440.
Steensgaard, Niels. 'The Seventeenth-century Crisis.' In *The General Crisis of the Seventeenth Century*. Edited by Geoffrey Parker and Lesley M. Smith. London: Routledge, 1978, pp. 26-56.
Storrs, Christopher. *War, Diplomacy and the Rise of Savoy, 1690-1720*. Cambridge: Cambridge University Press, 1999.
Swann, Julian. *Provincial Power and Absolute Monarchy: The Estates General of Burgundy, 1661–1790*. Cambridge: Cambridge University Press, 2003.
———, 'War Finance in Burgundy in the Reign of Louis XIV, 1661-1715.' In *Crises, Revolutions, and Self-Sustained Growth*. Edited by W.M. Ormrod, Margaret Bonney, and Richard Bonney. Stamford, UK: Shaun Tyas, 1999, pp. 294-322.
Symcox, Geoffrey. *Victor Amadeus II*. London: Thames and Hudson, 1983.
Temple, Nora. 'The Control and Exploitation of French Towns During the Ancien Régime.' In *State and Society in Seventeenth-Century France*. Edited by Raymond Kierstead. New York: New Viewpoints, 1975, pp. 67-93.
Tilly, Charles. *Coercion, Capital and European States: AD 900-1992*. Cambridge, Mass: Basil Blackwell, 1990.

Touzery, Mireille. *L'Invention de l'impôt sur le revenu: La taille tarifée, 1715-1789*. Paris: Comité pour l'Histoire Économique et Financière de la France, 1994.

Tracy, James. *A Financial Revolution in the Habsburg Netherlands*. Berkeley and Los Angeles: University of California Press, 1985.

Vannier, Jean. *Essai sur le bureau des finances de la Généralité de Rouen, 1551-1790*. Rouen: Lestringant, 1927.

Velde, François and Weir, David. 'The Financial Market and Government Debt Policy in France, 1746-1793.' *Journal of Economic History* 52 (1992): 1-39.

Wallon, Henri. *La Chambre de commerce de la province de Normandie, 1703-1791*. Rouen: Imprimerie Cagniard, 1903.

Wolf, John. *Louis XIV*. New York: Norton, 1968.

Index

absolutism 3–4, 8, 15–22, 96–7, 158, 182, 189–92
  and political change 4, 15–20, 22–3, 27, 194
  revisionist theories of 15–16, 18–19, 52
Alexandre, Pierre 150
augmentations de gages 11–12, 14, 37–9, 41–3, 46–7, 74, 78–80, 103, 110–13, 117–18, 121–2, 138, 141–2, 144, 156, 165, 175, 183–5, 203

Bardet, Pierre 123
Beik, William 15–16, 98, 136–7, 140, 146, 155
Bien, David 11–13, 78
Boisguilbert, Pierre le Pesant de 45–6
Bouchu, Claude 86
Brandenburg–Prussia, *see* Prussia
Brûlart, Nicolas 38
bureau des finances of Rouen 48, 100, 111–13, 164, 170, 203, 204
Burgundy 25–7, 48, 52–99, 100, 102–4, 106, 108, 110, 117, 138, 141–9, 167–74, 200–204
  sale of vacant offices in 43–45

capitation 58–9, 72–3, 81, 87, 104–8, 193
chambers of accounts 25, 176
  of Dijon 48, 67, 74, 78, 103, 145, 170, 176, 178, 203, 204
  of Rouen 44–5, 100, 113–17
chambers of justice 136, 140, 185, 189
Chamillart, Michel de 112–13
Chartraire, Antoine 142–4
Chartraire de Bière, François 142–4
Chaussinand-Nogaret, Guy 138
clienteles, *see also* patronage
  financial 27, 135, 138–42, 154, 158–81
clientelism, *see* patronage
coalitions 25–7, 54, 61–74, 80, 96–8, 100–101, 110, 124, 132, 145–46, 157
Colbert, Jean–Baptiste 8, 22, 30, 37–9, 41–2, 47, 76, 104, 106–7, 109, 137, 150, 177, 182, 189
Collins, James 19
Condé princes, governors of Burgundy 54–7, 64, 94–5, 99, 142–3, 145–6, 171, 178
corps 10, 23–4, 27, 38, 52, 65, 66, 73, 97, 80, 96, 97, 135, 149, 157, 189, 191; *see also* parlements; estates; chambers of accounts; receivers general
  as intermediaries 11–16, 19, 20–23, 26, 47–8, 110, 112, 130, 135, 158–81, 192
cour des comptes aides et finances of Rouen 48, 115, 154, 203
Cousin, Pierre 150–151

default, financial 12, 97, 170, 183, 185, 188–9
Desmaretz, Nicolas 39, 152, 183
Dessert, Daniel 140, 154, 177
Dijon 25, 53, 64–5, 67–8, 100–101
  municipal government of 68, 76–7, 167, 171, 176, 203–4
dixième 19, 72–3, 106, 146, 193
don gratuit 55, 57, 61, 69, 81, 95, 106, 143
Downing, Brian 17–18
droit annuel 33–4, 40–42, 46, 112–13, 156, 165
  renewal of 34, 36–40, 45, 189
Dutch Netherlands 20–21, 158, 160, 191

élections 46, 52–3, 101, 103–4, 118, 147, 151, 156, 203
England 20–21, 158, 160, 191–4
estates 6, 13–16, 18, 21, 24, 17, 47, 51–4, 102–3, 131–2, 138, 155, 157, 182, 189–91

of Burgundy 13, 25–7, 52–99,
100–103, 106, 118, 120, 124–5,
127, 130–132, 141–7, 155, 159,
166–8, 172–81, 187, 190, 203
and coalition building 61–73, 80,
98, 110, 191
élus généraux of 55–6, 68, 76,
95–6, 143, 171, 178
negotiation of taxes 54–61,
68–9, 70–73, 81, 95, 109
revenues under their control
70–72, 75, 90–96
of Normandy 26, 69, 101, 107
Estates-General 20, 33

financial revolution 20–21, 158, 190,
192–93
Fouquet, Nicolas 8, 37, 177
Fronde, the, *see* unrest

Grisel, Robert 153–4
Guyot, Pierre Jean Jacques 31, 34
Guyot de Chenizot, François 148

Hamscher, Albert 15
't Hart, Marjolein 16
Hoffman, Philip 176
Hurt, John 47

intendants 5, 51, 55–6, 72, 84, 86, 95,
102–4, 109, 118, 120–121, 155,
165, 193
intermediation 9–16, 19–21, 26, 31, 47–8,
74, 80–82, 90, 135, 138, 140, 142,
155–6, 182, 190–191

Jouanna, Arlette 62

Kettering, Sharon 15, 57, 98

Lamy, Edmé 92–4, 145–6
Law affair (or scheme) 162, 176, 185,
187–8
Law, John 185–6
Louis XIV
personal rule of 8, 15, 22, 25–6, 52,
136–7, 156
strategies of 8–11, 13–15, 19, 22–3,
25, 27, 31, 46–7, 126, 130, 157–8,
182, 188–9, 193–4, 202

Louis-Lucas, Paul 35–6

Major, J. Russell 15, 18, 57, 61, 98
Malet, Jean Roland 152
Marye, Nicolas 126, 196
Mazarin, Jules 5, 8, 14, 22, 30, 36–7,
156, 164, 189, 190
Médard, Claude 151–2
merchants 23–4, 27, 68, 72–3, 86, 92–3,
96, 100–101, 110, 118, 122–30,
132, 154, 174, 195
mortgages 162–7, 177, 179
conditions for 40–42
on offices 26, 40–42, 98, 163–5, 189
on revenues 90–95, 166
Mousnier, Roland 17–18, 136–7, 140–141,
155–6

Netherlands, *see* Dutch Netherlands
Nine Years' War 4, 71, 89–90, 149, 165,
174
Noailles, Adrien-Maurice de 183–4, 189
Normandy 25–7, 48, 53, 69, 100–132, 138,
147–55, 167–8, 173–4
sale of vacant offices in 43–4
North, Douglass 20
notaries 161–2

octrois 83, 98, 125–30, 184
de la Saône 83–95 97, 125, 145, 166,
187
farmers of 92–5, 145–7
offices 23–4, 29–48
heritability of 6, 26, 31, 33–41, 46,
112, 156, 164, 166, 189
sale or creation of 6–8, 13, 32, 42–4,
47, 69–72, 74, 78, 80, 90, 102, 110,
113–22, 138, 141–2, 156, 158, 184,
189, 190
suppression of 183–4
vacant 33, 42–5, 148
Oursin, Jean 152, 187

parlements 25, 28, 47, 162, 176
Parlement of Dijon 38–9, 40, 45, 48, 57,
67, 74, 97, 142–3, 146, 165, 170,
178
Parlement of Rouen 100, 110–113, 116,
153, 170, 195–6, 201

parties casuelles, bureau de 32–3, 41–2, 45, 148
patron–client networks, *see* patronage
patronage 15–16, 23, 54, 56–7, 62, 135, 191
paulette, *see droit annuel*
pays d'élection 26, 100–110, 130, 144, 147–57, 191
pays d'États, see estates
Pellot, Claude 195–6
Phélypeaux de Pontchartrain, Louis 47
Poisson de Bourvallais, Paul 154
Poulletier, Jacques 150–151
privilege 8, 10–14, 17, 20–26, 52–3, 55, 69, 73, 97–8, 103, 110, 131, 156–7, 183, 191–2, 200–202
    bargaining over 11–14, 26–7, 36–40, 48, 52, 70, 74–80, 90, 111–12, 117, 156, 189
    undermining of 5–6, 17–18
Prussia 17, 21, 192–4

receivers 158
    general 142, 144, 147–51
    particular of the *taille* 143, 145, 147–8, 150–52, 171
revolts, *see* unrest
Richelieu, Armand du Plessis, Cardinal 5, 7–8, 14, 22, 30, 36, 52, 156, 164, 189, 190
Rothkrug, Lionel 128–9
Rouen 25, 33, 35, 79, 80, 100, 153, 174, 195–6, 200, 203
    chamber of commerce of 127–30
    généralité of 100–132, 147–55, 167, 169–70, 203
    municipal government 101, 122–27, 129, 132, 195–6
Rouillé, Elisabeth 187–8

Savoy, Duchy of 192–4
Schaeper, Thomas 128
secrétaires du roi 13, 29, 33, 145–6, 153
Skocpol, Theda 18

Spanish Succession, War of the 4, 89, 93, 97, 105, 118, 159, 164, 169, 170, 174, 176, 183, 193
Swann, Julian 60, 76

taille 29, 57–8, 60, 70–73, 101–2, 106–7, 109, 136
tax farmers 17, 21, 92–5, 136, 138, 143, 147, 154, 158, 166
taxation 12, 16–17, 24–6, 51, 54–61, 70–73, 81, 109; *see also* capitation; *dixième; don gratuit; octrois; don gratuit*
    annual amounts of, kingdom-wide 5–6
    burden on Normany 104–110, 131
    collection of 27, 138, 140, 143–8
Temple, Nora 131
Thirty Years' War 4, 8, 9, 17, 30
Tocqueville, Alexis de 96
Tracy, James 20
traitants 102–3, 110, 118–21, 131, 137–9, 141–4, 146, 149, 152–4, 157–8, 200
traités 6–7, 118–20, 137–41, 144, 146, 148–9, 152–4, 156, 200

unrest 6–7, 26, 53
    Fronde, the 6, 36–7
uprisings; *see* unrest

venality 28–36, 42, 51, 73, 77, 110, 174, 183, 188, 190
    revenues from 13, 42

warfare 3–5, 8, 26–7, 182; *see also* Nine Years' War; Spanish Succession; Thirty Years' War
    impact on state development 16–23, 28, 30–31, 51–2, 189–92, 194
Weber, Max 17
Weberian sociologists 51, 192
Weingast, Barry 20

For Product Safety Concerns and Information please contact our EU representative GPSR@taylorandfrancis.com
Taylor & Francis Verlag GmbH, Kaufingerstraße 24, 80331 München, Germany

www.ingramcontent.com/pod-product-compliance
Lightning Source LLC
Chambersburg PA
CBHW052109300426
44116CB00010B/1588